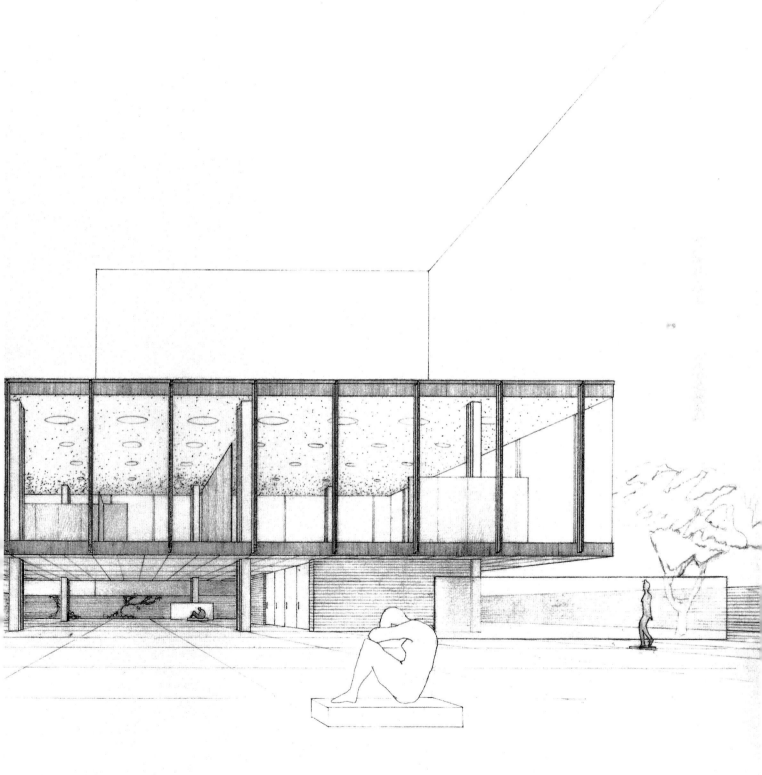

STUDIES IN MODERN ART 6

Philip Johnson
and The Museum
of Modern Art

THE MUSEUM OF MODERN ART, NEW YORK

Distributed by Harry N. Abrams, Inc., New York

Studies in Modern Art is prepared by the Research and Scholarly Publications Program of The Museum of Modern Art, which was initiated with the support of a grant from the Andrew W. Mellon Foundation. Publication is made possible by an endowment fund established by the Andrew W. Mellon Foundation, the Edward John Noble Foundation, Mr. and Mrs. Perry R. Bass, and the National Endowment for the Humanities' Challenge Grant Program.

Produced by the Department of Publications,
The Museum of Modern Art, New York
Edited by Barbara Ross
Design and typography by Emsworth Design, New York
Production by Marc Sapir
Printed by Herlin Press, West Haven, Connecticut
Bound by Acme Bookbinding Company, Inc., Charlestown, Massachusetts

Published annually by The Museum of Modern Art,
11 West 53 Street, New York, New York 10019

Distributed in the United States and Canada by
Harry N. Abrams, Inc., New York

Distributed outside the United States and Canada by
Thames and Hudson, Ltd., London

Contents

Philip Johnson (second from left) installing the
exhibition *Machine Art* at The Museum of Modern
Art in 1934

Preface

Philip Cortelyou Johnson's long association with The Museum of Modern Art originated in June 1929 when he first met Alfred H. Barr, Jr., the newly appointed director of the Museum, which would open that November. Johnson was then an undergraduate at Harvard University and, at best, an amateur of architecture, albeit an utterly passionate one. On very short acquaintance, Barr encouraged Johnson to become a member of the young institution's Advisory Committee, which he joined upon his graduation in 1930, and shortly afterward invited him to head the Museum's Department of Architecture. Johnson accepted, directing the department from 1932 to 1934, and again from 1949, when it was reorganized to encompass design as well as architecture, to 1954. In 1947, he was elected to the Board of Trustees, and subsequently served on eight trustee committees, including Painting and Sculpture (formerly Museum Collections), of which he has been a member since 1957; and Architecture and Design, which he chaired from 1954 to 1981 and continues to serve as honorary chair.

This volume, the sixth in the series *Studies in Modern Art,* is dedicated to the three principal aspects of Johnson's association with the Museum: as a patron, as a curator of exhibitions, and as an architect. (It does not treat his curatorial role in forming the Museum's collection of Architecture and Design or his role as a Museum trustee; neither does it examine any aspect of his work or life outside of the context of the Museum.) The volume thus continues the impetus of the preceding two issues of *Studies in Modern Art,* both devoted to the Museum at mid-century, in examining aspects of the Modern's own history.

Least known, at least outside the institution itself, of Philip Johnson's contributions to The Museum of Modern Art is his role as a patron of its various collections. Yet, he has been, unquestionably, one of the most generous donors in the Museum's entire history: between 1932 and 1966, he donated, or provided funds for, more than twenty-two hundred paintings, sculptures, drawings, prints, photographs, posters, design objects, and architectural models and drawings. (This total does not include some five hundred books and periodicals given to help establish the Museum Library in 1932–33.) As might be expected, Johnson's gifts to the Department of Architecture and Design have been many and significant, ranging from architectural drawings by the donor himself, to his partial gift of the Jan Tschichold Collection, comprising nearly eight hundred examples of early modern graphic design. But the most important of his donations have been those made to the Museum's Department of Painting and Sculpture. An overview of Johnson's role as donor, with particular reference to his gifts to that department's collection, is provided here by Kirk Varnedoe, Chief Curator of Painting and Sculpture, with an appendix that lists selected gifts to all departments of the Museum. While drawing attention to Johnson's early purchase (or provisions of funds for purchase) of what are now key historical works in the Museum's collection— including Otto Dix's *Dr. Mayer-Hermann* in 1932 and Oskar Schlemmer's *Bauhaus Stairway* in 1933—Varnedoe points out that it was Johnson's purchase of Jasper Johns's *Flag* in 1958, that opened the period of his most critical gift-giving, which included a number of radically new, mostly American works. Following his 1962 donation of Andy Warhol's *Gold Marilyn Monroe,* however, Johnson was no longer responding to Barr's initiatives but shaping the collection himself. As Varnedoe explains, the Museum would hardly have a collection of American painting and sculpture of the 1960s at all were it not for Johnson's own initiatives, for during that decade (and thereafter) he made gifts in the areas of Pop and Minimal art to which Barr, the other curators, and the acquisitions committee were largely inattentive.

If it took until the 1960s for Johnson to assert leadership with respect to the Museum's taste in painting and sculpture, in his own area of architecture and design it was quite a different story. The opening premise of "Portrait of the Curator as a Young Man," by Terence Riley, Chief Curator, Department of Architecture and Design, is that Johnson, more than any other curator at the Museum, shaped the public's image of the institution as a place that held daringly radical and controversial positions. This was the effect, Riley argues, of the seven exhibitions directed by Johnson during his first tenure as director of the Department of Architecture, including, most famously, *Modern Architecture—International Exhibition,* in 1932, and the *Machine Art* show of 1934. These seven exhibitions were evidently a form of public education in architecture and design for Johnson, who had no formal training in either architecture or architectural history. It is, therefore, all the more surprising, perhaps, to learn of the panache—indeed, the showmanship—with which they were carried out. (Having the pioneer aviator Amelia Earhart photographed holding a large steel spring to publicize *Machine Art* is but one example of the curator's skill in the then-new field of public relations.) Yet, what was being promoted, Riley makes clear, was of a severe, even puritanical, cast. Art Deco was neglected, and denigrated, in order to proselytise for the emergent International Style: in Johnson's view, "machine art" provided not merely pleasure, but *pure* pleasure.

Subsequent to Johnson's early role as curator, he became involved in a variety of architectural projects for the Museum, effectively becoming the institution's unofficial architect from the late 1940s to the early 1970s. This aspect of his association with the Museum is the subject of the final two essays in this volume. Johnson's Museum projects, from the Rockefeller Guest House, completed in 1950, to an expansion proposal of 1970, are examined by Peter Reed, Associate Curator, Department of Architecture and Design, in an essay that includes extensive visual documentation, among it previously unpublished materials, drawn from the Museum's Johnson archives. The Abby Aldrich Rockefeller Sculpture Garden of 1953, Johnson's best-loved architectural contribution to the Museum and a hallmark of modern urban garden design, is the subject of an essay by Mirka Beneš, Associate Professor of

Alfred H. Barr, Jr., Philip Johnson, and Margaret Scolari Barr in Corona, Italy, in fall 1932

the History of Landscape Architecture, Graduate School of Design, Harvard University—an essay that traces the garden's evolution within the context of international trends in landscape architecture from the nineteenth to the mid-twentieth century.

Reed's essay is of particularly topical relevance, given the Museum's present plans to embark upon an extensive expansion, for it confirms that building campaigns and expansion have been almost perennial concerns throughout the Museum's history. Certainly, by the time Johnson returned to the Museum in 1945 (and, concurrently, established his own professional architectural practice), it would not be long before its original building on Fifty-third Street, designed by Philip Goodwin and Edward Durell Stone and completed in 1939, was recognized to be inadequate to the needs of the institution. Reed documents how Johnson's various built additions successfully formed what could easily have been merely a rough assemblage of parts into a harmonious whole, and reveals the extent to which the example of Ludwig Mies van der Rohe carries through all of them, from the self-evidently Miesian Grace Rainey Rogers Annex of 1949–50, to the element of Miesian parody (what was called at the time "Camp Mies") in the East Wing Founders' Room of 1964. What will be particularly intriguing to many readers, though, will be the unbuilt projects that Reed documents: from the beautiful "House of Glass" envisaged for the garden in 1948, through the plans that the firm of Philip Johnson and John Burgee prepared for significantly expanding the Museum in 1970. And even those who have followed the Museum's architectural history most closely will be surprised to see not only Johnson's proposed 1959 Museum expansion but details of a 1960–61 counterproposal by Arthur Drexler, appointed director of the Department of Architecture and Design in 1956, that is distinguished by terraced rooftop gardens that in some ways prefigure the present Garden Hall, designed by Cesar Pelli and Associates in 1977–84.

Philip Johnson, and René d'Harnoncourt viewing the model of the proposed East Wing expansion of The Museum of Modern Art, installed as part of the exhibition *The Museum of Modern Art Builds,* 1962

Needless to say, Drexler's proposal asserted rivalry with what has long been regarded as both Johnson's most successful contribution to the architecture of the Museum and a most important landmark in the history of modern urban garden design, namely, The Abby Aldrich Rockefeller Sculpture Garden, conceived by Johnson in 1950 and constructed in 1952–53. As Beneš points out in her article, it was not, of course, the first sculpture garden built by the Museum. That garden—which was also the very first of all modern sculpture gardens—was concocted by Barr and John McAndrew, the curator of architecture under Johnson, in the two weeks before the Goodwin–Stone building opened in May 1939. It was manifestly a garden designed for sculpture, and the history that Beneš describes as leading up to Johnson's 1953 garden is a history of the transformation of that original concept, from a garden *for* sculpture into a garden *with* sculpture. That history is also, she demonstrates, an expansion of the Miesian courtyard garden concept that formed the original garden (its Alvar Aalto–influenced layout notwithstanding), and a grafting to that concept of elements of Japanese garden design, resulting in an original "sort of outdoor room" (as Johnson described his garden) whose settled graciousness is both fully modern and redolent of paved gardens of the classical past. Insofar as Johnson conceived a garden with sculpture, he made the character of the sculpture installed there subservient to the character of the garden. (Thus, we learn that his original installation of the garden concentrated on figurative, representational works, some with overt iconographical reference to gardens and water. His reinstallation of 1996 recapitulated that effect.) From the start, this has caused some curators to grumble about the inflexibility of the garden as an exhibition space for sculpture; but as an urban garden, an oasis in New York, it has always garnered the highest of praise. Indeed, it seems safe to say that Johnson's garden is the single most admired architectural feature of the Museum as it presently exists, a fact that will unquestionably be important as the institution prepares for expansion once again.

The series *Studies in Modern Art* is devoted to the encouragement of study of the collections and programs of The Museum of Modern Art. (A fuller description of its purposes appears in my preface to the first, 1991 issue.) I should like to record here my thanks to the individual and collective donors, acknowledged by name on page 4, who have made it possible for us to initiate and maintain the series; to the members of the Advisory and Editorial Committees of *Studies in Modern Art,* also named on that page; and to Beatrice Kernan, Executive Editor of the series, who, once again, supervised the detailed scholarly and editorial procedures involved in preparing this volume, in addition to reading and offering valuable commentary on the articles in their various drafts.

Ms. Kernan and I are indebted to those individuals, both inside and outside the Museum, who agreed to contribute their expertise and knowledge by serving as readers for individual articles within the volume, and in this context extend particular appreciation to Franz Schulze, as well as to Richard Koch, Richard E. Oldenburg, and Marc Treib. Particular thanks are due to Harriet Schoenholz Bee, Managing Editor, Department of Publications, for her crucial participation, as well as Jasmine Moorhead and Dale Tucker for proofreading. In addition, we are grateful to many other members of the Museum's staff for their support: Rona Roob, Chief Archivist, for not only sharing her own expertise but also, with the assistance of Leslie Heitzman and Michelle Elligott, providing invaluable documentation; Mikki Carpenter and Jeffrey Ryan of the Department of Photographic Services and Permissions, for securing important documentary images; Kathleen Curry, Virginia Dodier, Jodi Hauptman, Deborah Dewees, Janis Ekdahl, and Cora Rosevear, for assembling information on Johnson's many gifts to the Museum collections; and Elspeth Cowell, Bevin Howard, and Christel Hollevoet, for furnishing indispensable research assistance. Our work was aided by the essential administrative support of Sharon Dec and Amy Romesburg.

The editorial work for this volume was, once again, done by Barbara Ross, whose knowledge of the history of the Museum meant that her contribution was major and substantial; she was also responsible for compiling the list of selected gifts that comprises the volume's appendix. We thank her especially, as we do Antony Drobinski and Roberta Savage, who designed the volume; Marc Sapir, who supervised its production; and Jody Hanson, who oversaw the design process.

Finally, we are grateful to David Whitney for his support. And we thank most of all the subject of the volume, Philip Johnson, for the extraordinary achievement that we are pleased to be able to document here. He has been a most creative, energetic, erudite, and impatient champion of The Museum of Modern Art throughout its history.

John Elderfield
Editor-in-Chief
Studies in Modern Art

Philip Johnson, ca. 1962

Philip Johnson as Donor to the Museum Collections: An Overview

Kirk Varnedoe

Though he is by any estimate one of the most generous donors in the history of The Museum of Modern Art, and though we count among his gifts several of the most prized treasures of the Museum collections, Philip Johnson has always been extremely modest in assessing his own role as a tastemaker or connoisseur, especially in the areas of painting and sculpture. He has been particularly emphatic in insisting on the primacy of Alfred H. Barr, Jr. in shaping his knowledge of modern art and in guiding his purchases for the Museum—citing as a primary instance Barr's transoceanic plea, in 1933, that Johnson provide the funds for the purchase of Oskar Schlemmer's *Bauhaus Stairway* (pl., p. 18). Then under threat of the Nazi suppression of modern art, the Schlemmer is now an icon of our collection.[1] On another occasion of at least equal significance, it was also at Barr's behest that Johnson purchased Jasper Johns's *Flag* (pl., p. 21) in 1958. Confirming Barr's initial worries, the Trustees had expressed the opinion that the Museum's direct acquisition of this piece might provoke unwanted political controversy; hence Johnson was asked to buy the work with an eye to making it a future gift. That gift was made, in honor of Barr, in 1973—by which time *Flag* had come to be recognized as a work of seminal importance for all that followed in American art.

Even if Barr guided these two acquisitions, however, they point to areas of modern creativity with which Johnson became strongly, personally identified. The *Bauhaus Stairway* speaks for his keen interest, as architect and as historian, in that exceptional school, its faculty and its ideals. This interest echoed in his later gifts of Bauhaus photographs by T. Lux Feininger, of two works by László Moholy-Nagy, and of the first work of art Johnson ever bought for himself, a drawing by Paul Klee. The predilection is still more forcefully illuminated by Johnson's role as partial donor of the Jan Tshichold Collection, with its many hundreds of examples of Bauhaus-inspired modern graphic design. In similar fashion, the purchase of *Flag*, however it was initially instigated, now seems inseparable from Johnson's ardent engagement both with Johns's later art and with what we might see as *Flag*'s progeny in the new art of the 1960s, in Pop and Minimalism particularly.

Prior to *Flag*, Johnson had made, either directly or through funds provided at Barr's request, several key donations to the painting and sculpture collection—

notably, Otto Dix's *Dr. Mayer-Hermann* (pl., p. 17) in 1932, Piet Mondrian's *Composition II* (1929) in 1941, *Bauhaus Stairway* in 1942, and both a major Bradley Walker Tomlin (*Number 20,* 1949), and a beautiful Mark Rothko, *Number 10, 1950* (pl., p. 20), in 1952. But it was through the art of the 1960s that Johnson would play his strongest role in shaping the Museum's collection of painting and sculpture, beginning with his gift of Andy Warhol's unrivaled *Gold Marilyn Monroe* in the year it was painted, 1962 (pl., p. 25). This must have seemed a radically new, if not subversive work to most of Johnson's fellow trustees at that date, and those who were present at the board meeting when the work was first presented for accession still remember Barr's advocacy of the gift—conjuring its kinship to ancient imagery of "love goddesses"—as one of his finest, most inventive and persuasive, moments of rhetoric.[2]

Ironically, the 1962 Warhol gift marked the beginning of an intense period of Johnson's collecting in which Barr would no longer be the driving force. Often moving in advance of Barr's tastes (and certainly well ahead of the dominant pattern of collecting then being followed by the Museum's acquisitions committee and board), Johnson set out to acquire his own collection of advanced art of the 1960s. In this pursuit he was informed less by curatorial guidance than by his friendships with artists and dealers, and most especially by the advice of his companion, David Whitney. During the five or six years following his donation of *Gold Marilyn Monroe,* despite his very close engagement with the Museum as architect of its new East Wing, and despite his acquisition by gift or purchase of a cutting-edge collection of works by Donald Judd, Robert Morris, Andy Warhol, Frank Stella, Claes Oldenburg, and others, Johnson made virtually no gifts of paintings or sculptures to the Museum. It was only after the turbulent year of 1968 (and after Barr had officially retired, in 1967) that this drought ended, as Johnson donated more than forty works —almost all produced in the previous eight years—in 1969–70, followed by several more in 1971 (and, in 1972, by the key gift of what was for years the Museum's only significant combine-painting by Robert Rauschenberg, *First Landing Jump* of 1961).

It would be difficult to overemphasize what this spurt of giving meant, and still means, to the Museum's representation of postwar painting and sculpture. European patrons in many instances had been much swifter than all but a few American collectors to embrace advanced American art of the 1960s. As the end of the decade approached, neither Barr nor any other curator had proved attentive and acquisitive in the areas of Pop and Minimal art. With rare exceptions, the collection was relatively threadbare in these areas; and those exceptions—such as Oldenburg's *Two Cheeseburgers, with Everything* (pl., p.23), Robert Indiana's *Moon* (1960, acquired 1961), and George Segal's *The Bus Driver* (1962, acquired 1963)—had more often than not been purchased with Johnson's funds. Moreover, the years following René d'Harnoncourt's death in 1968 were markedly unsettled ones for the Museum, not only as regarded internal administration, but in terms of the mounting discontent, on the part of both younger staff and a vocal section of the visiting public, with what were perceived as the Modern's conservative, anachronistic failures to stay abreast of contemporary creativity. In very short order, Johnson's gifts brought the painting and sculpture collection up-to-date, and gave it a strength in representation of American art of the 1960s that, more than a quarter of a century later, remains virtually unrivaled among other museums in this country. The donations of 1969–71, coming at a perilous moment of transition for the institution, simultaneously cast a potent vote for contemporaneity and youth, countered the traditional perception of the Museum's bias toward European modernism, and allowed it almost instantly to "catch up" in areas where it had failed to seize initiatives.

Subsequent gifts have reinforced Johnson's unique role in forming this part of the painting and sculpture collection. Having given the funds for the purchase of Oldenburg's *Two Cheeseburgers, with Everything* in 1962, he added gifts of two important large, early soft floor pieces by Oldenburg, *Floor Cake* and *Floor Cone* (both 1962), in 1975 and 1981, respectively. Also in 1981, he reinforced his contribution to the purchase of Roy Lichtenstein's *Drowning Girl* in 1971 by giving the seminal *Girl With Ball* of 1962, the first Lichtenstein painting exhibited by Leo Castelli and one of Johnson's most adventurous and prescient acquisitions of the early 1960s. Similarly, to the exceptional group of small Robert Morris sculptures he gave to the Museum in 1970, Johnson added larger, more imposing Morris works of the 1960s, with donations in 1979 (*Rope Piece*, 1964), 1984 (Untitled, 1968), and 1995 (Untitled [Tangle]; pl., p. 22). The gifts of a monumental work by Frank Stella (*Abra Variation I*; pl., p 24) in 1980, as well as a photo-work by Bruce Nauman (*Composite Photo of Two Messes on the Studio Floor*, 1967) and a large early wood sculpture by Mark Di Suvero (*Ladderpiece*, 1961–62) in 1984, added dimensions to the representation of the American 1960s that had not been present in Johnson's initial, 1969–71 group.

Johnson's gifts seem just as critical to the Museum's representation of more off-center currents as to its concentration on New York–based, "mainstream" trends. California, for example, is represented by a Wayne Thiebaud, *Pink Cones* (1961–62), given in 1969, and a Bruce Conner, *Child* (1959–60), given in 1970. Looking back now over the Johnson donations in regard to the art of the 1960s, it also seems at least as important to stress what at first glance may seem (given Johnson's dominant, in-depth focus on the American art of that period) the international periphery— single works by foreign artists that, individually and collectively, enrich our representation of the 1960s with an aerating diversity of geography and style. A number of key European pieces in the Museum's collection were either given or funded by Johnson, beginning with works by Jean Tinguely and Daniel Spoerri accessioned in 1960 and 1961, respectively, and continuing through significant contributions of works by Arman, Pol Bury, Lucio Fontana, Raymond Hains, and Yves Klein; and a more extensive foreign presence is signaled by Johnson's donations of work by Jesús Rafael Soto, John Latham, Tomio Miki, and, in the Department of Drawings, Yayoi Kusama. As was proved by Robert Storr's handsome installation of a selection of Johnson's gifts to the Museum, in the summer of 1996, these pieces, while perhaps less widely known than the American works, are often of arresting quality, and add immeasurably to the importance of the donor's legacy.

It is hardly a secret to anyone associated with The Museum of Modern Art that the period during and following the renovation and expansion of the Museum in the early 1980s, overseen by the architect Cesar Pelli, was a period in which Philip Johnson felt relatively estranged from this institution. Although he then began, with David Whitney's guidance, an active new phase of collecting, focused on younger American painters, Johnson found himself once again exploring areas where the committee on painting and sculpture acquisitions was reluctant to tread, and none of the extensive purchases he made of 1980s art came to the Museum as gifts. In the latter part of that decade, Johnson arranged with the National Trust for Historic

Preservation to bequeath his Glass House in New Canaan, Connecticut, complete with its surrounding buildings and land, as an historic site. One might conjecture that, with a more continuously happy relationship, this estate might have come to the Museum in bequest; but under the new arrangement, Johnson's collection gallery on the New Canaan property, and the dominant part of his collection that then remained with him, was designated for the Trust. His ability to donate further works to this or any other institution obviously became sharply constrained. Nonetheless, when Agnes Gund, President of The Museum of Modern Art, and I went to plead with him in 1990 for one more key work from the 1960s, he responded to our expression of need. Having set the high standard for our Warhol holdings with the initial gift of *Gold Marilyn Monroe* in 1962, Johnson maintained it, and invaluably aided the Museum's representation of the artist, when he honored the request and offered the institution—as a kind of reverse birthday present, on his own birthday, in July 1991—the gift of Warhol's two-panel "disaster" canvas of 1963, *Orange Car Crash Fourteen Times* (pl., pp. 26–27).

Recently, the Museum has added some key pieces—the thirty-two-canvas array of Warhol's *Campbell Soup Cans* (1962) and James Rosenquist's billboard-size *F-III* (1966)—to its representation of the 1960s; and there are still gaping holes to be filled before we will consider that representation adequate. However, it would hardly be an exaggeration to say that we would not have a chance of assembling a comprehensive selection—indeed, that we would virtually not have a collection of American and European art of the 1960s at all—were it not for Philip Johnson's farsighted decisions as a collector, and his tremendous generosity as a patron. Ironically, it is in this area, where he first moved beyond the tutelage of Alfred Barr, that Johnson, through the empowerment and rejuvenation of the Museum Barr helped found, may have most amply repaid the debt he always felt to his early mentor.

Notes

1. For a discussion of these and other instances of Johnson's activities as collector/donor, see Jodi Hauptman, "Philip Johnson: MoMA's Form Giver," *MoMA Magazine,* no. 22 (Summer 1996), pp. 20–24.
2. Thanks to John Szarkowski, former director of the Museum's Department of Photography, for this reminiscence.

Otto Dix. *Dr. Mayer-Hermann*. 1926. Oil and tempera on wood, 58¾ x 39" (149.2 x 99.1 cm). Gift of Philip Johnson, 1932

Oskar Schlemmer. *Bauhaus Stairway*. (1932). Oil on canvas, 63⅜ x 45" (162.3 x 114.3 cm). Gift of Philip Johnson, 1942

Barnett Newman. *Abraham*. 1949. Oil on canvas, 6'10¾" x 34½" (210.2 x 87.7 cm). Philip Johnson Fund, 1959

Mark Rothko. *Number 10*. **1950. Oil on canvas, 7'6⅜" x 57⅛" (229.6 x 145.1 cm). Gift of Philip Johnson, 1952**

Jasper Johns. *Flag*. (1954–55; dated on reverse 1954). Encaustic, oil, and collage on fabric mounted on plywood, 42¼ x 60⅝" (107.3 x 153.8 cm). Gift of Philip Johnson in honor of Alfred H. Barr, Jr., 1973

Robert Morris. Untitled (Tangle). (1967). Felt, 9'8" x 8'10" x 58" (296.7 x 269.3 x 147.4 cm), variable. Gift of Philip Johnson, 1995

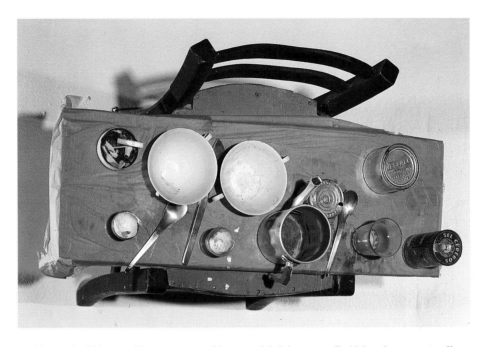

Daniel Spoerri. *Kichka's Breakfast I*. 1960. Assemblage: wood chair hung on wall with board across seat, coffee pot, tumbler, china, egg cups, eggshells, cigarette butts, spoons, tin cans, etc., 14⅜ x 27⅜ x 25¾" (36.6 x 69.5 x 65.4 cm). Philip Johnson Fund, 1961

Claes Oldenburg. *Two Cheeseburgers, with Everything (Dual Hamburgers)*. 1962. Burlap soaked in plaster, painted with enamel, 7 x 14¾ x 8⅝" (17.8 x 37.5 x 21.8 cm). Philip Johnson Fund, 1962

Andy Warhol. *Gold Marilyn Monroe*. 1962. Synthetic polymer paint, silkscreened, and oil on canvas, 6'11¼"
x 57" (211.4 x 144.7 cm). Gift of Philip Johnson, 1962

Opposite:
Frank Stella. *Abra Variation I*. (1969). Fluorescent alkyd on canvas, 10' x 9'11⅞" (304.8 x 304.5 cm). Gift of
Philip Johnson in honor of William Rubin, 1980

Andy Warhol. *Orange Car Crash Fourteen Times.*
(1963). Synthetic polymer paint and silkscreen
ink on canvas, two panels, overall 8'9⅞" x 13'8⅛"
(288.9 x 416.9 cm). Gift of Philip Johnson, 1991

Jean (Hans) Arp. *Squares Arranged According to the Laws of Chance*. (1917). Cut-and-pasted papers, ink, and bronze paint on paper, 13⅛ x 10¼" (33.2 x 25.9 cm). Gift of Philip Johnson, 1970

Max Burchartz. Poster: "Schubertfeier" (Schubert Celebration). 1928. Offset lithograph, 23¼ x 33" (59 x 83.8 cm). Gift of Philip Johnson, 1968

Hans Hollein. Highrise Building: Sparkplug, Project. Perspective view. 1964. Photomontage, 4¾ x 7¼" (12 x 18.4 cm). Philip Johnson Fund, 1967

Karl J. Jucker and Wilhelm Wagenfeld. Table Lamp. (1923–24). Glass, chromeplated metal, and silver-bronze wiring tube, 16¾" (42.5 cm) high x 5⅛" (14 cm) base diameter. Gift of Philip Johnson, 1953

Gerrit Rietveld. "Red and Blue" Chair. (ca. 1918).
Wood, painted, 34⅛ x 26 x 33" (86.5 x 66 x 83.8 cm).
Gift of Philip Johnson, 1953

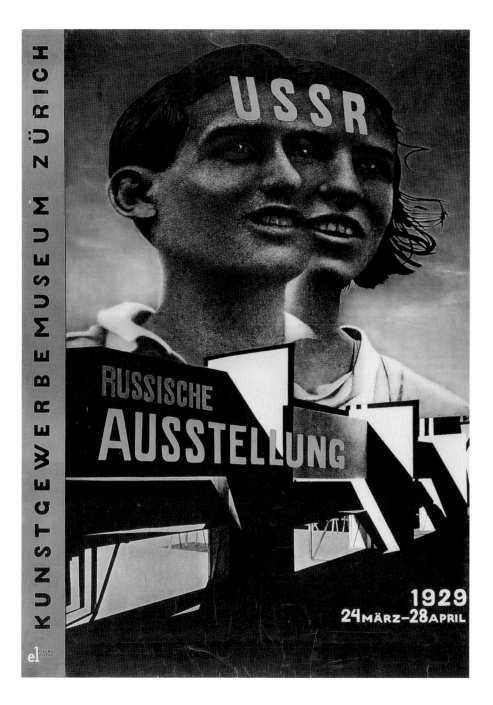

El Lissitzky. Poster: "Russische Ausstellung, Zurich" (Russian Exhibition, Zurich). 1929. Photomontage, 49 x 35¼" (124.5 x 89.5 cm). Gift of Philip Johnson, Jan Tschichold Collection, 1953

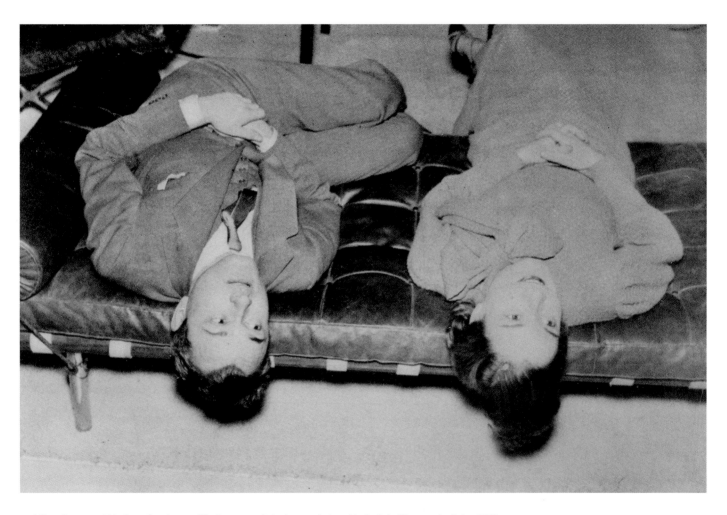

1. Philip Johnson and his sister Theodate upside-down on a chaise longue designed by Ludwig Mies van der Rohe, 1934

Portrait of the Curator as a Young Man

Terence Riley

On April 30, 1934, *Machine Art*—the seventh in a rapid-fire series of often brilliant exhibitions organized for The Museum of Modern Art by the young Philip Johnson in just under three years—closed, eight weeks after it opened to the public. Although the show would tour for many years, Johnson's relationship with the Museum would shortly, if temporarily, end: In December 1934, he resigned from the Museum to pursue a career in the populist currents of the far right of America's mid-Depression political spectrum, astonishing the media, which had followed his mercurial rise to prominence in the cultural world of New York.

Johnson's abrupt *démarche* created an eleven-year gap between his early career at the Museum and his return there in 1945. Thus, to write of this early career alone is, admittedly, to write the first chapter of a two-chapter professional history, and furthermore, it runs the risk of tacitly implying that Johnson's subsequent involvement in politics had no particular bearing on the matter at hand. Nonetheless, a shorter history need not be seen as indifferent to the benefits of a broader analysis of his life;[1] while this essay is necessarily more limited, it is bracketed by the genuinely significant moments of Johnson's earliest years at the Museum and the credible astonishment of his colleagues and the press at his leave-taking. From the point of view of his contemporaries, Johnson's action was not a logical extension or transformation of his career at the Museum but a puzzling, if not wholly inexplicable, turn of events.

The importance of Johnson's efforts in the early years of The Museum of Modern Art cannot be underestimated. In addition to their intrinsically challenging intellectual positions, the exhibitions he organized were also, in the words of an admiring critic, "ultra" events that caught the attention of the press and fired the imagination of the public.[2] Perhaps more than any other curator, Johnson was consistently able to shape the public's image of the Museum as a scrappy David in opposition to the Goliath of The Metropolitan Museum of Art, as a forum for challenging intellectual discourse leavened by wit and cleverness in an age that appreciated both.

"Modern Architecture—International Exhibition"

In January 1931, at the behest of Alfred H. Barr, Jr., founding director of The Museum of Modern Art, Philip Cortelyou Johnson was appointed director of the Museum's first architecture exhibition. Johnson, a twenty-four-year-old, recent graduate of Harvard University, had no formal training in architecture or the history of architecture, having taken an undergraduate degree in philosophy. His considerable knowledge of contemporary building was acquired principally on his own initiative, while traveling through Europe in the company of the young art historian Henry-Russell Hitchcock. Hitchcock would subsequently collaborate with Johnson on the development of the exhibition, which would be titled *Modern Architecture—International Exhibition.*[3]

Barr's faith in an unproven young man was not wholly unprecedented in the Museum's brief history. In selecting Barr as the Museum's first director, the founding trustees had shown a readiness to take certain risks in charting the course of the new institution. Of his proposed appointment, Barr wrote to trustee Paul J. Sachs: "The fact that you are even considering me as a possible participant in this great scheme has set my mind teeming with ideas and plans. This is something I could give my life to—unstintedly."[4] In turn, Barr extended the confidence placed in him to others, and necessarily relied on criteria other than academic credentials in selecting his lieutenants in the "great scheme." For example, Hitchcock, like Barr,[5] had no doctoral degree—not uncommon in the day for either an academic or a museum career—but his writings on modern architecture were among the few authoritative sources for American readers.[6] Johnson also had certain qualities that contributed to Barr's estimation of his capabilities: his instinctive critical sense, his wealth, and his willingness.[7]

Many young men of Johnson's generation with private means might have settled into a life of idle elegance. Johnson was certainly not one of them. Writing to Barr in 1931 in response to a dressing-down from the director regarding strategy, Johnson remarked: "I did not resent your sermon in the slightest. After all what I most want to do is be influential, and if there is a method why not learn it."[8] The precociousness, if not presumptuousness, of this statement is striking. However, it is clear that in the early 1930s, Johnson's desire to be influential was synonymous with his desire to promote what he believed to be the unrecognized genius of contemporary architecture. In a letter to the Dutch architect J. J. P. Oud he wrote: "I wish I could communicate the feeling of seeing the Bruenn house of Mies [the Tugendhat House in Brno, Czechoslovakia, designed by Ludwig Mies van der Rohe]. I have only had similar architectural experiences before . . . old things [like] the Parthenon."[9] While many critics' support for contemporary culture was ideologically or politically motivated, Johnson was clearly *moved* by modern architecture. From Berlin he related what was for him, at that point, an unusual experience: "Last night I hardly dreamt of buildings at all. It is a strange fact that not one night has gone by but that I have had some dream on architecture."[10] Johnson's subjective orientation—a sort of architectural rapture—combined with his keen intellect and formidable resources, created his activist mien.

Johnson's dedication in organizing the Museum's first architecture exhibition, now known popularly as the "International Style" show,[11] and his support of the selected architects is striking. Not only did he hire Mies van der Rohe to renovate his Manhattan apartment (fig. 2) and propose that he design the exhibition installation, he also sought commissions for the architect with the Rockefeller family and the Aluminum Company of America (ALCOA).[12] He personally loaned Bowman

2. Ludwig Mies van der Rohe. Apartment Interior (Philip Johnson Residence), New York. 1930. Included in *Modern Architecture—International Exhibition,* The Museum of Modern Art, New York, 1932

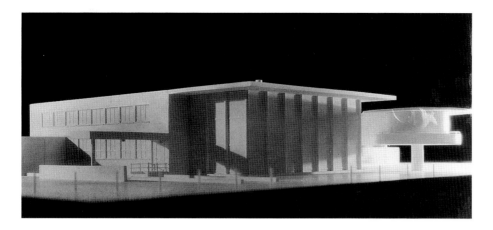

3. J. J. P. Oud. Johnson House, Pinehurst, North Carolina. Model. 1931. Included in *Modern Architecture—International Exhibition,* The Museum of Modern Art, New York, 1932

Brothers of Chicago money to complete their model for the exhibition.[13] In addition to donating his own time to the project for over a year, Johnson was largely responsible for its financing. He convinced his father, the patent attorney Homer H. Johnson of Cleveland, Ohio, to contribute funds and to serve on the exhibition committee; through his father, he also approached ALCOA for additional funding. At his urging, the Johnson family asked Oud to design a house for their property at Pinehurst, North Carolina[14] (fig. 3), a project for which the young New York architects Alfred Clauss and George Daub were also asked to submit designs; Clauss and Daub were also commissioned to design a series of service stations for The Standard Oil Company of Ohio, a client of the elder Johnson[15] (fig. 4). Although neither of the Pinehurst proposals was executed, Oud's project, Johnson's Mies-designed apartment, and one of the service stations would be featured in the exhibition. (Johnson's curatorial patronage extended beyond architectural commissions. A certain amount of his 1930 European trip with Hitchcock, during which they traveled extensively to study modern architecture, was devoted to negotiating purchases of drawings by Le Corbusier, a painting by Piet Mondrian, and, while in Germany, furniture and lighting fixtures for himself, his mother, and Alfred Barr.[16])

4. Clauss and Daub. Standard Oil Filling Station. 1931. Included in *Modern Architecture—International Exhibition,* The Museum of Modern Art, New York, 1932

Johnson's attempts to be influential on behalf of "the movement" were not limited to financial succor. He lent photographs to the Harvard Society of Contemporary Art's exhibition on the Bauhaus[17] and secured Oud a visiting professorship at Columbia University (Oud declined).[18] While planning the exhibition, both he and Barr, independent of the Museum, involved themselves in a dispute surrounding the Architectural League Annual by organizing a counter-event, *Rejected Architects,* an exhibition of work by younger architects who were not included in the League's show.[19] Before *Modern Architecture* opened, Johnson also attempted to organize the "rejected" architects and a number of other young designers in the short-lived American Union for New Architecture.[20] Moreover, his duties as director of the exhibition were not entirely exalted. With a staff of one, he frequently found himself packing crates, hanging photographs, and rushing off to Buffalo and elsewhere when the exhibition ran into logistical problems while on tour. Plainly, Johnson's earnestness, ambition, and money, more than any other factors, made the Museum's first architecture exhibition possible.

In early December 1930, preceding his appointment as director of the exhibition, Johnson submitted a three-page memorandum to the Museum's president, A. Conger Goodyear, proposing an exhibition comprising three sections: (1) models by the "most prominent architects in the world," (2) an "industrial" section, and (3) an international competition for young architects.[21] For the first section, "Modern Architects," nine designers were to be invited to submit models of their work. With one exception (the substitution of Richard Neutra for Norman Bel Geddes) the proposed roster would remain the same throughout the entire year of curatorial planning: from the United States, Bel Geddes, Bowman Brothers, Howe and Lescaze, Raymond Hood, Frank Lloyd Wright; from Germany, Walter Gropius and Mies van der Rohe; from France, Le Corbusier; and from the Netherlands, Oud.

The industrial section, eliminated during the exhibition planning phase, was to focus on three areas: an exhibit on large-scale urban construction, a presentation of an "advanced" factory prototype, and an example of an "industrial housing project." As in the "Modern Architects" section, these exhibits would be presented in model form, augmented by detailed reports published separately from the catalogue, incorporating plans and construction and cost information. Interestingly, Johnson suggested that two of the exhibits be organized by builders, the exhibit on urban construction by the Starrett Brothers and Eken Company of New York, which had recently completed the masonry-and-steel construction for the Empire State Building; and a prototype representing "the most advanced development of factory design" designed by the Austin Company. The industrial housing exhibit, which was described as being "of great significance" and "incorporating the most recent and scientific theory on the subject in America," was proposed without specifying who would lead the effort, although Johnson did contact the well-known architectural and social critic Lewis Mumford immediately after the project was approved.[22] (The third exhibition component, a competition for young architects, was little elaborated, and is not mentioned in later proposals.)

In the spring of 1931, *Built to Live In,* an updated prospectus for the exhibition authored by Johnson, was published by the Museum.[23] Slightly coy, it does not identify publicly the architects chosen for the exhibition, although a certain amount of reading between the lines gives a clue as to the names of the world's "most prominent architects." The text, an expanded version of earlier, internally circulated proposals, repeats the account of "modern activity" in America and abroad: Wright, Hood, Bowman Brothers, and Le Corbusier are mentioned by name, as is Neutra, an Austrian émigré and the newcomer to Johnson's original list of nine. Neutra effectively replaced Bel Geddes, whose name does not appear in this or any subsequent documents related to the exhibition.[24] Furthermore, all nine, with the exception of Bowman Brothers, are represented in the illustrations. (The Bowmans had not yet constructed a single project other than their own offices. Johnson's reluctance to include an illustration of one of their proposed works can be explained by the pamphlet's title: The particular emphasis on built work clearly indicates the curators' preference for "actual monuments."[25])

In addition to being a prospectus for the exhibition, *Built to Live In* served another purpose. The various articles published by Johnson around this time, along with the *Rejected Architects* exhibition, increased the Museum's visibility and served to introduce Johnson to the architectural community. Hitchcock and Barr previously had published various works in which they identified themselves with the "new" architecture. Beyond his book *Modern Architecture: Romanticism and Reintegration,* published in 1929, Hitchcock frequently reviewed American and European books and periodicals for the *Architectural Record.* A review by Barr of the Necco factory in Cambridgeport, Massachusetts, had appeared in *Arts* magazine in 1928, shortly followed by his survey of the Russian architectural scene.[26] Both men had also been regular contributors to *Hound and Horn.* Within the interlocking circles of the Museum and the "crimson connection"—the national network of Harvard University graduates—Johnson was certainly the newcomer, as was the Museum itself, among the traditional venues of architecture exhibitions. Although anyone who knew Barr would not have been surprised at the proposal for such an exhibition, the Museum's (not to mention Johnson's) first forays into propagandizing modern building must have raised certain expectations as well as trepidations within the New York architectural establishment.

If the December proposal and *Built to Live In* were somewhat coy about the curators' views on modern architecture, the *Rejected Architects* exhibition and Johnson's writings were decidedly partisan. In his review of Joseph Urban's design for The New School for Social Research in New York, published in March 1931, Johnson based his critique on the principles of the "International Style," a new term coined by Barr, Hitchcock, and Johnson[27] that did not appear in the earlier exhibition proposals. While remarking that the building, "at first glance, gives the impression" that it embodies elements of the new "International Style, with which the names of Le Corbusier, Oud, Gropius, and Mies van der Rohe are associated," Johnson concluded: "In the New School we have an anomaly of a building supposed to be in a style of architecture based on the development of the plan from function and façade from plan but which is as formally and pretentiously conceived as a Renaissance palace. Urban's admiration for the New Style is more complete than his understanding."[28]

Rejected Architects—essentially a stalking horse for the International Style show—opened in April 1931. Although neither its organizers nor The Museum of Modern Art were mentioned by name in the exhibition pamphlet, the event was widely identified with Barr and Johnson. The pamphlet, which again refers to the International Style, is a précis of their shared views: "[T]he style is characterized by flexibility, lightness and simplicity. Ornament has no place, since hand-cut ornament is impracticable in an industrial age. The beauty of the style rests in the free composition of volumes and surfaces, the adjustment of such elements as doors and windows, and the perfection of machined surfaces."[29]

Implicit in Johnson's doctrinaire proscriptions was a critique of the Architectural League's stylistic catholicity—a critique that was not confined to the text materials for *Rejected Architects.* Men hired by Johnson paraded outside the League show wearing sandwich boards that proclaimed, "SEE REALLY MODERN ARCHITECTURE, REJECTED BY THE LEAGUE, AT 907 SEVENTH AVENUE." While *Rejected Architects* might have been dismissed by some as a stunt, the architects criticized in print by Johnson in his flurry of articles in 1931—Urban and Walker among them—were no doubt nonplussed by the twenty-four-year-old tastemaker's sharp remarks. In the June 1931 issue of *Creative Art,* Johnson offered his own "review" of the exhibition's critics. Taking Ely Jacques Kahn, Deems Taylor, and Douglas Haskell specifically to task,

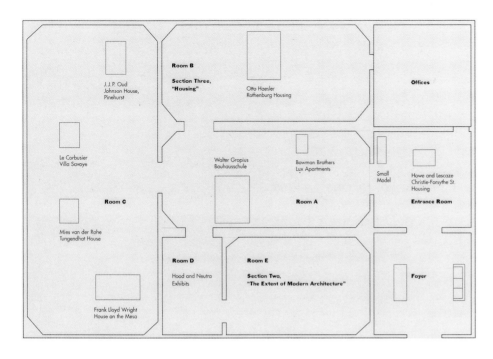

5. Installation plan, *Modern Architecture—International Exhibition*, in the Heckscher Building galleries, The Museum of Modern Art, New York, 1932. Reconstruction by Terence Riley

he insisted that the "critics of both the Rejected Architecture and the League Show have been uncritical."[30]

Modern Architecture—International Exhibition, which opened on February 9, 1932, was the final exhibition to be held in the Museum's first galleries, located on the twelfth floor of the Heckscher Building (now known as the Crown Building) at 730 Fifth Avenue.[31] Unfortunately, no architectural plans of the galleries remain in the Museum Archives; however, by examining installation photographs of the various exhibitions held there and newspaper coverage of the Museum's opening in 1929, the principal gallery spaces can be credibly reconstructed. Furthermore, a post-installation memorandum and seven extant installation photographs housed in various archives indicate the layout of the *Modern Architecture* exhibition (fig. 5).

The "Modern Architects" section opened the exhibition, with the work of Howe and Lescaze installed in the Entrance Room (so designated in the memorandum); a large model of the firm's Chrystie-Forsyth St. project was visible from the Museum's foyer. The exhibits of Gropius and Bowman Brothers, featuring the Bauhausschüle and a midrise metal-construction housing block, respectively, were installed in the next gallery (Room A), the central space that connected all the others (fig. 6). In the largest gallery (Room C) were the exhibits of Le Corbusier (fig. 7), Mies van der Rohe, Oud, and Wright (fig. 8), establishing them as the most important of the "Modern Architects." Of these, Le Corbusier and Mies were further distinguished in that their exhibits were immediately to the right and left, respectively, of the gallery's principal axis and visible from the anterior rooms. To underscore the importance of their work, the featured models—Corbusier's Villa Savoye and Mies's Tugendhat House (figs. 31, 32, p. 64)—were illuminated by small electric lights attached to the display stands. Of "the nine," the work of Hood and Neutra, installed in a smaller space to the left of the central gallery (Room D), was given the least prominence. Their projects—Hood's Apartment Tower in the Country (1932)

6. Installation view, Walter Gropius exhibit (Room A), *Modern Architecture—International Exhibition*, The Museum of Modern Art, New York, 1932. In foreground: Model of the Bauhausschüle, Dessau, Germany, 1926

Left:
7. Installation view, Le Corbusier exhibit (Room C), *Modern Architecture—International Exhibition,* The Museum of Modern Art, New York, 1932. At center: Model of the Villa Savoye, Poissy-sur-Seine, France, 1930

Right:
8. Installation view, Frank Lloyd Wright exhibit (Room C), *Modern Architecture—International Exhibition,* The Museum of Modern Art, New York, 1932. At right: Model of Project for a House on the Mesa, Denver, 1932

and a school design from Neutra's proposed Rush City Reformed (1928–31)—were oddly mismatched: While both projects were exurban, Hood's Tower was essentially a highrise development, while Neutra's scheme was both low-rise and low-density.

The forty-one photographs in section two, "The Extent of Modern Architecture," added to the show at the last minute, were displayed in Room E, an out-of-the-way gallery beyond Room D. All of the exhibits comprising section three, "Housing," were contained in a single gallery to the right of the central space (Room B; fig. 9), mirroring Rooms D and E. The relatively less important positions of the second and third sections were predicted in the statements made by the curators throughout the exhibition's development, specifically: "Distinct from the models, there are two sections which should be laid out so as to be more or less separate from the rest of the show."[32]

Despite hopes that Mies might come to New York to "arrange" the exhibition, Johnson spent considerable time planning the installation. Before leaving again for Europe in June 1931, he had already determined the size of the photographic enlargements. Furthermore, in response to a series of questions from Howe and Lescaze regarding the installation design, his assistant wrote in July that Johnson had "set the maximum number of photographs for the Exhibition at 50. . . . I know that Mr. Johnson wants to keep the Exhibition as a whole as consistent as possible in design. Hence, I doubt that he would want each architect to design his individual layout of photographs."[33]

Even as Mies was being invited to design the installation, Johnson appears to have been formulating his own proposals: "Explanatory plans, elevations and perspectives will be placed on the wall behind each model. Enlarged photographs of actual buildings by these architects will also be shown."[34] In this manner the model served more-or-less to define the area of each architect's exhibit. Beyond this vague definition of territory, the installation was indeed, in Johnson's words, "consistent":[35] "We will at least have a simple and understandable arrangement."[36] This remark was made in relating to Alfred Barr his impressions of the Frank Lloyd Wright exhibition installed in the Preussische Akademie der Kunst in Berlin by H. Th. Wijdeveld,

9. Installation view, "Housing" section (Room B), *Modern Architecture—International Exhibition,* The Museum of Modern Art, New York, 1932. At right: Model of the Rothenberg Housing Development, Kassel, 1930–32, designed by Otto Haesler

10. Installation view, exhibit of wood veneers, *Die Wohnung Unserer Zeit (The Dwelling in Our Time)*, Deutscher Werkbund, Berlin, 1931. Installation design by Ludwig Mies van der Rohe

which Johnson visited during the summer of 1931.[37] The Wijdeveld installation was organized around a series of tall freestanding partitions with "wings" on each end. On the partitions and on the walls of the exhibition hall were drawings and photographs of varying scales, mounted salon-style. Nor was there any uniformity of scale or materials in the architectural models, which were placed at odd angles throughout. Johnson termed this freely composed arrangement "frightful."[38] His own installation, in contrast, was the very model of the stylistic "discipline" that he, Barr, and Hitchcock urged on American architects. In an ironic reference to classical architecture Johnson instructed that the photographs "be placed in a frieze around the room, allowing about 2 ft. in between."[39] The uniformity of the mediums, the scale of the models and photographs, the spacing, and the hanging height all contributed to a composed character.

Johnson's installation did not go unnoticed, particularly in New York, where viewers of architectural exhibitions were accustomed to salon-style installations, frequently on a grand scale. Yet we should not assume that Johnson's installation was simply a reaction to the status quo. The installation of *Modern Architecture* recalls the simplicity of Mies's and Lilly Reich's installations for the Deutscher Werkbund exhibition *Die Wohnung Unserer Zeit* (*The Dwelling in Our Time*), which Johnson had seen in Berlin the previous summer[40] (fig. 10). Furthermore, photographs of Barr's relatively minimalist installations of painting and sculpture suggest a more immediate model. Not only did Johnson adapt the generous spacing and uniform hanging height that characterized Barr's installations, but even the size of *Modern Architecture*'s photographic enlargements was consistent with the scale of the Post-Impressionist works championed by Barr in the Museum's earlier exhibitions (see, for example, fig. 11). The installation photographs support a reading of the models and photopanels as independent *objets d'art* rather than documentary materials. Johnson, tellingly, instructed subscribers to the exhibition's tour to hang the photographs "in the same manner as paintings."[41]

Given Johnson's extremely personal involvement with the exhibition, it is unlikely that any review could have lived up to his expectations. While he had hoped to cause a coast-to-coast sensation, he afterwards remarked, "I may safely say that there was not one really critical review of the Exhibition."[42] Johnson's comment does not account for the fact that the show was treated very seriously in a good number of important, principally New York–based, journals and papers,[43] and he was more likely speaking of the national popular press, which carried notices like this one in the Hartford *Courant:* "An exhibition of advanced housing models, made of little pieces of metal, glass, and wood, will be opened Saturday afternoon, April 20, with a tea to the members of the Wadsworth Athenaeum."[44] The preceding hardly portended the broad-based stylistic Armageddon envisioned by Barr, Hitchcock, and Johnson. Perhaps most disappointing, however, was the apparent inability of the popular press and the public at large to discern the finely wrought stylistic messages of the exhibition. The curators might have been shocked further to find how loosely their exhibition statement was interpreted. A reporter for the Worcester (Massachusetts) *Sunday Telegram* (who also referred to "Miss van der Rohe, famous German draftsman") wrote that Hood's Tower in the Country "well exemplifies the theory held by most modern architects that rural districts are best for skyscraper homes"[45]—a somewhat mystifying statement, to say the least. Yet another surprising observation was: "The most extreme development of the International Style which has yet been suggested is the Dymaxion house, proposed but not yet built by Buckminster Fuller."[46] (Although Fuller's Dymaxion Deployment Unit would be shown at the Museum in 1942, it was not included in *Modern Architecture,* and understandably so: Fuller was by no means sympathetic to the International Style.)

Nonetheless, within the architectural community the curators' message was quite clear and caused extended debate. Hitchcock noted: "As the epithets fly about my own head . . . I can only recall the British battles over the Houses of Parliament and the Government Offices in Whitehall."[47] Much of the criticism centered on the formulation of the International Style, which even Oud (who generally supported the curators) referred to as "school mastering."[48] The émigré California architect Rudolph Schindler was more explicit: "I am not a stylist, not a functionalist, nor any other sloganist. Each of my buildings deals with a different *architectural* problem, the existance [sic] of which has been entirely forgotten in this period of rational mechanisation. The question of whether a house is really a house is more important to me, than the fact that it is made of steel, glass, putty or hot air."[49]

The foregoing is from a letter in which Schindler asked, rather undiplomatically, to be included in the Los Angeles venue of the exhibition. Even as Schindler and others sought to be included, Wright insisted on being taken out. In addition to various misunderstandings throughout the planning of the exhibition, Wright was displeased with certain aspects of the show and the publicity surrounding it, including the curators' reference to Wright as a past master in the catalogue, and reports of disparaging remarks made by Hood about his work. Wright cabled Johnson: "MY WAY HAS BEEN TOO LONG AND TOO LONELY TO MAKE A BELATED BOW TO MY PEOPLE AS A MODERN ARCHITECT IN COMPANY WITH A SELF ADVERTISING AMATEUR AND A HIGH POWERED SALESMAN NO BITTERNESS AND SORRY BUT KINDLY AND FINALLY DROP ME OUT OF YOUR PROMOTION."[50] Mumford attempted to persuade Wright to reverse his decision, and he eventually did so—on the condition that copies of Wright's essay "Of Thee I Sing" be distributed at the exhibition in New York.[51] The curators ultimately compromised, including the essay in a special issue of *Shelter*

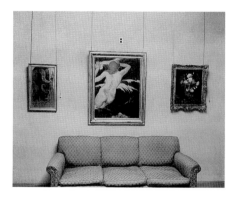

11. Installation view, *Cézanne, Gauguin, Seurat and van Gogh,* The Museum of Modern Art, New York, 1929. Installation design by Alfred Barr

magazine devoted to the exhibition and making reprints available to the public throughout the show's tour.[52]

In addition to Wright's essay and the transcripts of the Architects' Symposium held in conjunction with the exhibition, three opposing viewpoints, by Kurt Lönberg-Holm, Arthur T. North, and Chester Aldrich, were printed in the magazine.[53] For his critique, Lönberg-Holm excerpted all of the curators' references to "style" in the catalogue and juxtaposed them with an advertisement for toilet fixtures and a manifesto by Mies in which he rejected "all aesthetic speculation," "all dogma," and "all formalism." North's and Aldrich's critiques were similarly negative, the former titled "Old New Stuff" and the latter "Modernism and Publicity." William Adams Delano, a partner in Aldrich's architectural firm, added this coda in a subsequent issue of *Shelter:* "After centuries of struggle to evolve a culture worthy of his position in the animal kingdom, is this to be man's end? No better, no worse than the insects, ants and caterpillars."[54]

"Early Modern Architecture: Chicago, 1870–1910"

Based on the success of his initial efforts, the Museum named Johnson chairman of its newly constituted Department of Architecture in the summer of 1932, shortly after the Museum moved into new quarters in a Beaux-Arts townhouse at 11 West Fifty-third Street. The creation of a permanent curatorial position devoted to architecture was the first step toward realizing Barr's dream of a multidisciplinary program encompassing a broad spectrum of modern culture.

While Johnson took naturally to the proactive role Barr created for him, Hitchcock's scholarly ambitions set him on a different course. In 1928, he wrote: "My appetite for the Avant garde will carry me through the book [*Modern Architecture: Romance and Reintegration*], I hope, then back in to the past. I have really enjoyed making analyses of Late Gothic and Baroque, etc."[55] Thus, the second architecture exhibition at the Museum, *Early Modern Architecture: Chicago, 1870–1910,* seems at first glance to have been tailored to Hitchcock's taste for history. Even so, Barr had developed a twofold mission for the young institution: not only to present the best of the art of the day but also to establish a history of modern art that supported contemporary artistic theory. Furthermore, Johnson (as well as Barr) had an interest in skyscrapers, as was evident in his original proposal for the *Modern Architecture* exhibition, which had included a section on urban building. Thus, the multifold emphases in *Early Modern Architecture*—critical history, the skyscraper, and contemporary theory—were not wholly unpredictable.

Early Modern Architecture was a much more modest affair than the Museum's first architecture exhibition. The mimeographed catalogue features a collection of the various installation texts rather than a lengthy expository essay.[56] More of a distilled historical sketch, the catalogue interweaves, with little in-depth elaboration, a technical history of the development of the skyscraper and a more traditional architectural history that includes various building types. Henry Hobson Richardson, Louis Sullivan, and Frank Lloyd Wright, all three of whom figure greatly in Hitchcock's previous and subsequent historical works, are positioned as the principal protagonists in the aesthetic development of the Chicago school of architecture, running parallel to the technical accomplishments of Dankmar Adler, William Holabird, and William Le Baron Jenney. In fact, the exhibition may even be considered a work-in-progress or as a prologue to the Museum's publication, in 1935, of *Louis Sullivan—Prophet of Modern Architecture* by Hugh Morrison, who was to some extent consulted by the curators in preparing the exhibition;[57] and, in 1936, Hitchcock's *The Architecture of Henry Hobson Richardson and His Times.*

Hitchcock and Johnson traveled to Chicago after the opening of the International Style show to study the buildings that would be presented in *Early Modern Architecture.* Even so, it is unlikely that all of the research represented by the exhibition texts, as brief as they are, could have been undertaken in the short ten months between the openings of the two shows. No doubt much of the work on Richardson, Sullivan, and Wright was drawn from Hitchcock's longstanding and ongoing interest in the work of those architects, including his 1928 monograph on Wright. Nonetheless, the slim bibliographies cited by Hitchcock and Johnson and the nature of their correspondence indicate a considerable amount of digging for essential information. Johnson's letters are filled with queries seeking basic facts: biographical data on Holabird and Martin Roche; the name of the architect of New York's World Building (also known as the Pulitzer Building; designed by George B. Post, 1889–90), whether or not the Reliance Building (D. H. Burnham and Company, 1890–95), in Chicago, still existed, etcetera.[58]

Given the learning curve implied in such queries, it may be assumed that Hitchcock and Johnson consulted with other researchers in compiling the detailed chronology of the technical development of the skyscraper. A highly specialized analysis, the chronology encompasses the first use of cast iron as a façade, in the Bogardus Building in New York (James Bogardus, 1848); the introduction of wrought-iron girders, in the Harper Building in New York (John B. Corlies with James Bogardus, 1854); and the issuance of the patent for fire-resistant hollow tile floors in 1871. The Home Insurance Company Building (William Le Baron Jenney, 1883–85; fig. 12) and the Tacoma Building (Holabird and Roche, 1887–89; fig. 13), both built in Chicago, are presented as the first skyscrapers. Indeed, extant correspondence shows that the curators had been in contact not only with Morrison but also with Thomas E. Tallmadge, an architect from Chicago who wrote about skyscrapers for the *Architectural Record.*[59] Tallmadge was also a respected amateur historian, advising the Governor of Illinois on historic architecture and helping to establish the Burnham Library of Architectural History at The Art Institute of Chicago.

The timing of the Museum's exhibition suggests that the interest of Hitchcock, Johnson, and Tallmadge in the significance of these early modern structures was caused by the same events: In 1929 and 1931, respectively, the Tacoma and the Home Insurance buildings were demolished. It is evident from Tallmadge's *Architecture in Old Chicago* (1941) that the historical importance of the structures was not widely known at the time of their demolition.[60] The Marshall Field Estate, which owned the property beneath the Home Insurance Building, was apparently surprised when the American Metallurgical Society (*not* the American Institute of Architects) asked permission to place a plaque at the site commemorating the structure as the first skyscraper. The estate allowed a commission of architects and historians, chaired by Tallmadge, to study the fabric of the building during its demolition to ascertain its exact method of construction. The commission confirmed in a 1931 report that the Home Insurance Building was "the first high building to utilize as the basic principle of its design the method known as skeleton construction."[61]

12. William Le Baron Jenney. Home Insurance Company Building, Chicago. 1883–85. Included in *Early Modern Architecture: Chicago, 1870–1910,* The Museum of Modern Art, New York, 1933

13. Holabird and Roche. Tacoma Building, Chicago. 1887–89. Included in *Early Modern Architecture: Chicago, 1870–1910,* The Museum of Modern Art, New York, 1933

By 1933, when *Early Modern Architecture* opened, the commission's conclusions no doubt were more widely known in Chicago. Yet in New York, which took considerable pride in the profiles of the Empire State Building, the Chrysler Building, and Rockefeller Center, the press was somewhat taken aback by the curators' revision of popular history. An unidentified clipping states that "the purpose of the show" was "to assure us that the skyscraper was born, not as is usually supposed, in New York, but in Chicago."[62] Henry McBride, writing for the New York *Sun,* was a bit more dramatic: "Philip Johnson, I very much fear, is destined to die young. Some New Yorkers will probably massacre him—and shortly. Do you know what his latest is? He has arranged an exhibition in the Museum of Modern Art that tends to prove Chicago invented skyscrapers. He snatches the one aesthetic glory we have left, snatches it in broad daylight with every one looking—and takes it to Chicago. Talk about gunmen!"[63]

McBride's mock horror aside, the idea that the skyscraper might have been invented in Chicago rather than in New York was not a new one and had a fair amount of currency, at least in professional circles, much earlier on. In 1910, the New York architect Peter B. Wight observed: "Chicago is sometimes spoken of as the birthplace of the skyscraper. . . . If Chicago is not the birthplace of 'skyscraper', it is the first city in which office buildings for renting purposes, ten, twelve and fourteen stories in height, were built. New York was close second."[64] Similarly, John Taylor Boyd, Jr., writing in the *Architectural Record* in 1922, stated: "The beginnings of tall building design go back to about 1890, when, in Chicago, the first steel skyscraper was erected."[65] Even so, the purpose of the show should not be seen simply as an indulgence of Hitchcock's historical interests, nor solely as the creation of a local sensation by revising Gotham's self-image as the city of skyscrapers. Barr, Hitchcock, and Johnson, individually, had been critical of New York's contemporary skyscrapers, and the exhibition should not be seen as unrelated. In the foreword to Hitchcock and Johnson's *The International Style: Architecture Since 1922* (1932) Barr wrote sarcastically of the city's "aesthetic glory": "Romanesque, Mayan, Assyrian, Renaissance, Aztec, Gothic and especially Modernistic—everything from the stainless steel gargoyles of the Chrysler Building to the fantastic mooring mast atop the Empire State. No wonder that some of us who have been appalled by this chaos turn with the utmost interest and expectancy to the International Style."[66]

In this respect, Tallmadge's and the curators' points of view diverged. While all concerned looked to Chicago as the birthplace of the skyscraper, and each similarly decried the historicist "New York skyscraper school," Tallmadge alone was sympathetic to the recent development, in Europe, of the Art Deco style, to which Barr was referring derisively with the term "modernistic." Somewhat defensively, Tallmadge wrote: "The [Paris] Decorative Arts Exposition of 1925 cannot be ignored. For better or worse, a wealth of new detail which we had not the time, patience and ingenuity to evolve, was laid at our doors."[67]

Johnson found little in twentieth-century skyscraper design to be admired. In a sharply critical article published in *The Arts* in May 1931, he negatively compared Cass Gilbert's Woolworth Building (1910–13), Ralph Walker's Telephone Building (1923–26), and the drawings by Hugh Ferriss with the unadorned 1891 Monadnock Building in Chicago. Ferriss, Johnson pointedly noted, "is not an architect," and described his drawings as "falsely lighted renderings that picture fantastic crags rising high above dark caverns."[68] Johnson also departed from standard architectural criticism in that he directed his comments to other critics. Using their own remarks, he rather undiplomatically rebutted the writings of the supporters of the New York skyscraper school: Tallmadge (on whose research he would rely for the skyscraper exhibition); C. H. Edgell, dean of the Graduate School of Architecture at Harvard University; and Fiske Kimball, director of the Pennsylvania Museum of Art (now the Philadelphia Museum of Art). As Kimball's support of the *Modern Architecture* exhibition had been critical—as had Edgell's, to a lesser degree, in launching its national tour—Johnson's remarks were particularly daring. (Kimball had the last word: A document in the Philadelphia Museum archives indicates that when the show reached Philadelphia, he added dozens of projects, including the Woolworth Building; Hood's Chicago Tribune Tower [1923–25]; Josef Hoffmann's Palais Stoclet, Brussels [1905–11]; Eric Mendelsohn's Einstein Tower, Potsdam [1920–24]; and Hans Poelzig's Grosses Schauspielhaus, Berlin [1919–20], all of which had been criticized by Barr, Hitchcock, and Johnson.[69])

Unlike Hitchcock, Johnson's principal interest in the skyscraper exhibition was critical rather than historical. His intention was not to glorify the past but to cut back the skyscraper's history to its roots; its new growth might thus reflect the tenets of the International Style as demonstrated in Howe and Lescaze's PSFS Tower, Philadelphia (1928–32; fig. 14), exhibited previously in *Modern Architecture*. Hood's McGraw-Hill Building, New York (1931), among other of his skyscraper designs, was also included in that show but less out of real conviction: Johnson had hopes that Hood could be converted to the "true" style. In describing his inclusion of the various projects, he revealed his critical program: "Raymond Hood [was included] because some day he may be attracted into the fold by his opportunism."[70] Johnson's appreciation of the structural clarity of the early Chicago skyscraper is evident, yet it is not solely a historical appreciation. In a publicity photograph that accompanied the press release, he is shown standing next to three diagrammatic scale models of eight, fourteen, and twenty stories, commissioned to illustrate the transition from "Low, Heavy Masonry Building to the Light, Airy, Steel Tower of Today"[71] (fig. 15). While the models were intended to show the implications of the structural system on relative mass and volume, the "light, airy, steel tower" bore an uncanny, prophetic resemblance to Mies's American towers of the 1950s and 1960s.

"Objects 1900 and Today"

Following his first two exhibitions, Johnson embarked on a project that would significantly expand his brief at The Museum of Modern Art. Sometime before the end of 1932, he submitted a proposal for, not another architecture exhibition, but an "Art in Industry Exhibition."[72] In January of the new year, trustee Nelson A. Rockefeller responded to Johnson's questions regarding the outcome of the Exhibition Committee's deliberations on his proposal: "The question of an industrial exhibition was discussed at the Trustees' meeting of the Museum of Modern Art and while the general idea of the Museum going into the field of industrial art met with approval, the idea of opening up with a big show was decidedly frowned upon."[73]

The trustees' comments can be taken at face value. The Metropolitan Museum of Art had been staging annual exhibitions of "American industrialist art" since 1917, which in the 1920s grew to be very large installations.[74] Given the precedent,

14. Howe and Lescaze. PSFS Tower, Philadelphia. 1928–32. Included in *Modern Architecture—International Exhibition,* The Museum of Modern Art, New York, 1932

15. Philip Johnson standing next to scale models commissioned for *Early Modern Architecture: Chicago, 1870–1910,* The Museum of Modern Art, New York, 1933

16, 17. Installation views, *Objects 1900 and Today*, The Museum of Modern Art, New York, 1933

the hesitancy of the Museum's trustees should be seen as arising, most likely, from fiscal concerns rather than as an objection to the exhibition per se. Nor is it so surprising that Johnson's proposal was referred to as "big": At this point in his career he seems to have had few small ideas, particularly when they concerned architecture and design, himself, and The Museum of Modern Art.

In place of the "big show" was a more modest affair with a double focus. Johnson's two previous shows were, respectively, a contemporary survey and a historical retrospective—each a well-known exhibition format. His third exhibition, which occupied an upper floor of the Museum's Beaux-Arts townhouse, was both a historical retrospective *and* a contemporary survey. Titled *Objects 1900 and Today,* it consisted of approximately thirty pairs of objects—"Lamps, bowls, boxes, tables, spoons, wall hangings, designed in the 'Art Nouveau' or 'Jugendstil' style of the early 1900's . . . exhibited side by side with similar objects inspired by the principles of the modernists of today"[75] (figs. 16, 17).

Given Hitchcock and Johnson's emphasis on a lack of ornament as a defining characteristic of the International Style, reflected in the pristine surfaces and planar compositions of Johnson's own Mies-designed apartment, the exhibition may have been assumed to be yet another vehicle for advancing the cause of modernism. The potentially confrontational nature of the installation and the exhibition wall labels—"A Style of Ornament vs. An Unornamented Style," "Decorative Objects of 1900 vs. Useful Objects of Today"—echoed the young curator's taste for the polemical. In his choice of title and in the text materials, however, Johnson took a softer tone. For example, the exhibition was originally titled "Decorative Objects of the Art Nouveau vs. Useful Objects of Today."[76] In sharp contrast, the language of the final edit is neutral: "Decorative" and "useful" are no longer opposed, and the conjunction "and" is diplomatically substituted for "versus," avoiding the confrontation the latter implied. Similarly, in his introduction to the mimeographed, unillustrated catalogue Johnson demurred, "This exhibition of decorative and useful objects is arranged with the purpose of contrasting the design, and the attitude toward design, of two modern periods. One is not necessarily better than the other."[77] Thus, a bronze table lamp in the form of a draped female figure was exhibited side-by-side with a 1923 Bauhaus desk lamp designed by Wilhelm Wagenfeld and K. J. Vucker, a typical turn-of-the-century wall sconce mounted adjacent to a chromeplated tubular-steel light fixture. The press picked up on the evenhandedness of Johnson's remarks: "Without praising or attacking either style, the museum has placed side by side objects of both periods so that the public may study the divergent trends."[78]

On the face of it, the exhibition seemed to represent a wholly different curatorial demeanor than Johnson had displayed previously, a clue to which can be found in the provenance of the loans. The wall sconce was borrowed from one of the many midtown properties owned by the Rockefeller family. The chromeplated light fixture came from Johnson's own apartment, as did the Wagenfeld lamp; the contrasting bronze table lamp was borrowed from his mother.[79] Other "objects of 1900" included personal property of Abby Aldrich Rockefeller, furniture and china from The Metropolitan Museum of Art, and various pieces from Tiffany Studios. As a result, Johnson's instinct for both ardent support of the modern and withering criticism of all else was sharply curtailed. It is not hard to imagine the reaction (and the political fallout) had he borrowed pieces from the Museum's trustees or from other museums and subsequently ridiculed them, particularly as so many of the pieces that would have benefited from such criticism were, in fact, his. (In addition to the broader political implications, negatively contrasting his mother's and his own taste would have had a personal cost.)

Given such obvious difficulties, why did Johnson not simply mount an exhibition of contemporary design, with the same International Style edge as the *Modern Architecture* show? The answer may lie in some of the press comments: "The new exhibition in the Museum of Modern Art is a little masterpiece in the art of showmanship."[80] Indeed, the very conception of such a public confrontation (albeit a genteel one) had an implicit element of spectacle, a crowd-pleasing exhibition that was both didactic *and* entertaining. Johnson and (no doubt) Barr were clearly aware of this. In his first proposal for *Objects 1900 and Today,* Johnson described the exhibition as "historical and critical" but felt it necessary to state that he did not intend it to be "humorous."[81] Nevertheless, a viewer who approached the purely decorative, tulip-shaped objet d'art produced by Tiffany Studios and, unlike all the other exhibits, found no comparable contemporary object beside it, merely a card with the somewhat haughty inscription *Ornamental* objets d'art *are avoided in modern interior architectural schemes,*[82] very likely would have found it historical, critical, *and* humorous. As Aaron Marc Stein noted in his review, "This contrast of an exhibit with no exhibit . . . is rather more significant than a simply amusing stunt."[83]

Objects 1900 and Today was the Museum's first modern design exhibition and should be seen as pivotal within Barr's overall plans for the institution. As such, one might have expected its focus to be Barr, Johnson, and Hitchcock's shared antipathy for Art Deco rather than the relatively value-neutral "comparison" of Art Nouveau and the modern. It can be supposed that the desire to stage a showdown between "real" and "pseudo" modern design was actually the genesis of the project, reflecting the same bias evident in the Museum's first architecture exhibition. Still, Johnson would have been constrained by the same politesse required in light of his lenders' generosity. Worse, had he substituted Art Deco for Art Nouveau within the more neutral format of simple contrast, the results could have been vastly different.

Art Deco was indeed very popular, having been introduced in the United States at The Metropolitan Museum of Art's annual industrial arts show in 1926, which featured items from the Paris Exposition d'arts décoratifs and, as such, had been eagerly adopted by many of America's industrial designers. The ideological distinctions between the constructivist composition of Le Corbusier, Pierre Jeanneret, and Charlotte Perriand's adjustable chrome armchair of 1929 (fig. 18) and, say, the streamlined styling of Donald Deskey's tubular-steel and leather furniture of the early 1930s (see, for example, fig. 19) may not have been as apparent to the Museum's visitors as Johnson would have liked.

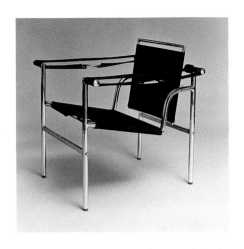

18. Le Corbusier (Charles-Edouard Jeanneret), in collaboration with Pierre Jeanneret and Charlotte Perriand. Armchair with Adjustable Back. 1929. Chrome-plated tubular steel and black canvas, 26⅛ x 25⅝ x 26" (66.3 x 65 x 66 cm). The Museum of Modern Art, New York. Gift of Thonet Brothers, Inc. Included in *Objects 1900 and Today*, The Museum of Modern Art, New York, 1933

Ultimately—the decorative arts of 1900 were less of a threat than Art Deco. They were, firstly, historical, three decades or more removed from the contemporary moment. Less of a vital contest, the "objects of 1900" assumed an almost Darwinian function, demonstrating an inescapable evolution toward the modern—at least, the modern as Johnson saw it. Moreover, Art Nouveau and Jugendstil were, conveniently, out of fashion. Stein, who clearly was disposed toward the arts of the day, wrote: "[T]he Museum must have been confronted with almost an impossible task of locating collectors of Jugendstil and of persuading owners of decorations in the 1900 manner to confess to ownership."[84]

Nonetheless, Johnson allowed himself to be, somewhat perversely, a defender of the *un*fashionable: "These objects are now regarded with fashionable horror. Such shudders are, however, unjustified. It is only that the proper perspective on the period is lacking. . . . Jugendstil, or as it is called in French (and English!), Art Nouveau, is one that merits reevaluation."[85] The "proper perspective" was, of course, a safely historical one: "[T]here is no going back except in the spirit of adventure and fantasy to the creations that were so acceptable at the beginning of the century."[86]

19. Donald Deskey. Tubular-steel couch, chair, and side tables designed for the Ypsilanti Reed Furniture Co., Ionia, Michigan. ca. 1930. Courtesy Cooper-Hewitt National Design Museum, Smithsonian Institution

Of the "objects of today" exhibited, no comprehensive critical assessment can be made. As with the section of the *Modern Architecture* exhibition titled "The Extent of Modern Architecture," financial constraints rather than fully developed curatorial positions ruled, and the selections for exhibition were made from sources at hand: A third of the modern objects were owned by Johnson, the balance borrowed from New York department stores and showrooms and from U.S. manufacturers.

A much noted aspect of the exhibition was its installation. In contrast, it might be said that the installation of *Modern Architecture,* despite its success as a first effort, was a somewhat amateurish demonstration of the *absence* of Mies as the proposed designer. In his third show Johnson demonstrated his own growing talents, radically transforming the top floor of the Museum's Beaux-Arts townhouse. According to a press review: "The background will be of white beaverboard. The larger objects will be placed on tables of curly maple edged in light blue and supported by chromium posts. The smaller objects will be placed on black Carrara glass shelves, protected by sheets of plate glass six feet high. Materials will be hung from the ceiling and the panes of translucent glass will be set into the beaverboard against the light."[87] Recalling the ingenious exhibits designed for the Deutscher Werkbund by Reich and Mies (fig. 10, p. 42; fig. 20), which Johnson admired, the installation of *Objects 1900 and Today* illustrated his rapid transformation from connoisseur to impresario.

Reviewers were enthusiastic, one referring to Johnson's "latest adventure in smart installation" as "lively," "effective," and as making "the rest of the museum look rather stodgy and forlorn."[88] Johnson could not have been but pleased at the

20. Installation view, glass exhibit, *Die Wohnung Unserer Zeit (The Dwelling in Our Time)*, Deutscher Werkbund, Berlin, 1931. Installation design by Lilly Reich

personal recognition he received: "Johnson, who is the *genius loci*, has entirely remade two of the smaller galleries in the modern way, with simple shelves and ingenious glass cases."[89] Another reporter gamely foretold the future, "Philip Johnson . . . is obviously a man to be reckoned with. . . . I trust that those in authority will see to it that sooner or later he gets a free hand on the other floors in the way of backgrounds and decorative accessories."[90]

"Work of Young Architects in the Middle West"; "Project for a House in North Carolina"; "A House by Richard C. Wood"

Johnson mounted three additional exhibitions at the Museum in 1933, one of which—*Work of Young Architects in the Middle West*—was held concurrently with *Objects 1900 and Today.* Opening just six weeks after the close of the skyscraper exhibition, *Young Architects,* in Johnson's words, was "a worthy continuation of the exhibition of the pioneers of modern architecture held at the museum last year and serves as a further proof of the value and vitality of the international style."[91]

While the aesthetic criteria revealed in *Modern Architecture* certainly were in evidence in *Young Architects,* the former exhibition's relationship to the latter was most clearly seen in its inversion of the relative emphasis on "style" and the more technical and functional aspects of housing. While the technical clearly took a backseat to the aesthetic in Johnson's first exhibition, it was nonetheless part of the initial concept. Despite the fact that most historians have seen the International Style as purely formal in conception (or at least in terms of effect), the *Young Architects* exhibition is further evidence of the ambitiously broad agenda Johnson set for himself in his early years at the Museum. In Johnson's words: "The problem in housing goes far beyond architecture into industry, economics, sociology and politics. In the end many experts will have to have a hand in solving it. But it is the peculiar province of the architect, in other words, the artist, not only to co-ordinate the work of city planners, politicians, engineers and economists, but to imagine new solutions

[to] old problems and new ways of living."[92] The technocratic works presented in *Young Architects* were a true reflection of Johnson's description, even to the extent that a viewer would have questioned his sincerity regarding the artist's role. Many of the projects, such as Hamilton and Gwenydd Beatty's proposal for a Contemporary Satellite Community (1933; fig. 21), are so functionalist in appearance that they seem to flaunt Hitchcock's concern that "there should be a balance between evolving ideal houses for scientific living and providing comfortable houses for ordinary living."[93]

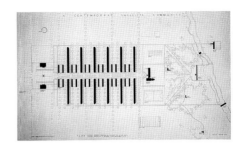

21. Hamilton and Gwenydd Beatty. Contemporary Satellite Community, Madison, Wisconsin. 1933. Included in *Work of Young Architects in the Middle West*, The Museum of Modern Art, New York, 1933

The Midwestern architects presented in the 1933 exhibition were, and for the most part are to this day, relatively unknown figures. George Fred Keck was the exception. Thirty-eight years old at the time, he was the most accomplished and promising of the group and acted as its unofficial leader, regularly corresponding with Johnson concerning details of the exhibition. (Although there are no extant documents related to the genesis of the *Young Architects* exhibition, it may be that Johnson met Keck in Chicago when he and Hitchcock were researching the skyscraper exhibition.) From Keck's rather modest oeuvre Johnson selected the Cruger Apartments, Elmhurst, Illinois (1926); Miralago (1929), a multiuse development (with more than an uncharacteristic whiff of Art Deco) in Wilmette, Illinois; and the "country house" that Keck had been commissioned to design and construct for the 1933–34 Century of Progress Exposition in Chicago. The house, as eventually built, displeased Johnson, not for its overtly functionalistic ethos but for its octagonal plan, reminiscent of Fuller's Dymaxion Deployment Unit. Keck also submitted a housing project in association with R. Paul Schweikker. Schweikker, who had spent a year traveling throughout Germany and was thus familiar with the new functionalism, was further represented by two commissions for private houses and a project for a "small suburban house adaptable to row houses."[94]

Hans Oberhammer, an ethnic German émigré from Czechoslovakia, was, like most of his co-exhibitors, younger than Keck at twenty-nine; like Keck, he had worked for the Chicago firm of Schmidt, Garden and Erikson. Oberhammer was represented by four unbuilt projects designed for various German cities, and his rhetoric in the exhibition catalogue is notable for its didactic tone: "I want to mention the fact that I am a trained *bricklayor* [sic], my *first* step to study architecture. . . . Training based upon this principle should be advocated in America. It would do away with the draftsman-designer type."[95] As severe in aspect was the Beattys' Project for a Contemporary Satellite Community, consisting of 288 living units in twelve apartment blocks laid out in double rows flanking a central axis connecting a commercial center and a school.[96] Intended for a fifty-acre site outside Madison, Wisconsin, with an additional one hundred acres serving as a green belt— "so that other communities could not encroach"[97]—the "community" resembles a military encampment in its straightforward efficiency. Educated in Wisconsin and London, Hamilton Beatty, then twenty-six, had also worked briefly for Le Corbusier. Equally young was Wallace G. Teare, who with his partner William H. Conrad, had teamed up with Joseph L. Weinberg to develop a "slum clearance" project for Cleveland, Johnson's hometown. Weinberg, the senior member of the trio at forty-three, had worked for Albert Kahn in Detroit as well as various Cleveland firms before opening his own practice in 1930.[98]

Virtually all of the architects, though younger than Weinberg, had similar career patterns: a college education, employment by various professional firms, and

Left:
22. Howard Fisher. Page House, Chicago. Southwest view. ca. 1930. Included in *Work of Young Architects in the Middle West,* The Museum of Modern Art, New York, 1933

Right:
23. Interior of the Page House, with the "offensive" valance at rear

the recent establishment of an independent practice, fulfilling small commissions while generating larger, more ambitious projects on their own initiative. Their common career paths are important, for reasons beyond professional development. It is no coincidence that most of them began "practicing independently" shortly after the stock market crash of 1929, an event that had a devastating effect on the architectural profession. In this historical context, an independent practice was frequently the only option as the larger and more established firms shrank or closed altogether.

Harvard-educated Howard T. Fisher stands apart from his colleagues in the *Young Architects* exhibition in this regard. Once professional employment became scarce, Fisher joined General Houses, of Chicago, a business created to manufacture and erect mass-produced, prefabricated housing. Two houses he designed for General Houses were featured in the exhibition, one a prototype built for Ruth Page, a prominent Chicago dancer-choreographer; the other, a show house to be built at the Century of Progress Exposition in 1933. The Page House (fig. 22), while interesting for its use of a prefabricated steel frame and composite panels as both the interior and exterior finish, was as spatially awkward, gloomy, and technically crude as Mies's Tugendhat House was spatially refined, expansive, and well-crafted. Even so, Johnson was enthusiastic about the potential application of this technology during the Depression, when a housing shortage and lack of capital demanded new solutions. In this instance, Johnson's aesthetic concerns were all but suspended, except for what might be called nitpicking over an apparently offensive scalloped curtain valance (fig. 23). The only real emphasis on aesthetic innovation in *Young Architects* could be found in the catalogue: The projects were chosen to demonstrate "not only research into new problems but great strides away from the Beaux Arts classical (not to mention the Beaux Arts 'modernistic')."[99]

While Johnson's selection of such highly functional schemes may seem unusual to contemporary readers, the conception of *Young Architects* is now a familiar one. Even so, at a museum that loudly proclaimed its mission as "the conscientious, continuous, resolute distinction of quality from mediocrity,"[100] the exhibition was not only proactive but extraordinarily speculative. While most curators seek to identify and encourage up-and-coming artists, including their work in exhibitions when appropriate, Johnson was the first to conceive an entire exhibition on the basis of promise rather than performance and to place it within a museum context, reversing the preferences displayed in *Modern Architecture,* which featured, almost exclusively, architects whose reputations were based on built works. The suspension of certain levels of critical judgment inherent in such an undertaking presents both opportunities and risks, which Johnson appears to be addressing in this description of the exhibition's premise: "The younger generation, now beginning their independent practice, have broken away from academic design. They have not as much opportunity to build as their predecessors, but more to observe and study. As a result this exhibition consists mainly of projects."[101]

Clearly, Johnson was hoping to deflect potential criticism regarding the architects' somewhat modest achievements while using the Museum as a platform from which this younger generation might vault to the fore in a traditionally conservative profession. A similar motivation, with similar risks, was undoubtedly behind his decision to include Bowman Brothers in the *Modern Architecture* exhibition and, further, to install their more modest works alongside those of the much more accomplished and distinguished Walter Gropius. In that instance, Johnson's proactive stance had almost no positive effect. The press made little note of the young architects and their subsequent careers never matched the high expectations generated by Johnson's speculative attention. Nevertheless, his failure with the Bowmans did not shake Johnson's belief that the Museum had a responsibility not only to recognize young architects but to actively promote their careers.

The unusual premise of the exhibition did not go unnoticed by the press. One reporter, who found the work presented "persuasively," nonetheless remarked with more than a little tongue-in-cheek attitude, "The artists are modernists because— Mr. Johnson explains this with the utmost tact—they have not had as many opportunities to build as their predecessors and consequently have had more time to observe. Therefore, they are more in tune with actual requirements. This, which has heretofore been their misfortune, may ultimately prove to have been their good luck."[102] Another critic, while admitting he could "not find anything to get excited about" in the work presented, was more willing to endorse Johnson's speculative curatorial position: "Under the ardent leadership of Philip Johnson, the fresh and vital currents of new thought in the architectural life of Europe and America are being directed toward the Modern Museum and given a liberal representation, and I am inclined to believe that it is this very liberal attitude towards the newer phases of our architectural life that will, in time, help to give the Modern Museum a truly definitive and properly American form."[103]

Johnson's liberality in promoting the younger generation of American architects was also apparent in two smaller shows mounted in the summer and fall of 1933, *Project for a House in North Carolina,* featuring a design by William T. Priestley,[104] and *A House by Richard C. Wood.*[105] The extant, unillustrated press clippings tell us little about the North Carolina house. Priestley had been studying at the Bauhaus under Mies van der Rohe, and he collaborated on the project (apparently an actual commission) with interior designer Lila Ulrich, a student of Lilly Reich. The only indication of the house's formal characteristics is in the description of the two wings of the house being joined by a "gallery enclosed in glass on both sides,"[106] which is suggestive of Mies's influence. No records of the Wood project survive in the Museum's archives. Johnson's recollections of these two shows, over sixty years later, are far fewer than those of his other efforts. The architects were, in his words, "worthy and able" and had produced "two very fine home designs," which he cites today as reason enough to encourage their fledgling careers.[107] As he himself was only twenty-seven at the time, the birth of the "young architects" genre may be seen as having derived from personal empathy as much as any other influence.

"Machine Art"

The "large" industrial arts show Johnson had proposed to the Museum's Board of Trustees in late 1932 was most likely the same exhibition that opened to the public on March 7, 1934. *Machine Art,* installed on all three floors of the Fifty-third Street townhouse (figs. 24–26), was the largest of Johnson's exhibitions to date, with hundreds of objects listed in a fully illustrated catalogue. The myriad objects selected were uniform in only one regard: They were wholly products of the Machine Age. Nonetheless, the relationships between the individual objects and the machine were various. At two extremes, some were products of serial machine processes (cylindrical containers made from rolled aluminum, #120), while others were essentially hand-built objects whose components were mechanically produced, rendered, and/or finished, (Desk Lamp, designed by Howe and Lescaze, #273). Similarly, some of the objects were finished consumer products (Glass Bowl, designed by Walter Dorwin Teague for Steuben, #228), some were tools or devices with industrial purposes (Vernier Depth Gauge, Brown and Sharpe, #289), and some were machine-made components of what would become yet other machines (Bearing Spring, American Steel and Wire Company, #1). Given the overwhelming metaphorical omnipresence of the machine, it might even be said that including actual examples of machinery—such as the gasoline pump designed for The Standard Oil Company (#54)—was redundant.

24. Installation view, *Machine Art,* The Museum of Modern Art, New York, 1934

25, 26. Installation views, *Machine Art*, The Museum of Modern Art, New York, 1934

The works presented necessarily constituted a similarly broad range in terms of who devised them and for what reason. A number of the pieces were produced by well-known architects and designers of the day, including Marcel Breuer, Le Corbusier, and Gilbert Rohde. Principally, these objects—interior furnishings produced in limited quantities and often finished by hand—had for decades, if not centuries, been classified as decorative arts, fusing aesthetic and utilitarian concerns. A second group of objects, primarily mass-produced office and household equipment—for example, the automatic electric waffle baker manufactured by the McGraw Electric Company (#77)—were not formally grounded in the history of the decorative arts. Though little information exists regarding who designed them, objects of this kind were often devised by what are now called "industrial designers," many of whom were employees of large manufacturing concerns who had little, if any, formal arts education. Distinct from this latter group of objects were the tools and components of industrial production itself, devised by product engineers and highly-skilled laborers—such as the machinists who would have perfected the self-aligning ball bearing (#50) featured on the cover of the exhibition catalogue[108] (fig. 27)—who probably had never been called, or thought of themselves as, designers in the sense of either of the above categories. Even so, if "designer" refers to a person who is involved in determining an object's form, dimensions, materials, and means of production, they certainly were so.

It is interesting to consider how the show might have been perceived without the explication of Barr's and Johnson's catalogue texts. Given the exhibition's whole-cloth approach, and minus the didactic texts, the public could have been excused for mistaking it for a conflation of three more familiar exhibition genres: a decorative arts exhibition (not unlike *Objects 1900 and Today*), a department store exhibit (as were popular at the time), and an industrial fair of the kind the Deutscher Werkbund promoted. However, the curatorial presumption was daring, and the viewer was left with little possibility of mistaking Barr's and Johnson's intentions. *Machine Art* was precisely that: art, regardless of the intended use of the object. As the Museum's press release announced, "Beauty—mathematical, mechanical and utilitarian—has determined their selection for display in the

Exhibition, regardless of whether their fine design was intended by artist or engineer or was merely the unconscious result of the efficiency compelled by mass production."[109] The release cautioned that it would not be an art exhibition "in the usual sense," but Barr's and Johnson's arguments concentrated on the high-art metaphor with little regard for that which distinguished *Machine Art* from the "usual sense" of a fine arts exhibition.

In his various exhibitions Johnson, as did Barr and Hitchcock, continued to grapple with the apparently intransigent problem of the relative importance of the aesthetic and the functional in modern architecture and design. The balance of "form" and "function" was, of course, a shared philosophical problem of Johnson's generation, and of the preceding generation as well. In 1901, Frank Lloyd Wright wrote critically of the Arts and Crafts movement, particularly its rejection of the machine and the culture of industrialization: "Artists who feel toward Modernity and the Machine now as William Morris and Ruskin were justified in feeling then, had best distinctly wait and work sociologically where great work may still be done by them. In the field of art activity they will do harm. Already they have wrought much miserable mischief."[110]

Wright's words reflected the transformation of his own work from the earlier hand-sketched, Sullivanian ornamental detail to the mechanically drafted, more geometric and abstract work of the first decade of this century. In many ways, Johnson's essay picked up where Wright left off, with a critique of handcraft's "irregularity, picturesqueness, decorative value and uniqueness"[111]—qualities Wright attempted to rationalize mechanically without abandoning. Moreover, Johnson sought to introduce values beyond those Wright was willing to endorse, qualities that were nonetheless the inevitable result of Wright's valorization of the machine: "precision, simplicity, smoothness, reproducibility."[112]

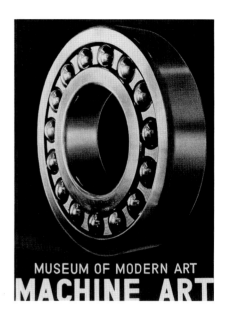

27. Cover of the *Machine Art* exhibition catalogue (1934), designed by Josef Albers

If *Machine Art* had been but a more ardent and less sentimental declaration by Johnson of his generation's devotion to the machine, it may have been more readily dismissed. The journalist Joseph W. Alsop, Jr., who wrote a generally positive review, said of the objects displayed: "[T]hey were handsome enough and plentiful enough to make that eccentric inhabitant of the artistic world of pre-war Paris, the Baroness Elsa von Freytagh-Loringhoven, who used to promenade the boulevards wearing a cook-pot exterior brassiere and a frying-pan hat, swoon with delight."[113] Barr and Johnson were aware of the mix of sensationalism and seriousness that the show carried. As in *Objects 1900 and Today,* the possibility that the exhibition might be perceived as lively, or even entertaining, was not undesirable—provided the curatorial message was clear. *Machine Art,* with its broad-stroke approach, clearly had the potential for both, as observed by the critic Helen Appleton Read: "[T]he exhibition has many sound reasons for being shown in a museum of modern art, although it is necessary to analyze them lest it be regarded as a somewhat precious and ultra stunt."[114]

Johnson's essay provided a concise historical analysis of the role of the machine in architecture and design, from Joseph Paxton's Crystal Palace, London, of 1850–51 through the Arts and Crafts movement, Art Nouveau, and Art Deco, criticizing everything since Paxton's initial achievement. While Johnson sought to position *Machine Art* firmly within the context and continuum of the decorative arts, along with an established relationship to the architecture of its time, Barr, in his introduction, provided an overview that was at least as provocative, if not more so: "The Italian futurists, Russolo and Balla, and their English and Russian followers were romantically excited by the power and speed—the *dinamismo*—of machines. Painters such as Léger and Baumeister have been interested in the decorative and formal qualities of machines. Malyevitch, Lissitsky, and Mondriaan have used technicians' tools, the compass and the square, to achieve 'abstract' geometrical paintings of machine-like precision. Picabia and Grosz used machines to invoke the mirthless laughter of dadaism."[115]

Barr knew, however, that the presence of the machine as an inspiration in the work of these artists was not in itself a rationalization for bringing the machine into a museum, any more than exhibiting oranges because Cézanne and Matisse had painted them. It could even be argued that, in the eyes of some conservative critics, a roll call of machine-influenced modern artists would have been evidence of the exhibition's weakness. Indeed, the tremendous reaction to the show in the press was less related to Barr's invocation of modern painters and sculptors than to his references to Plato. His introduction opens with a particularly well-chosen quote from the philosopher's *Philebus:* "'By beauty of shapes I do not mean, as most people would suppose, the beauty of living figures or of pictures, but, to make my point clear, I mean straight lines and circles, and shapes, plane or solid, made from them by lathe, ruler and square. These are not, like other things, beautiful relatively, but always and absolutely.'"[116] Barr elaborated: "In Plato's day the tools were simple handworker's implements but today, as a result of the perfection of modern materials and the precision of modern instruments, the modern machine-made object approaches far more closely and more frequently those pure shapes the contemplation of which Plato calls the first of the 'pure pleasures.'"[117]

The implications of Barr's words were clear, and provocative. Much of the new thinking in art, architecture, and design had agitated for a stronger role for abstraction, utility, and geometry in creating a work of art, as opposed to academic notions of beauty. Barr's argument stood many others, such as those put forth by the adherents of the New Objectivity, on end, arguing that the more objective, abstract, utilitarian, and geometrical an object became the closer it was to Plato's classical notion of *absolute* beauty. In other words, beauty was a natural product of the machine's functional processes: Objects were not functional *as opposed to* beautiful, but beautiful *because* they were functional, or at the least because they embodied the dynamic functional ethos of the machine.

John Dewey, the American pragmatist philosopher, considered Barr's point: "I think it somewhat extraordinary that modern machine production for industrial purposes should illustrate as well as it does the statement of Plato regarding the abstract beauty of geometric forms, made before any such thing as machinery existed. I hope that all those who are skeptical about the aesthetic possibilities of machine production will see the Exhibition. To my mind there is convincing proof that there is no essential opposition between production for utility and for beauty."[118]

Ironically, Barr's simple rhetorical equation is not unlike Ralph Waldo Emerson's speculations on aesthetics. Each in their own way argued that beauty derived from utility—that the two were, in fact, inseparable. Even so, their points of view could not have been more opposed. Emerson believed the equation of form and function derived from nature: "Beauty must come back to the useful arts, and distinction between the fine arts and the useful art be forgotten. . . . In nature all is useful, all is beautiful."[119] Furthermore, his concerns about the ill-effects of the machine on the landscape led him to call for an integration of the machine and nature, while Barr's concerns were principally about the integration of the machine and culture. In addition to Plato (and St. Thomas Aquinas), Barr included the words of the contemporary critic Lawrence Pearsall Jacks in his foreword: "'Industrial civilization must either find a means of ending the divorce between its industry and its "culture" or perish.'"[120]

If the relatively brief texts by Barr and Johnson raised a great number of issues, they also left a great number of questions unanswered. Indeed, it is unclear how Barr might have sustained his highly selective references to Plato and the machine in a longer, more detailed analysis. Plato himself did not elaborate at length on the topic in the *Philebus;* the quote is actually a rather isolated observation. It could even be said that the interjection of Plato somewhat obscured a more interesting and potentially more provocative point. As if taking a cue from Le Corbusier's dictum to heed the engineers but beware the architects, Barr had suggested in 1928, in his review of the Necco factory (fig. 28), that engineers were creating new architectural forms precisely because they were ignoring established aesthetic rules.[121]

As such, the Necco factory (which Barr had visited with his students as part of his seminar on modern art at Wellesley College) represented a kind of indigenous architecture of industrialized culture—an unfortunately underdeveloped thesis of the *Machine Art* exhibition. Nonetheless, it may be argued that the open-ended nature of the debate surrounding the Platonic ideal provided the press with a clear opportunity to participate in the exhibition's premise. After what he perceived as lackluster coverage of the *Modern Architecture* show, Johnson had remarked: "For the most part the critics either make excerpts from the catalog, or if they are constitutionally opposed to modern architecture, they merely remark that the Exhibition displeases them."[122] Neither he nor Barr could say the same about the media reaction to *Machine Art.* Some of the most prominent journalists of the day weighed in with long and thoughtful articles, both positive and negative, none missing the opportunity to deal with Plato. Henry McBride's article for the New York *Sun* led with a populist edge: "[I]f you should happen to be a plumber—gracious heavens! how this show will set you up! It's the first real 'break' the plumbers have ever had."[123] (A cartoon in *The New Yorker* made a similar point; see fig. 29.) But McBride quickly got serious, taking on Barr's reference to Plato and citing Friedrich von Schiller, Henri Stendhal, and Samuel Butler as he wrote critically of the show: "I refuse to pretend . . . that a machine is a human and that its children can be works of art."

Helen Appleton Read's reaction was more positive, and passionate: "Atavistic emotions are stirred by the precise, shining, geometric shapes of the spheres, cubes and cylinders of metal and glass."[124] Her article fairly plunged into the exhibition, drawing on William Morris, the Bauhaus, and Thorstein Veblen's influential *Theory of the Leisure Class* (1899). Anita Brenner of *The Nation* also wrote of the show at length in the *Nation,* urging artists to take it seriously: "There is no reason, except perhaps business, why artists should not be served by the machine instead of only serving it. At present, however, it still comes hard to the manual craftsman, such as every painter and sculptor still is, to make his peace with higher mechanics. In order to do so he must learn his trade all over again, and people

28. Lockwood and Greene. Necco factory, Cambridge-port, Massachusetts. ca. 1928

"Recognition at last! The Museum of Modern Art wants to give me a one-man show."

29. Cartoon published in the April 14, 1934, issue of *The New Yorker* **on the occasion of the** *Machine Art* **exhibition**

tend to defend what they know against what they don't know. Besides, the artist is sentimentally attached to the palette and chisel and quiet studio and easel and Greek fragment. Spray-guns, electric drills, and laboratories imply a terrifying new world, and it takes brave men to master it."[125]

Machine Art certainly did not serve as a final word on the difficult theoretical issues it raised, but, as a good exhibition should, it served as a catalyst, prompting serious discourse in both the popular and the critical press. The debate was so extended that critics began quoting other reviews, such as the *New York Literary Digest*'s citation of Royal Cortissoz's negative assessments of *Machine Art*, previously published in the *New York Herald Tribune*;[126] and the *Richmond News-Leader*'s quotation of both Edward Alden Jewell's review in *The New York Times* and McBride's review in the *Sun*.[127] In fact, Jewell wrote not only a review but a preview piece as well. In the former he wrote: "Nearly everything in the exhibition seemed to me beautiful . . . yet I found it . . . impossible to perceive beauty as not inextricably bound up in the function of the object. Nor, somehow, did this fascinating show seem to me less significant on that account."[128]

The reactions of the popular press were often fueled by the impossible-to-pass-up opportunity to mock the Museum's high-brow stance: the *New York Herald Tribune*'s headline read: "Pots and Sinks Going on View as Art at Machinery Exhibit." The *Los Angeles Times:* "Is Beauty the Same Thing in Auto's Lines and in Sunset?" And again, the *Herald Tribune:* " Piece of Spring Wins Art Show Beauty Award."[129] The last refers to an aspect of the exhibition that came as close as can be imagined to Ms. Read's definition of an "ultra stunt." A committee—consisting of John Dewey; Amelia Earhart; Charles R. Richards, director of the Museum of Science and Industry, Chicago; and U.S. Secretary of Labor Frances Perkins—was asked to select the three most beautiful objects in the exhibition. Earhart, having gained fame as one of America's aviation pioneers, was a media star in her own right, and many of the show's notices included a photograph of her posed with a section of a large spring made by the American Steel and Wire Company, of which she said: "I chose this section of spring because it is satisfactory from every angle. One doesn't have to know what it is to appreciate its form"[130] (fig. 30). Another popular aspect of the show was the balloting system by which museum-goers could cast a vote for their favorite exhibit—a rather dramatic example of what the Museum had signaled in stating that *Machine Art* would not be an art exhibition in the usual sense.

As opposed to many of the Museum's early exhibitions, the proportion of by-lined, rather than wire-copy, reviews was extraordinarily high. The length and personal nature of the media's reaction had as much to do with the vast amount that was left unsaid as that which was explicitly laid out by Barr and Johnson in their texts. Certainly the exhibition struck a nerve and, given Barr and Johnson's growing talents for doing so, that was no doubt intentional. Even so, the most negative critiques reserved some positive comment for the installation, designed by Johnson in collaboration with Jan Ruhtenberg, a young architect who had been introduced to Mies van der Rohe by Johnson and who had subsequently worked for him. The more effusive accounts were unstinting in their admiration. Jewell of *The New York Times* wrote: "First of all, the exhibition is splendidly installed. To make possible this elaborate yet in its elements severely simple installation, the interior of the museum has had virtually to be built over. Backgrounds have been carefully planned, so that

30. Amelia Earhart with the bearing spring she selected as the "most beautiful object" included in the *Machine Art* exhibition, 1934

the most telling effect might be contrived."[131] Margaret Breuning of the *Post* stated simply: "The installation can be unreservedly praised."[132]

Epilogue

Johnson's success as a curator lay in his ability to fulfill a potential that Barr (and undoubtedly he) saw in exhibitions of architecture and design, above and beyond their intrinsic curatorial messages. Freed from many of the constraints that surrounded the exhibition of painting and sculpture, Johnson had wide latitude to promote Barr's views in a more populist, and often more ardent, fashion than was otherwise possible within a museum context. Barr not only supported Johnson's unorthodox methods but was himself freed to suggest, for example, the picketing of the Architectural League's exclusion of what the two men called "real modern architecture"—a public demonstration that furthered the "cause" of modernism without the possible backlash had Barr and Johnson picketed, say, the Metropolitan for not showing "real modern art." Nor is it easy to imagine Barr installing a borrowed sculpture on the steps of the Fifty-third Street townhouse in the manner of Johnson placing an eight-foot-diameter marine propeller at the Museum's entrance during the *Machine Art* exhibition. Similarly, it is hard to conceive of Barr staging painting exhibitions similar to *Objects 1900 and Today,* in which lenders might have found their works installed in such a way that the viewer was invited, however tacitly, to criticize them.

Johnson has said, self-deprecatingly, of the International Style project: "[Barr] coined the phrase, Russell Hitchcock wrote the book, and I was the drummer and screamer-arounder."[133] On other occasions he has referred to his early role at the Museum as that of "a propagandist."[134] Beyond the colorfulness of this self-characterization, Johnson's statements in this regard merit some attention. In the late 1920s and early 1930s, the United States and Europe were adjusting to the realities of mass communications. The newly discovered ability to use the media to champion a cause publicly was both exciting and alarming to various cultural and political pundits. Edward L. Bernays, in his influential book *Crystallizing Public Opinion* (1923), noted: "The only difference between 'propaganda' and 'education,' really, is in the point of view. The advocacy of what we believe in is education. The advocacy of what we don't believe in is propaganda."[135]

Bernays had worked for the U.S. Office of War Information during World War I and subsequently went to work in New York, calling himself (and coining a new term) a "public relations counsel."[136] Quite early in its history, the Museum paid a retainer to Bernays for advice on public relations.[137] Given Johnson's remarkable ability to use the media to broadcast the Museum's message, one wonders if Bernays's services were really necessary. Johnson was articulate, passionately motivated, rich, and media-savvy—qualities that created a symbiotic relationship between the young curator and the burgeoning mass media.

Bernays could have been describing Johnson when, writing about various ways of influencing public opinion, he cited a psychologist's list of seven primary instincts, expounding at length on one of these: pugnacity. "The public relations counsel uses this continually in constructing all kinds of events that will call it into play. . . . He stages battles against evils in which the antagonist is personified for the public."[138] The difference between Bernays's rather cynical attitude and Johnson's youthful ardor aside, the latter's proactive stance is reflected in the former's writings. Johnson consistently endeavored to ensure that "the antagonist" was "personified for the public" in each of his exhibitions: In the International Style project, the antagonists were "modernistic" Art Deco designers in the United States and *sachlich* functionalists in Europe; in *Young Architects,* academia and Art Deco "stylists"; in *Early Modern Architecture,* the New York skyscraper school; and in *Machine Art,* the Arts and Crafts movement and, yet again, Art Deco. In Bernays's terms, *Objects 1900 and Today* stands out as Johnson's sole effort where pugnacity gave way to politesse and criticism to neutral appreciation.

Everett Dean Martin, director of the Cooper Union Forum, a prominent New York venue for public debate, provided additional insight into the public reaction to Johnson's exhibitions: "Nothing so easily catches general attention and creates a crowd as a contest of any kind."[139] The extent to which Johnson was willing to engage the contestants in his world was demonstrated by his arranging to send the *Young Architects* exhibition to the Chicago Century of Progress Exposition, an exploit akin to sending a modern Daniel into the lion's den of Art Deco. Certainly, Johnson's ability to draw a crowd had a lot to do with his tendency to conceive of his exhibitions as showdowns between the "good guys" and the "bad guys." The introduction of a literal contest—that is, the celebrity jury for *Machine Art*—and reaction to it in the press further validates Martin's observation as an element of Johnson's style.

In assessing the substance and long-term effects of Johnson's early shows, there is as much evidence of their critical success as there is of their stylishness. Some of these successes were mixed, however. The careers of Priestley and Wood, as well as those of the participants in *Young Architects,* did not fulfill the expectations raised by Johnson's attention. Even so, the concept of proactive, speculative exhibitions of younger designers' early works is now widely accepted by professional and cultural organizations. Various other Museum exhibitions, such as *Hidden Talent* in 1949 and *Visionary Architecture* in 1960, can be traced to this precedent.[140] Moreover, book publishers today are more than willing to issue monographs on younger architects, covering relatively brief careers that are long on unrealized projects and short on built work.

The impact of *Objects 1900 and Today* is not as easily assessed. Ironically, given Johnson's implied preference, the only objects from that exhibition to remain in the permanent design collection of The Museum of Modern Art—the ornate silver box designed by Archibald Knox and the floral art-glass lamp by Tiffany Studios—are "decorative" rather than "useful." These pieces formed the nucleus of what would become a substantial collection of Art Nouveau holdings during the tenure of Arthur Drexler, director of the Department of Architecture and Design from 1956 to 1987. In this light it might be said that Johnson's relatively benign, if not wholly positive, assessment of Art Nouveau in *Objects 1900 and Today* paved the way for the eventual embrace of that "style of ornament." (Needless to say, the arm's-length approach to Art Deco has remained as virtual policy at the Museum for six decades, although somewhat recent acquisitions of work by Eileen Gray and René Herbst push the definition.) The exhibition's emphasis on "useful" design may also have influenced the series of annual design exhibitions initiated by Johnson's immediate successor, John McAndrew, in 1938. Titled "Useful Objects," the series stressed functionality as well as economy, the majority featuring consumer products costing no more than five to ten dollars each.[141]

More than *Objects 1900 and Today* could have, *Machine Art* firmly launched the idea of a curatorial department devoted to design and a permanent collection of design objects within the Museum. While other institutions had staged contemporary design exhibitions, the Museum's establishment of the Department of Architecture (in 1932), the design collection (1935), and the Department of Industrial Design (1940) was truly innovative, and widely imitated. Many of the objects exhibited in *Machine Art* remain in the design collection today. Beyond these broadreaching effects, it must be said that the exhibition, with all of its Platonic associations, was more an art-critical sensation than a lasting influence on the development of design as a discipline. Even so, *Machine Art* effectively established The Museum of Modern Art as the place where contemporary design was most visibly presented and vigorously debated, and was implicitly a challenge to The Metropolitan Museum of Art's annual industrial arts show. In 1934, Mumford acknowledged this rivalry: "Except in details, the exhibition now at the Metropolitan Museum is marking time. There has been no substantial advance over the forms that were on view five years ago. What is lacking in this exhibition is at least one modest room, composed of run-of-the-mill products, such as Mr. Philip Johnson recently showed at the Museum of Modern Art."[142]

The show that Mumford was reviewing might even be considered the Metropolitan's final attempt to influence contemporary design, effectively ceding the field to Johnson and his successors at the Museum. Yet, notwithstanding the virtual hegemony McAndrew, Eliot Noyes, Edgar J. Kaufmann, Jr., and Drexler would enjoy over design exhibitions through the 1960s, no single accomplishment of Johnson's curatorial career can rival his identification of Mies as the pivotal figure of modern architecture. In fact, it may be said that such an accomplishment is what all curators aspire to: the singular, prescient identification of the significance of the present and the direction of the future. In this respect Johnson's estimation of Mies's import was wholly independent of Hitchcock's or Barr's. In his book *Modern Architecture: Romanticism and Reintegration* Hitchcock's opinion of Mies's work was certainly secondary to that of Gropius. Hitchcock described Mies as successful in his "technical experimentation" but decried the residual expressionism, as he saw it, in the architect's steel-and-glass towers.[143] He was more positive about the Weissenhof Housing Settlement and the Barcelona Pavilion, but ended his remarks with only a cautious endorsement: Mies was "primarily a man of promise."[144] Likewise, before Johnson's advocacy of Mies, Barr frequently cited Oud, Le Corbusier, and Gropius as the leaders of the new architecture, with no mention of Mies.[145]

By the time *Modern Architecture—International Exhibition* opened in 1932, both Barr and Hitchcock had revised their estimations of Mies's work; the turning point appears to have been Johnson's photographs and descriptions of his visit to the Tugendhat House in Brno (figs. 31, 32) in August 1930, after which they added Mies to their list of the three leading new architects, eliminating Gropius. At this later date, Hitchcock also wrote more admiringly of the Barcelona project and referred to Mies as an aesthetic, as opposed to technical, "innovator,"[146] although it was Johnson who wrote Mies's entry in the *Modern Architecture* catalogue (Hitchcock wrote those of the eight others).

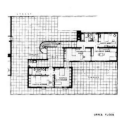

It is clear that Johnson was impressed by his first, somewhat modest encounter with Mies's built work, a series of apartment renovations in Berlin designed with Lilly Reich. He immediately wrote to his mother seeking permission to hire Mies to redesign his own apartment in New York. Johnson's response to Mies's interior work, which he characterized as "elegant" and "simple,"[147] was enthusiastic, but it paled next to his later description of, and instinctive rapport with, the Tugendhat House (figs. 31, 32): "He has one room, very low ceilinged, one hundred feet long, toward the south all of glass from the ceiling to the very floor. Great sheets of plate glass that go into the floor electrically. The side of the room is at least thirty feet and is glass to the east. This room is divided into dining room, library and living room by partial walls which do not in the least destroy its size, but rather magnify it."[148] The building's complex spatial qualities, so immediately grasped by Johnson, in a sense exceeded Hitchcock's own expectations for the International Style. For Johnson's part, his visit to Brno confirmed his intent to commission Mies; he would write of his meeting with the architect: "Mies is the greatest man that . . . I have ever met. Oud I like better, I almost love Oud, such a dear man he is besides being a genius, but Mies is a great man."[149]

Certainly the *Modern Architecture* show would have had lasting significance whether or not Johnson had included Mies. First and foremost, it established the precedent of mounting contemporary architecture exhibitions within a museum context, creating a model that not only influenced the Museum's course over the succeeding six decades but also had an effect on the programs of museums throughout the world. Furthermore, Gropius's appointment to head the Graduate School of Design at Harvard, a watershed in American architectural education, is hard to imagine without the introduction of his work to a broad segment of the profession via the *Modern Architecture* exhibition. The longevity of the term "International Style" is further evidence of the curators' acuity in introducing various aspects of European modernism in the United States. While Hitchcock would come to realize that the work presented in *Modern Architecture* was in fact somewhat dated by 1932, the elasticity of their definition of the International Style served to prescribe the course of postwar American (and, to an extent, European) architecture for nearly thirty-five years after the term was coined. Still, it is hard to imagine that the Museum's first architecture exhibition would have had the same vitality had it not been for Johnson's "great man," Mies van der Rohe.

Left:
31. Ludwig Mies van der Rohe. Tugendhat House, Brno, Czechoslovakia. Garden façade. 1930. Included in *Modern Architecture—International Exhibition*, The Museum of Modern Art, New York, 1932

Right:
32. Ludwig Mies van der Rohe. Tugendhat House, Brno, Czechoslovakia. Plans. 1930.

Of Johnson's many other achievements, a final curatorial accomplishment, one that would have a direct impact on the future, must be noted. Johnson's near self-invention, at the age of twenty-four, as an influential voice in the world of architecture and design was unprecedented, and remains unmatched to this day. It is probably too much to expect that in his early years—which Johnson described then as the first time he had known "enough about anything . . . to be boring to people"[150]— his message would be clearly defined, which it was not. For example, no issue seems to have vexed him more than the relative roles of functional and aesthetic criteria in the design process. In his early exhibitions Johnson continuously sought to define a position that would represent his conflicting desires to be equally influential in the two worlds to which he had access: the intellectual and highly aestheticized milieu of The Museum of Modern Art, and the more pragmatic arena of commerce and industry of his midwestern roots.

In the *Modern Architecture* exhibition, Johnson argued that the two were not mutually exclusive, that the aesthetic dimension of modernism was not irreconcilable with utilitarian and commercial concerns. In his subsequent shows it could even be said that greater emphasis was placed on the utilitarian. The skyscraper show lauded the "engineer-architects" for concentrating on the development and refinement of steel-framed, nonload-bearing, curtain-wall construction over the formal sensations and predilictions of the New York skyscraper school. In *Objects 1900 and Today* the essential difference between the two periods was an emphasis on ornament rather than utility, the former being characterized as old-fashioned. In *Work of Young Architects in the Middle West* the balance between the aesthetic and the utilitarian, as presented in *Modern Architecture,* was fundamentally reversed: If that first exhibition might be characterized primarily as a formal exercise, with accommodation made for the various functional mechanisms related to politics, economics, and sociology, *Young Architects,* more than any other exhibition organized by Johnson, placed practical concerns above aesthetic distinction. With *Machine Art* Johnson came full circle, in that the function was shown to be inseparable from formal beauty.

Johnson's efforts in the early years of the Museum therefore cannot be seen as having a single underlying theme. Rather, they reflected a vast panoply of the issues of the day: the shifting relationships between European and American modernism, high and low culture, architecture and design, the machine and craft, the aesthetic and the pragmatic. What unites his efforts is a young man's self-assurance, a belief that all challenges could be met, that every assumption should be questioned, and that no limits should be placed on the pursuit of the Art of the Now.

Notes

Portions of this text were originally published in Terence Riley, *The International Style: Exhibition 15 and The Museum of Modern Art* (New York: Trustees of Columbia University and Rizzoli International Publications, 1992). Bevin Howard, Research Assistant in the Department of Architecture and Design, and intern Elspeth Cowell located many of the archival materials used to expand the original text; I am indebted to them both. Rona Roob, Chief Archivist, and her staff in the Museum Archives also provided invaluable research assistance. Readers of an early draft included Franz Schulze and Harriet Schoenholz Bee, Managing Editor in the Department of Publications, whose thoughful comments were extremely helpful. I also want to thank my assistant, Caren Oestereich, for her help in preparing the final manuscript.

The Museum of Modern Art Archives will be abbreviated throughout these notes as *MoMA Archives*. The designations *Architecture and Design archive* and *Registrar's archive* refer to uncatalogued source material housed in the Museum's Department of Architecture and Design and Department of Registration, respectively.

1. See Selected Bibliography, in Franz Schulze, *Philip Johnson: Life and Work* (New York: Alfred A. Knopf, 1994), pp. 444–50.
2. Helen Appleton Read, "Machine Art: Modern Museum Provides Long-Awaited Last Chapter in Machine Age Esthetics—Social and Economic Aspects Convincingly Set Forth," *Brooklyn Eagle,* March 11, 1934 (clipping). MoMA Archives: Public Information Scrapbooks, no. 13.
3. Hitchcock was never formally on the Museum's staff, although he consulted on the curatorial aspects of several important shows. While Johnson was designated chairman of the Museum's Department of Architecture, he, like Barr before him, has repeatedly credited Hitchcock for his curatorial acumen.
4. Letter, Alfred H. Barr, Jr., to Paul J. Sachs, July 1, 1929; cited in Russell Lynes, *Good Old Modern: An Intimate Portrait of The Museum of Modern Art* (New York: Atheneum, 1973), p. 33.
5. Barr's own lack of a doctorate had more to do with circumstance than academic ambition. At the time he was chosen to head The Museum of Modern Art in 1929, he had completed the coursework for his Ph.D. and was slated to begin work on his dissertation at New York University's Institute of Fine Arts. Other members of the early Museum's staff had academic backgrounds, but Barr did not consider it a prerequisite. None of Johnson's successors held advanced degrees, and in fact, most were professionally trained as architects rather than historians. Arthur Drexler, director of the department from 1956 to 1987, had no university degree at all.
6. Examples of Hitchcock's published works include *Frank Lloyd Wright* (Paris: Cahiers d'Art, 1928), *Modern Architecture: Romanticism and Rein-* *tegration* (New York: Payson and Clarke, 1929; rpt., New York: Hacker, 1970), and *Architecture: Nineteenth and Twentieth Centuries* (Baltimore: Penguin Books, 1958).
7. Barr had first met Johnson in 1929 at the graduation of Johnson's sister Theodate from Wellesley College, where Barr was then teaching his famous course on modern art. Within a month of their meeting, Barr was approached by Mrs. John D. (Abby Aldrich) Rockefeller, Jr., to head The Museum of Modern Art. Johnson subsequently became a frequent visitor to New York and a member of the Museum's Junior Advisory Committee, with which he was involved at the time of his appointment as director of the *Modern Architecture* exhibition.
8. Letter, Johnson to Barr, undated [July 1931] Department of Registration exhibition files: MoMA Exh. #15, Johnson–Blackburn/Barr Correspondence.
9. Letter, Johnson to J. J. P. Oud, August 30, [1931]. Department of Registration exhibition files: MoMA Exh. #15, J. J. P. Oud Correspondence. Bruenn is the German name for Brno.
10. Letter, Johnson to Mrs. Homer H. Johnson, August 6, 1930. Architecture and Design archive: 1932 Project.
11. *Modern Architecture—International Exhibition* (New York: The Museum of Modern Art and W. W. Norton, 1932), catalogue by Henry-Russell Hitchcock, Philip Johnson, and Lewis Mumford, was published in a paperback edition for sale at the Museum and in a hardcover trade edition under the title *Modern Architects*. At roughly the same time, Hitchcock and Johnson published another book, *The International Style: Architecture Since 1922* (New York: W. W. Norton, 1932; rpt. 1966, 1995), which is frequently taken to be the catalogue of the *Modern Architecture* exhibition. To confuse matters further, the exhibition's title is very similar to that of Hitchcock's 1929 book, *Modern Architecture: Romanticism and Reintegration.*
12. "With the Aluminum Company and with private people I have tried to arrange work for you. In January a prominent New Yorker, wishing to have his apartment done, was willing to pay for your passage and to engage you to do this work" (letter, Johnson to Ludwig Mies van der Rohe, undated [March 1931]). Architecture and Design archive: 1932 Project. Despite the gender reference, the "prominent New Yorker" was Mrs. John D. Rockefeller, Jr., and the commission was to design an art gallery for her New York apartment. The commission ultimately went to Donald Deskey.
13. Letter, Elizabeth B. Mock to Monroe Bowman, June 14, 1944. Department of Registration exhibition files: MoMA Exh. #15, Bowman Brothers Corporation.
14. Johnson mentioned Oud to his mother in a letter of June 20, 1930: "And if we ever, ever build, I would have perfect confidence in him even on the other side of the ocean, something which I cannot say of Corbusier." Architecture and Design archive: 1932 Project.

Johnson discussed the project with Oud soon thereafter; in a letter to Johnson of November 12, Oud responded: "I think I could do now a big thing after so many experiences with other things and it must be 'herrlich,' to make important buildings in good material. To make 'Raum' has also to do something with architecture and now 'Raum' I could make were nearly only streets: interesting also of course but it has to be combined with 'Raum' inside also and the labourer dwellings of very low prices are not the best objects for this." Department of Registration exhibition files: MoMA Exh. #15, J. J. P. Oud Correspondence.
15. It is not clear whether the senior Johnsons seriously considered Clauss and Daub for the Pinehurst project or whether Johnson encouraged them to use the proposal as a propaganda piece. It was published in the November 1931 issue of *Architectural Record* and displayed at the *Rejected Architects* exhibition. In addition to the Pinehurst proposal, Clauss and Daub exhibited a house for "Mrs. Charles Lindberg," which apparently had not been commissioned and which drew an angry letter from Delano and Aldrich, who had been commissioned by Charles Lindberg to design their house; see letter, Johnson to Delano and Aldrich, February 2, 1932. Department of Registration exhibition files: MoMA Exh. #15, Blackburn Correspondence—Incoming. Alfred Clauss also built the models exhibited in Johnson's subsequent exhibition, *Early Modern Architecture: Chicago 1870–1919,* in 1933.
16. Johnson's attempt to purchase some of Le Corbusier's drawings was unsuccessful: "He had some plans to sell at what I thought would be around a hundred dollars, so we dickered and dickered only to find out that he was talking dollars and I francs" (letter, Johnson to Mrs. H. Johnson, June 20, 1930). Architecture and Design Archive: 1932 Project.

Some of the pieces of furniture Johnson purchased that summer can be seen in photographs of his apartment that appeared in the exhibition and in *The International Style* and are now part of the Museum's permanent collection. The painting by Mondrian (*Composition,* 1925) is also in the Museum's collection and was purchased on Johnson's behalf out of Mondrian's studio by Hitchcock.
17. *The Staatliches Bauhaus, Dessau,* held at the Harvard Society of Contemporary Art in Cambridge, Massachusetts, December 13, 1930–January 17, 1931, included paintings by Lyonel Feininger, Wassily Kandinsky, Erich Borchert, and Johannes Itton, as well as photographs (from Johnson's own collection) of the work of Walter Gropius and of Mies van der Rohe's Barcelona Pavilion.
18. "The Museum of Modern Art and Columbia University would like to invite you to come to this country for two months in late winter or early spring to give lectures and perhaps to work with architectural students" (letter, Johnson to Oud, November 23, 1933). This was Johnson's second attempt to get Oud to come to America. Oud's first response apparently did not discourage Johnson's efforts: "What about the business you wrote about?

I am not a man for teaching and also a 'princely salary.' . . . I like the real work of 'building' and only if I could get building-possibilities [sic] by it I should think a bit of teaching—a little. Naturally it would be another question to work a month or so with students on projects. But lecturing as a rule in schools and so—Brr!" (letter, Oud to Johnson, May 3, 1932). All correspondence, Department of Registration exhibition files: MoMA Exh. #15, J. J. P. Oud Correspondence.

19.   The exhibited architects were younger practitioners whose work had not been chosen for the 1931 Architectural League annual: Clauss and Daub, Stonorov and Morgan, Hazen Sise, William Muschenhiem, Walter Baermann, Elroy Webber, and Richard C. Wood (who was subsequently given a one-man exhibition at the Modern—organized by Johnson; see pp. 54–55). The exhibition was held in a West Fifty-seventh Street storefront near Seventh Avenue, in a building owned by the art dealer Julian Levy's father. See Robert A.M. Stern, Gregory Gilmartin, and Thomas Mellins, *New York 1930: Architecture and Urbanism Between the Two World Wars* (New York: Rizzoli, 1987), pp. 343–44, for further references.

20.   The organization seems to have had only one formal meeting, on January 25, 1932. The Temporary Committee is listed in the minutes (file 8036, Lewis Mumford Papers, University of Pennsylvania, Philadelphia) as Clauss, Johnson, Alfred Kastner, Norman Rice, and Richard C. Wood. Other attendees listed are Catherine Bauer, Walter Baermann, Simon Brines, George Daub, Albert Frey, Hitchcock, K. Löndberg-Holm, George Howe, Percival Goodman, Frederic Kiesler, William E. Lescaze, John Moore, William Muschenheim, Lyman Paine, Lewis Stone, Kenneth Stowell, and Julian Whittlesey. The principal business discussed at the meeting were plans for an exhibition in April of that year and a long discussion about the group and its purpose. Bauer provided a somewhat critical account of the evening: "I confined myself (almost) to an occasional sneering: 'But *is* it a group?' But I don't mean to be *quite* so nasty . . . it wasn't altogether disheartening to see so many people ready to fight for *something*, even though they hadn't the faintest idea what (except that in some way every sentence of their public credo must be worded so as to convey to Mr. Hood that not if he came on his hands and knees would he be allowed in)" (letter, Bauer to Mumford, January 16, 1932). University of Pennsylvania, Philadelphia: Mumford Papers, file 8036.

21.   Typescript, "The Proposed Architectural Exhibition for the Museum of Modern Art," undated [December 1930]. Department of Registration exhibition files: MoMA Exh. #15, Program, Checklist, Model Information.

22.   See Letter, Johnson to Mumford, January 3, 1931. University of Pennsylvania, Philadelphia: Mumford Papers, file 8036.

23.   Philip Johnson, *Built to Live In* (New York: The Museum of Modern Art, 1931).

24.   Bel Geddes apparently fell out of favor with Johnson during this time, possibly due to his participation in the Architectural League annual exhibition: "The trips of Norman Bel-Geddes and Joseph Urban to Europe have made ribbon windows the mode, even if these men have never fully understood the new architecture" (Philip Johnson, "Rejected Architects," *Creative Art* 8, no. 6 [June 1931], p. 435).

25.   "Architecture is always a set of actual monuments, not a vague corpus of theory" (Hitchcock and Johnson, *The International Style*, p. 21).

26.   Alfred H. Barr, Jr., "The Necco Factory," *The Arts* 13, no. 5 (May 1928), pp. 292–95; and "Notes on Russian Architecture," *The Arts* 15, no. 2 (February 1929), pp. 103–06.

27.   For a more detailed discussion of the term, see Terence Riley, *The International Style: Exhibition 15 and The Museum of Modern Art* (New York: Rizzoli, 1992), pp. 89–93.

28.   Philip Johnson, "The Architecture of the New School," *The Arts* 17, no. 6 (March 1931), pp. 393, 398.

29.   "Rejected Architects," exhibition pamphlet, 1931; reprinted in Riley, *The International Style: Exhibition 15 and The Museum of Modern Art*, p. 215.

30.   "Rejected Architects," op. cit., p. 434. Ely Jacques Kahn was the president of the Architectural League. Deems Taylor, who was himself a musician and wrote mostly on music, apparently reviewed the exhibition, although it is not known for which publication. Douglas Haskell reviewed both *Rejected Architects* and the League exhibition; see Haskell, "The Column, The Gable and Box," *The Arts* 17, no. 9 (June 1931), pp. 63–69.

31.   Lawrence Wodehouse's footnote indicating that the museum remained in the Heckscher Building until 1939 is incorrect (Wodehouse, *The Roots of International Style Architecture* [West Cornwall, Conn.: Locust Hill Press, 1991], n. 1, p.xiii). In 1932, the Museum was relocated to a townhouse at 11 West Fifty-third Street, where it remained until 1939, when a new building was erected on the site of the townhouse and three adjacent rowhouses.

32.   "Exhibition of Modern Architecture with Models," exhibition pamphlet (1934). Department of Registration exhibition files: MoMA Exh. #15, Program, Checklist, Model Information.

33.   Letter, Alan Blackburn to Howe and Lescaze, July 8, 1931. Department of Registration exhibition files: MoMA Exh. #15, Blackburn Correspondence—Incoming.

34.   Philip Johnson, "The Architectural Exhibition," typescript, February 10, 1931. Department of Registration exhibition files: MoMA Exh. #15, Program, Checklist, Model Information.

35.   Letter, Blackburn to Howe and Lescaze, July 8, 1931, op. cit.

36.   Letter, Johnson to Barr, July 11, 1931. Department of Registration exhibition files: MoMA Exh. #15, Johnson—Barr/Blackburn Correspondence. Johnson, like many members of the educated upper class, had a certain paternalistic sympathy with the plight of the impoverished working class, although this sympathy rarely involved a critique of the financial and social status quo. Before proposing his plans for involving industry and capital in solving the housing crises he remarked: "And now I notice that Hoover is to appoint a committee to see about building some Siedlungen, at least that is what our papers tell us. I hope it is true and that they will study the American situation as regards the housing of the worker. But isn't it rather socialistic of our dear president. The U.S. Government to build houses! I only hope they do" (letter, Johnson to Mrs. Homer H. Johnson, August 6, 1930). Architecture and Design archive: 1932 Project.

37.   Letter, Johnson to Barr, July 11, 1931, op. cit.

38.   Ibid.

39.   Philip Johnson, interoffice memorandum, September 24, 1931. Department of Registration exhibition files: MoMA Exh. #15: Program, Checklist, Model Information.

40.   See Matilda McQuaid, "Lilly Reich and the Art of Exhibition Design," in McQuaid, *Lilly Reich, Designer and Architect* (New York: The Museum of Modern Art, 1996), pp. 26–39.

41.   Shipping memorandum, undated (pre-installation). Architecture and Design archive: 1932 Project. *Modern Architecture—International Exhibition* was originally conceived, for a number of reasons (not least of all, financial), as a traveling exhibition. The venues on the exhibition's tour were referred to as subscribers.

42.   Letter, Johnson to Oud, March 17, 1932. Department of Registration exhibition files: MoMA Exh. #15, J. J. P. Oud Correspondence.

43.   See Schulze, *Philip Johnson: Life and Work,* pp. 80–81.

44.   "Miniature Apartment Dwellings to Be Included in Display at Wadsworth," *Courant* (Hartford, Conn.), April 22, 1932.

45.   "Modern Architecture at Art Museum," *Sunday Telegram* (Worcester, Mass.), June 18, 1933 (clipping). MoMA Archives: Public Information Scrapbooks, General X.

46.   "International Type Architecture to Be Shown at Morgan," *Courant* (Hartford, Conn.), April 21, 1932.

47.   Henry-Russell Hitchcock, "Architectural Criticism," *Shelter* 2, no. 3 (April 1932), p. 2.

48.   "The text seems to me (as far as I read it) excellent. The school mastering under the illustrations I don't like" (letter, Oud to Johnson, April 6, 1932). Department of Registration exhibition files: MoMA Exh. #15, J. J. P. Oud Correspondence.

49.   Letter, R. M. Schindler to Johnson, March 9, 1932. Department of Registration exhibition files: MoMA Exh. #15, Johnson, Philip—Correspondence.

50.   Letter, Wright to Johnson, January 18, 1932. Department of Registration exhibition files: MoMA Exh. #15, Frank Lloyd Wright Correspondence. It should be noted that it is not clear from the preceding nor the subsequent correspondence whether "amateur" and "salesman" refer to the curators or Wright's colleagues in the exhibition, Hood and Neutra.

51. "But being in some degree essential to the propaganda as the promoters of the exhibition see it I have consented to go along with them if I might state my own feelings in plain terms alongside their own statements. 'Of Thee I Sing' is that somewhat ungracious statement" (Frank Lloyd Wright, "Of Thee I Sing," draft preface, February 26, 1932). Department of Registration exhibition files: MoMA Exh. #15, Frank Lloyd Wright Correspondence.

52. Frank Lloyd Wright, "Of Thee I Sing," *Shelter* 2, no. 3 (April 1932), pp. 10–12.

53. K. Löndberg-Holm, "Two Shows: A Comment on the Aesthetic Racket"; Arthur T. North, "Old New Stuff"; and Chester Aldrich, "Modern and Publicity," *Shelter* 2, no. 3 (April 1932), pp. 16–17, 12–16, and 24–26, respectively.

54. William Adams Delano, "Man Versus Mass," *Shelter* 2, no. 4 (May 1932), p. 12. Also cited in Stern, Gilmartin, and Mellins, *New York 1930*, p. 344.

55. Letter, Hitchcock to Barr, August 12, 1928. MoMA Archives: Alfred H. Barr, Jr., Papers, I.16.

56. *Early Modern Architecture: Chicago, 1870–1910* (New York: The Museum of Modern Art, 1933; second edition [revised],1940).

57. See letter, Johnson to Stewart Leonard, November 26, 1932. Department of Registration exhibition files: MoMA Exh. #23. W. W. Norton was copublisher of Morrison's monograph on Sullivan.

58. See Johnson correspondence, June–December 1932. Department of Registration exhibition files: MoMA Exh. #23.

59. See letter, Thomas E. Tallmadge to Johnson, December 16, 1932. Registrar's archives. See also letter, Tallmadge to Johnson, December 23, 1932. Department of Registration exhibition files: MoMA Exh. #23.

60. Thomas E. Tallmadge, *Architecture in Old Chicago* (Chicago: University of Chicago Press, 1941), pp. 195–96.

61. Ibid. p. 196. The controversy of whether Chicago or New York was the birthplace of the skyscraper continues; see also Christopher Gray, "Streetscapes: The Idea That Led to New York's First Skyscraper," *The New York Times,* May 5, 1996, Real Estate Section, p. 7.

62. Malcolm Vaughan, "Skyscrapers' Story Is Told," unidentified newspaper, January 1933 (clipping). MoMA Archives: Public Information Scrapbooks, no. 2.

63. Henry McBride, "Philip Johnson's Architectural Show Presents the Case Fully," *Sun* (New York), January 21, 1933 (clipping). MoMA Archives: Public Information Scrapbooks, no. 2.

64. Peter B. Wight, "Additions to Chicago's Skyline: A Few Recent Skyscrapers," *Architectural Record* 28 (July 1910), p. 15.

65. John Taylor Boyd, Jr., "A New Emphasis in Skyscraper Design: Exemplified in the Recent Work of Starrett & Van Vlek," *Architectural Record* 52 (December 1922), p. 499.

66. Alfred H. Barr, Jr., Preface to Hitchcock and Johnson, *The International Style*, p. 12.

67. Thomas E. Tallmadge, "The Development of the Office Building," *Architectural Record* 67 (June 1930), p. 780. The Exposition internationale des arts décoratifs, now known popularly as the "Art Deco Exposition," was held in Paris in early 1925. A selection of four hundred objects from the exhibition began an eight-city U.S. tour at The Metropolitan Museum of Art in 1926.

68. Philip Johnson, "The Skyscraper School of Modern Architecture," *The Arts* 17, no. 8 (May 1931), p. 569.

69. "The Exhibition of Modern Architecture," checklist, undated. Philadelphia Museum of Art: Registrar Archives.

70. Letter, Johnson to Oud, April 16, 1932. MoMA Archives: Philip Johnson Papers, IV.1.

71. MoMA press release no. 1, January 16, 1933. Department of Communications, The Museum of Modern Art, New York.

72. Letter, Nelson A. Rockefeller to Johnson, December 30, 1932. Department of Registration exhibition files: MoMA Exh. #23.

73. Letter, Rockefeller to Johnson, January 13, 1933. Department of Registration exhibition files: MoMA Exh. #23.

74. R. Craig Miller, *Modern Design in the Metropolitan Museum of Art 1890–1990* (New York: The Metropolitan Museum of Art and Harry N. Abrams, 1990), pp. 8–12.

75. "Museum of Modern Art Contrasts Esthetic Creeds of 1900 and 1933," *Republican* (Springfield, Mass.), April 2, 1933 (clipping). MoMA Archives: Public Information Scrapbooks, no. 2.

76. "Report from The Sub-Committee on Industrial Arts to the Junior Advisory Committee of the Museum of Modern Art Prepared by Philip Johnson," January 20, 1933. Department of Registration exhibition files: MoMA Exh. #27.

77. Philip Johnson, *Objects 1900 and Today: An Exhibition of Decorative and Useful Objects Contrasting Two Periods of Design* (New York: The Museum of Modern Art, 1933), unpaginated, [p.1].

78. "Art Show Contrasts 1900 and The Present," *The New York Times*, April 5, 1933 (clipping). MoMA Archives: Public Information Scrapbooks, no. 2.

79. See correspondence, Johnson to Jeanette Dempsey, March 7, 1933; and Nelson Rockefeller to W. J. Demarest, undated. Department of Registration exhibition files: MoMA Exh. #27.

80. *Sun* (New York), April 8, 1933 (clipping). MoMA Archives: Public Information Scrapbooks, no. 2.

81. Johnson, "Report from The Sub-Committee on Industrial Arts," [p.1].

82. Johnson, *Objects 1900 and Today*, [p. 14].

83. Aaron Marc Stein, "Art Nouveau: Museum of Modern Art Presents Design of 1900 and That of Today for Comparison," *New York Post*, April 8, 1933 (clipping). MoMA Archives: Public Information Scrapbooks, no. 2.

84. Ibid.

85. Philip Johnson, "Decorative Art a Generation Ago," *Creative Art* 12, no. 4 (April 1933), p. 297.

86. "Exhibitions in New York: Objects 1900 and Today," unidentified newspaper, April 8, 1933 (clipping). MoMA Archives: Public Information Scrapbooks, no. 2.

87. "Museum of Modern Art Contrasts Esthetic Creeds of 1900 and 1933" (clipping), op. cit.

88. "Exhibitions in New York" (clipping), op. cit.

89. *Sun*, April 8, 1933 (clipping), op. cit.

90. "Museum of Modern Art Contrasts Esthetic Creeds of 1900 and 1933" (clipping), op. cit.

91. Quoted in "Hamilton, Gwenydd Beatty Exhibit at N.Y. Show," *Journal* (Madison, Wisc.), April 4, 1933 (clipping). MoMA Archives: Public Information Scrapbooks, no. 2.

92. Philip Johnson, *Work of Young Architects in the Middle West* (New York: The Museum of Modern Art, 1933), unpaginated, [p. 1].

93. Hitchcock and Johnson, *The International Style,* p. 92.

94. Johnson, *Work of Young Architects in the Middle West,* [p. 9].

95. Ibid., [p. 8].

96. Gwenydd Beatty is not cited in the catalogue, but is credited as having collaborated on the project with her husband in the bibliographical material provided by the architect.

97. "Hamilton, Gwenydd Beatty Exhibit at N.Y. Show" (clipping), op. cit.

98. Johnson undoubtedly met these architects through some hometown connection, although the circumstances are unclear; with Hubert C. Bebb, even less clear, although he may have met him through Keck or even through Bowman Brothers, whose low-cost prefabricated housing schemes were included in *Modern Architecture.* Curiously, Bowman Brothers failed to reappear in *Work of Young Architects in the Middle West,* despite Johnson's earlier support of their work.

99. Johnson, *Work of Young Architects in the Middle West,* [p. 1].

100. Quoted in *A Memorial Tribute: Alfred H. Barr* (New York: The Museum of Modern Art, 1982), n.p. [p. 32].

101. Johnson, *Work of Young Architects in the Middle West,* [p. 1].

102. "Attractions in the Galleries," unidentified journal, undated (clipping). MoMA Archives: Public Information Scrapbooks, no. 2.

103. "Work of Young Architects in the Middle West: Museum of Modern Art," *Art News*, April 15, 1933 (clipping). MoMA Archives: Public Information Scrapbooks, no. 2.

104. Johnson denies that this was yet another project commissioned for his family, although the proposal suggests a client much like himself (interview with the author, March 25, 1996). The exhibition was held July 10 through September 30, 1933.

105. The exhibition was held at the Museum from October 3 to 27, 1933.

106. "Modern Museum Shows a Modern Home," *Boston Transcript*, July 31, 1933 (clipping). MoMA Archives: Public Information Scrapbooks, no. 2.

107. Philip Johnson in interview with the author, March 25, 1996.

108. Philip Johnson, *Machine Art* (New York: The Museum of Modern Art, 1934; rpt., 1994).

109. MoMA press release no. 26, undated [March 1934]. Department of Publication Information, The Museum of Modern Art, New York.

110. Bruce Brooks Pfeiffer, ed., *Frank Lloyd Wright: Collected Writings* (New York: Rizzoli in association with The Frank Lloyd Wright Foundation, 1992), Vol. 1, 1894–1930, p. 64.

111. Philip Johnson, "History of Machine Art," in Johnson, *Machine Art,* [p. 13].

112. Ibid.

113. Joseph W. Alsop, Jr., "Pots and Sinks Going on View As Art Works," *New York Herald Tribune,* March 5, 1934 (clipping). MoMA Archives: Public Information Scrapbooks, no. 13.

114. Read, "Machine Art" (1934), op. cit.

115. Alfred H. Barr, Jr., Foreword to Johnson, *Machine Art,* [pp. 11–12].

116. Ibid., [p. 8].

117. Ibid., [p. 9].

118. Quoted in MoMA press release no. 31, March 1934. Department of Communications, The Museum of Modern Art, New York.

119. Ralph Waldo Emerson, "Essays XII: Art," *Essays, First and Second Series* (New York: First Vintage Books/The Library of America Edition, 1990), p. 210.

120. Quoted in Barr, Foreword to Johnson, *Machine Art,* [p. 9].

121. Barr makes the point that it is important, if not always possible, to distinguish between "consciously architectural effects" and the "involuntary effects of structural or utilitarian requirement"—a distinction that calls into question any definition of architecture. He offers a historical analogy as answer: "Whether or not the Gothic master-builder was primarily an engineer or an architect, his cathedral by general consent [is] architecture. Similarly . . . the Necco factory is architecture even though it be as far removed from the Beaux-Arts tradition as a Frigidaire refrigerator is from a *Louis Quinze* Victrola." Barr concludes: "F. C. Lutze, engineer and chief designer of the Necco factory, has achieved architecture positively by manipulation of proportions and masses, and by the restrained use of handsomer materials than were structurally necessary; negatively by the utmost economy in decorative motive and by the frank acknowledgment of utilitarian necessity both in plan and elevation." Barr, "The Necco Factory," pp. 293–94.

122. Letter, Johnson to Oud, March 17, 1932. Department of Registration exhibition files: MoMA Exh. #15, J. J. P. Oud Correspondence.

123. Henry McBride, "Museum Shows Machine Art In a Most Unusual Display," *Sun* (New York), March 5, 1934 (clipping). MoMA Archives: Public Information Scrapbooks, no. 13.

124. Read, "Machine Art" (1934), op. cit.

125. Anita Brenner, "Art: Frontiers of Machine Art," *The Nation,* March 28, 1934 (clipping). MoMA Archives: Public Information Scrapbooks, no. 13.

126. See Royal Cortissoz, "Can There Be Machine Art?," *Library Digest,* March 31, 1934 (clipping). MoMA Archives: Public Information Scrapbooks, no. 13.

127. "Machine Art Exhibit," *News-Leader* (Richmond, Va.), March 24, 1934 (clipping). MoMA Archives: Public Information Scrapbooks, no. 13.

128. Edward Alden Jewell, "The Realm of Art: Introducing Plato, 1934," *The New York Times,* date unknown (clipping). MoMA Archives: Johnson Papers, III.1.

129. "Pots and Sinks Going on View as Art at Machinery Exhibit," *New York Herald Tribune,* March 5, 1934; "Is Beauty the Same Thing in Auto's Lines and in Sunset?," *Los Angeles Times,* March 25, 1934; and "Piece of Spring Wins Art Show's Beauty Award," *New York Herald Tribune,* March 6, 1934 (clippings). MoMA Archives: Public Information Scrapbooks, nos. 12, 13.

130. MoMA press release no. 31, March 1934. Department of Communications, The Museum of Modern Art, New York. The spring was awarded first place. An outboard propeller manufactured by the Aluminum Company of America and the SKF ball bearing featured on the cover of the exhibition catalogue were awarded second and third place, respectively.

131. Edward Alden Jewell, "Machine Art Seen in Unique Exhibit," *The New York Times,* March 6, 1934 (clipping). MoMA Archives: Public Information Scrapbooks, no. 13.

132. Margaret Breuning, "Modern Museum Puts on Machine Art Exhibit," *New York Post,* March 10, 1934 (clipping). MoMA Archives: Public Information Scrapbooks, no. 13.

133. Quoted in *A Memorial Tribute: Alfred H. Barr* (1981), [p. 28].

134. Hitchcock and Johnson, *The International Style,* p. 14.

135. Edward L. Bernays, *Crystallizing Public Opinion* (New York: Liveright, 1923), p. 212.

136. Ibid., pp. 11–12.

137. Minutes of the meeting of the Board of Trustees, The Museum of Modern Art, New York, October 25, 1929. MoMA Archives: Board of Trustees Minutes, V.1.

138. Bernays, *Crystallizing Public Opinion,* p. 153.

139. Quoted in ibid., p. 155.

140. *Hidden Talent* was organized by Johnson. *Visionary Architecture* was directed by Drexler.

141. The series was held annually from 1938 to 1943 and again from 1945 to 1948. It was continued under the direction of Eliot Noyes, who succeeded John McAndrew as curator of architecture. For a description of this series and subsequent Museum programs promoting the "good design" of consumer products, see Terence Riley and Edward Eigen, "Between the Museum and the Marketplace: Selling Good Design," in *Studies in Modern Art 4. The Museum of Modern Art at Mid-Century: At Home and Abroad* (New York: The Museum of Modern Art, 1994), pp. 150–79

142. Miller, *Modern Design in the Metropolitan Museum of Art 1890–1990,* p. 28.

143. Hitchcock, *Modern Architecture,* p. 190.

144. Ibid., p. 192.

145. See, for example, Barr's "Mode in Architecture," *The Hound and Horn* 3, no. 3 (April–June 1930), pp. 431–45.

146. Hitchcock and Johnson, *The International Style,* p. 33.

147. Letter, Johnson to Mrs. Homer H. Johnson, July 21, [1930]. Architecture and Design archive: 1932 Project.

148. Letter, Johnson to Mrs. Homer H. Johnson, August 22, 1930. Architecture and Design archive: 1932 Project.

149. Letter, Johnson to Mrs. Homer H. Johnson, September 1, 1930. Architecture and Design archive: 1932 Project. This correspondence seems to contradict an unsigned note in the Mies van der Rohe Archive, The Museum of Modern Art, New York, that suggests J. B. Neumann introduced Johnson to Mies.

150. Letter, Johnson to Mrs. Homer H. Johnson, July 7, 1930. Architecture and Design archive: 1932 Project.

1. Philip Johnson and René d'Harnoncourt viewing the model of the proposed East Wing and Garden Wing expansion of The Museum of Modern Art, installed as part of the exhibition *The Museum of Modern Art Builds*, 1962

The Space and the Frame: Philip Johnson as the Museum's Architect

Peter Reed

Purely aesthetically speaking, the museum is an architect's dream. He has—as in a church—to make the visitor happy, to put him in a receptive frame of mind while he is undergoing an emotional experience.
—Philip Johnson[1]

Since its founding in 1929, The Museum of Modern Art's building campaigns and expansions have been of almost perennial concern to its trustees and staff. It is a rare moment when the Museum is not planning capital campaigns of remarkable ambition to keep pace with its phenomenal growth. The combination of a popular exhibition program, a continually expanding collection, and increases in attendance fuels the demands for additional space. Thus even after the 1939 opening of its permanent home at 11 West Fifty-third Street designed by Philip L. Goodwin and Edward Durell Stone (fig. 2),[2] generous benefactors regularly attended groundbreaking and ribbon-cutting ceremonies with philanthropic zeal, as the Museum replaced its neighboring brownstones with modern galleries. For more than two decades, from the late 1940s until the early 1970s, Philip Johnson's involvement in the Museum's expansion was so continuous as to make him its unofficial architect. What could have been an awkward assemblage of parts surrounding the original Goodwin–Stone building—the Grace Rainey Rogers Annex (built 1951), The Abby Aldrich Rockefeller Sculpture Garden (1953), the Whitney Museum of American Art (1954), the East Wing, Garden Wing, and reconfigured Lobby (1964)—developed into a harmonious composition with Johnson's guidance. Although each part retained its own identity, the consistency of materials, colors, massing, and general architectural expression resulted in a cohesive, urbane architecture. While the much-celebrated Abby Aldrich Rockefeller Sculpture Garden may be, very deservedly, one of his best known and most acclaimed designs (see p. 104 in the present volume), Johnson's other buildings and projects for the Museum—which range in date from the House of Glass pavilion of 1948 to the initial studies, executed in 1969–70, for the Museum Tower and Garden Hall—reflect both his own development as an architect and the Museum's evolution from a relatively modest gallery to a preeminent international institution with the only synoptic collection of modern art in the world. The ideas explored by Johnson in giving architectural form to The Museum of Modern Art is the subject of this essay.

Johnson's return to the Museum in 1945 and his resumption of a curatorial role

2. Philip L. Goodwin and Edward D. Stone, Architects. The Museum of Modern Art, New York. Aerial view. 1939. Photograph by Andreas Feininger

3. Philip Johnson. The House of Glass, The Museum of Modern Art Sculpture Garden, Project. Perspective view. 1948. (Whereabouts of original unknown)

coincided with the establishment of his professional architectural practice.[3] In 1947, two years before becoming director of the Department of Architecture and Design, he organized an exhibition on the German architect Ludwig Mies van der Rohe, whose vision had informed so much of Johnson's emerging career.[4] The reductive aesthetic of Mies's architecture—elegant simplicity and flowing space achieved with spare but often rich materials, especially the extensive use of glass in steel-framed structures—became the recurrent motif in much postwar international architecture, including Johnson's early additions to The Museum of Modern Art. The minimalist, abstract design underlying the gridded curtain wall was seen as emblematic of a technologically advanced, sophisticated society—an appropriate expression for a museum dedicated to modern art.

Glass, more than any other material, captured Johnson's attention in the postwar era. His enthusiasm both for Mies and for glass was celebrated privately in the Glass House (1946–49), the architect's retreat in New Canaan, Connecticut.[5] A more public demonstration was envisioned for The House of Glass (fig. 3), an astonishing proposal for a permanent glass pavilion in the Museum's original sculpture garden, designed in 1939 by founding director Alfred H. Barr, Jr., and curator of architecture John McAndrew. The garden had served as the setting, in 1942, for an architectural installation of R. Buckminster Fuller's Dymaxion Deployment Unit, and in later years temporary demonstration houses by Marcel Breuer (in 1949), Gregory Ain (1950), and Junzo Yoshimura's Japanese Exhibition House (1954–55) would be featured there. Johnson's first project for the Museum, never realized, would have been an extraordinary example of the new aesthetic he wholeheartedly embraced. In a written statement accompanying the proposal he described the purpose of the pavilion:

[It will demonstrate] that glass is the lightest, most flexible, and most completely modern material available to architects today. The building . . . will have the appearance of a huge crystal floating above the Museum's garden space in the center of Manhattan. . . . Its effect in revolutionizing the building industry and all facets of related design should be compared to that of the first steel frame skyscrapers.[6]

The design had been inspired by several unbuilt projects by Mies that had been included in Johnson's exhibition and catalogue on the architect the previous year.

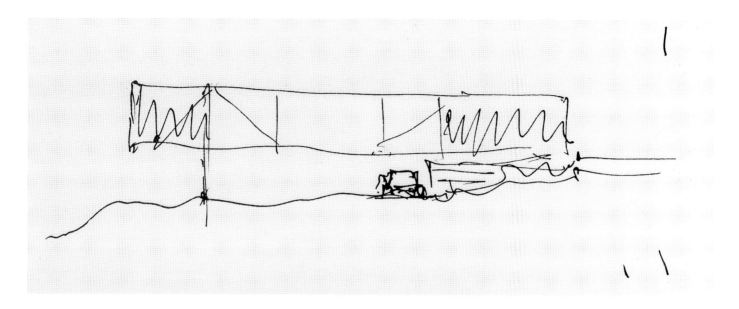

Above:
4. Ludwig Mies van der Rohe. House on a Hillside, Project. Elevation. ca. 1934. Ink on paper, 4¼ x 8" (10.5 x 20.3 cm). Mies van der Rohe Archive, The Museum of Modern Art, New York. Gift of the architect

Left:
5. Philip Johnson. Mr. and Mrs. Robert C. Leonhardt House, Lloyd's Neck, New York. 1956

Mies's sketch for a House on a Hillside (ca. 1934; fig. 4) shows a house supported on columns above a sloping ground.[7] In the 1942 project Museum for a Small City, he envisioned glass walls against a dramatic landscape, "a place for the enjoyment of art not its interment."[8] The building was defined exclusively by a floor slab, supporting columns, and roof plate, with walls of glass defining the otherwise flowing space.

Raised above the garden on steel columns, Johnson's proposed House of Glass "floats" in an almost ethereal sense, rising a full story aboveground—a concept he revived in 1956 in the house he designed for Mr. and Mrs. Robert C. Leonhardt (fig. 5). The Museum pavilion appears all the more striking if one compares it with the 1939 Goodwin–Stone building and with Goodwin's own 1946–47 proposal for a new wing, the style of which so closely follows the earlier building that it appears as an almost seamless extension (see model, fig. 6). Goodwin's design seems more ponderous, lacking the drama, simplicity, and evanescent quality embodied in The House of Glass. Whereas Goodwin and Stone had used glass brick to great effect, Johnson envisioned entire walls of plate glass—a smooth, uninterrupted, virtually unarticulated and textureless façade. The dematerialization of the wall revealed a modern, reductive aesthetic, a trend toward minimalization of structural mass and greater transparency.

Plans for the Goodwin addition, which would have nearly doubled the space of the Museum, had been publicly announced on February 9, 1947.[9] The new wing was to extend from Fifty-third to Fifty-fourth Street on a plot just west of the original building, replacing the townhouse at 21 West Fifty-third Street. By fall 1947, however, the project had been squelched. Despite the enthusiasm of the young and energetic Nelson A. Rockefeller (President of the Museum and son of cofounder Abby Aldrich Rockefeller), whose lifelong zeal for building campaigns was legendary, other trustees were not convinced that they could raise the $3,650,000 necessary to its realization.[10] Nor was The House of Glass realized, also perhaps owing to a lack of potential funding.[11] But Johnson's close connections and friendships with Nelson Rockefeller, Mrs. John D. Rockefeller 3rd (Blanchette Hooker Rockefeller), and the architect Wallace K. Harrison, a trustee who was closely allied with the Rockefellers, would guarantee his participation in the Museum's future architectural endeavors.[12] From 1948 until 1977, when Cesar Pelli and Associates, Edward Durell Stone Associates, and Gruen Associates were commissioned to design the Museum Tower, Johnson would be the Museum's architect.

Rockefeller Guest House

Johnson's talent and enthusiasm for modern architecture caught the attention of an important patron and friend, Blanchette Rockefeller, founding chairman of the Museum's Junior Council (now the Contemporary Arts Council)[13] and later chair-

6. From left to right: Philip Goodwin, James Thrall Soby, Mrs. Simon Guggenheim, Alfred Barr, Stephen C. Clark, René d'Harnoncourt, John E. Abbott, and Nelson Rockefeller with model of the Museum building and projected Fifty-fourth Street wing, designed by Goodwin in 1946

Below, from left to right:
7. Philip Johnson. Rockefeller Guest House, New York. 1948–50

8. Philip Johnson. Rockefeller Guest House, New York. Street façade, perspective view. 1948–50. Pencil on vellum, 48 x 36" (122 x 91.5 cm). The Museum of Modern Art, New York. Gift of Philip Johnson

9. Ludwig Mies van der Rohe. IIT Library and Administration Building, Chicago, Project. Southeast corner, perspective view. 1944. Pencil on illustration board, 44 x 34" (111.7 x 86.3 cm). Mies van der Rohe Archive, The Museum of Modern Art, New York. Gift of the architect

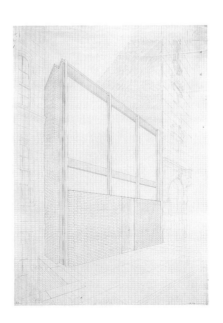

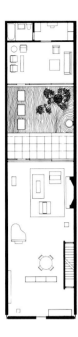

Left:
10. Philip Johnson. Rockefeller Guest House, New York. Plan. 1948–50. (Whereabouts of original unknown)

Right:
11. Philip Johnson. Rockefeller Guest House, New York. Interior. 1948–50

man of the board and president. In 1948, Johnson designed for Mrs. Rockefeller a guest house that was also conceived as a place to entertain and showcase her modern art collection.[14] Completed in 1950, the Rockefeller Guest House, located a few blocks from the Museum at 242 East Fifty-second Street was nothing less than a modern, urban Petit Trianon (fig. 7). It soon became the favored setting for Museum-related entertaining.

Although relatively modest in size, the commission nevertheless permitted Johnson to display his talent for tasteful interiors, dramatic architectural procession, and garden design in what was one of the city's first modern townhouses. Sandwiched between two older buildings, the site was similar to those of Johnson's later commissions for the Museum, which were, in effect, infill projects as well. An exterior rendering not only effectively portrays the townhouse's startling contrast with its neighbors but also clearly illustrates the elegant and precise articulation of the structure's own materials: brick, steel, and glass (fig. 8). Its Miesian sources are underscored by the close association of this rendering to Mies's drawing for the corner of the Library and Administration Building at IIT (1944), which Johnson had chosen to illustrate his 1947 exhibition catalogue on Mies's work (fig. 9).

Johnson's large, loftlike interior of exposed brick walls painted white, white linoleum floor, and simple furnishings is an uncluttered, spacious setting for works of art.[15] A walnut sectional storage cabinet screens the entryway from the expansive living area, a flowing space that is made to feel even larger by the unbroken view to the atrium and bedroom beyond (figs. 10, 11). Floor-to-ceiling glass walls in the living room and bedroom, which are separated by the outdoor garden and pool, mirror each other. Light from the atrium fills the interior.

In this tight urban setting, Johnson effectively maximized the available light and space by bringing the outdoors in, a pervasive theme in modern postwar residential architecture, and one which ran contrary to the traditionally dark and narrow New York townhouse. The approach to the master bedroom was deliberately intended to awaken "a sense of adventure":[16] It was necessary to pass through the outdoors, traversing a pool on travertine stepping stones illuminated by underwater lighting. Indeed, Johnson's flare for dramatic and romantic settings has rarely been surpassed, and is only heightened by the intimacy of scale. While there is a debt to Mies's court-house studies, which we know fascinated Johnson in the 1940s, the historical resonance of the townhouse's Roman atrium has also been observed.[17] His interests were, however, eclectic: The slightly precarious stepping stones evince his admiration for Japanese garden design—an affinity that would be manifest to an even greater degree in Johnson's design for the Museum's Abby Aldrich Rockefeller Sculpture Garden a few years later.[18]

In 1954, the public was invited to the Rockefeller Guest House for the first time to see a special exhibition sponsored by the Junior Council. The works of art on display were owned by the Council's young members, and were described in the press as "a freewheeling and unusually venturesome collectors' collection."[19] Not surprisingly, the Guest House quickly became a popular setting for Museum functions, and in 1958, the Rockefellers donated the property to the Museum, which lacked sufficient space for entertaining. When the Founders Room in the East Wing was added in 1964 precisely for this purpose, the Guest House was sold.[20]

Grace Rainey Rogers Annex

Although the Museum had cancelled its 1947 plan to construct a new wing by Goodwin, the need for additional space remained. Two years later, plans were underway for a more modest addition: the Grace Rainey Rogers Annex at 21 West Fifty-third Street, immediately west of the Goodwin–Stone building (figs. 12, 13). In 1949, while designing the Rockefeller Guest House, Johnson was chosen as the architect of the annex—his first building commission for the Museum itself.[21] The seven-story annex, also known as the "21" building, replaced a 1905 townhouse designed by C. P. H. Gilbert that the Museum had purchased in 1946.[22] The Rogers Annex did not contain galleries but housed the People's Art Center (the Museum's program for children's and adult's art classes), storage areas, additional library stacks, and staff offices, including an office for the Department of Architecture and Design, which until then had shared space with Painting and Sculpture.[23] Construction began in July 1950 and was completed the following summer. A sliver of a building roughly twenty feet wide, it was sandwiched between the Museum and an adjoining townhouse; its rear wall abutted the new Whitney Museum of American Art building at 22 West Fifty-fourth Street, the design of which was contemporaneous with the annex. The glass façade was defined by a Miesian grid of thin, decorative iron mullions expressive of the underlying steel skeleton and displayed a clarity and discipline typical of Mies's Chicago projects of the same period. To underscore the fact that the applied beams were not structural, they spanned only from the second to the seventh floor, above the sheer glass wall of the entrance. The quiet rhythm of the façade and vertical emphasis formed a stark contrast to neighboring buildings: a French Renaissance townhouse to the west, and the marble- and Thermolux-sheathed Museum to the east, whose strict horizontality, underscored by ribbon windows and the sixth-floor balcony, was terminated by the vertical lines of the annex. Reflecting on the little building many years later, Johnson would claim that "there was no architecture to it. It was just a sliver and I didn't want to make an

12. Philip Johnson. Grace Rainey Rogers Annex, The Museum of Modern Art, New York. 1949–51

architectural statement."[24] However small and insignificant the annex may have seemed to the architect in hindsight, its design was nevertheless a statement. It was insistently modern, and an appropriate expression for the institution.[25] The annex was built at approximately the same time as two other significant New York buildings boasting remarkable curtain walls of metal and glass: the Secretariat of the United Nations Headquarters (1947–50), designed by a team of international architects directed by Wallace K. Harrison; and Lever House (1950–52), designed by Gordon Bunshaft of Skidmore, Owings and Merrill.

Other than the façade, the architect seems to have received the most satisfaction from designing the new Architecture and Design office on the building's fifth floor, which Johnson shared with his young assistant, Arthur Drexler. Rather than divide the narrow space into two small offices, he and Drexler shared one large, comfortable room (fig. 14). Johnson later recalled: "We made one office and both sat in it, which was always considered very strange. We got along fine."[26] (Of course, he was then dividing his time between work at the Museum and his studio office.) The wood-paneled office, with couch and chairs arranged around a coffee table, could easily have been mistaken for a living room. The wrought-iron furniture, upholstered in black cloth, was designed by Darrell Landrum for Avard, and was consonant with the architecture. Matching worktables for curator and director completed the suite. A Miró tapestry from Johnson's personal collection adorned one wall, adding to the sophisticated "residential ease" observed by a writer for *Interiors* magazine.[27] Johnson lavished the same attention on the old sixth-floor Members' Lounge at the top of the Goodwin–Stone building, which was turned into a regular cafeteria at this time. Using a palette of cool grays, he wove together contemporary fiberglass chairs by Charles Eames, Avard's wood-topped wrought-iron tables, and Marie Nichol's airy Dynel "Fishnet" curtains, which were strung along the glass walls—in all, a minimalist setting of the most contemporary design (fig. 15).

Unlike the 1947 Goodwin proposal, the Rogers Annex did not stretch from

13. Philip Johnson. Grace Rainey Rogers Annex, The Museum of Modern Art, New York. Perspective view. 1949–51. (Whereabouts of original unknown)

Left:
14. Philip Johnson. Office of the Department of Architecture and Design, Grace Rainey Rogers Annex, The Museum of Modern Art, New York. 1949–51

15. Philip Johnson. Members' Lounge, The Museum of Modern Art, New York. 1952

Fifty-third to Fifty-fourth Street; much of that site had been sold to the Whitney Museum for its new home. However, because the east façade of the Whitney bordered the sculpture garden, then being redesigned by Johnson, the Museum maintained a sliver of space on the ground floor for a garden café. The architect of record for the Whitney was Auguste L. Noel of Miller and Noel, but Johnson designed the café and the garden façade.[28] Although design was begun in 1949, the building was not completed until 1954.[29] Johnson explored numerous variations on a Miesian grid, studying the proportions and rhythm of the façade (figs. 16.a–e). Above the glass wall of the ground-floor café, a light-gray brick wall punctuated by vertical black-painted steel piers rose two-and-a-half stories to a crowning band of ribbon windows. The composition was a subtle backdrop for the new Abby Aldrich Rockefeller Sculpture Garden, completed in 1953, and its palette complemented the gray Vermont marble with which the garden was paved (fig. 17).

The "New" Museum of Modern Art: "A Problem Created by Success"[30]
While the Rogers Annex provided space for offices and educational programs, gallery space in the Museum was not increased. During the celebration of the Museum's twenty-fifth anniversary in the fall of 1955, the critical gallery shortage was addressed by René d'Harnoncourt, Director, and William A. M. Burden, Chairman of the Board. Their recognition of the Museum's physical shortcomings set the stage for a "new" Museum of Modern Art, one that would not be unveiled until nearly a decade later, with the opening of the East Wing, the Garden Wing, and a renovated lobby in 1964. In a long memorandum to Burden on October 3, d'Harnoncourt reflected on the Museum's growth and changing mission in its first twenty-five years, and outlined its future needs. Although the Museum had become an institution of international importance, one whose annual attendance had reached nearly seven hundred thousand visitors,[31] perhaps the most astonishing fact was that there were no permanent galleries for the installation of its important collections of photographs, architectural models and drawings, design objects, and graphic art. Furthermore, only about fifteen percent of the painting and sculpture collection was on view. D'Harnoncourt explained:

The need for additional gallery space to exhibit the Museum's collections is becoming more and more important. When the Museum of Modern Art was founded it had no collection, and its entire program consisted of temporary exhibitions designed to acquaint the New York public not only with current events in contemporary art, but also to bring before them the work of the great masters of the 19th and 20th Century. . . . During the last twenty-five years the Museum has been exceedingly successful in building up its permanent collection and is today recognized as owning the most representative collection of modern art in the world. At its inception no space was provided for the collection. . . . In 1945 it was decided that this collection had reached such an importance that the Museum had to set aside a space for its permanent showing. Since then the collection has steadily grown both in number and importance but no more space could be assigned to it without crippling the Museum's program of temporary exhibitions. . . .

We are at present completely unable to answer the ever growing public demand to see a representative and important selection of our holdings, and are constantly disappointing donors of masterworks who find that their gifts are not on view.[32]

In his reply to d'Harnoncourt three weeks later, Burden concurred with the director's initial projections for a new wing. The goal was to increase the nine thousand square feet available for exhibition of the permanent collection to twenty-three thousand, and to expand ancillary office, storage, and support space as well. Without specifying the exact location, Burden's memorandum approximated the dimensions of the new building at forty-five by eighty-eight feet, with a total of ten stories, three below-ground and seven above, the floor lines corresponding to those of the existing building in order to achieve a more unified appearance.[33] By these calculations, the Museum would nearly double in size, accommodating its collection and befitting its growing international reputation.

Burden's description of the new building matches Johnson's 1956 studies for a new wing situated between the main building and St. Thomas' Church to the east,

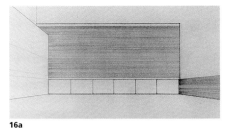

16a

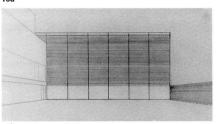

16b

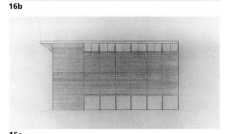

16c

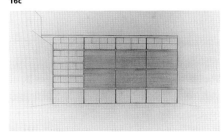

16d

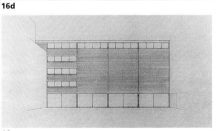

16e

16.a–e. Philip Johnson. Studies for East (Garden) Façade of the Whitney Museum of American Art, New York. ca. 1949–50. Pencil on vellum, a) 16¾ x 21⅛" (42.5 x 53.7 cm); b) 16¾ x 21⅛" (42.5 x 53.7 cm); c) 14⅞ x 21⅛" (37.8 x 53.7 cm); d) 15" x 21⅛" (38.1 x 53.7 cm); e) 13¾ x 21⅛" (34.9 x 53.7 cm). Philip Johnson Archive (110.3, 110.2, 110.7, 110.8, 110.17), The Museum of Modern Art, New York

Left:
17. Philip Johnson. The Abby Aldrich Rockefeller Sculpture Garden, The Museum of Modern Art, New York. 1953. In background: The Whitney Museum of American Art

at 5 and 7 West Fifty-third Street—precisely the location of the East Wing that would open in 1964. In his preliminary studies, the façade, with its applied I-beams, was modeled on the Miesian, rectilinear grid of the Rogers Annex.[34] The ground-floor lobby was relocated from the original building to the new wing, and in some studies was rendered as an impressive double-height space. In others, an upper-floor gallery was designed as a balconied double-height space for the display of large works of art.

The site for which these studies were made was then occupied by two five-story brownstones, built in the 1880s, which were owned and occupied by Mrs. E. Parmelee Prentice (daughter of John D. Rockefeller). Perhaps Mrs. Prentice showed no signs of relinquishing her townhouses in the immediate future. (Not until 1960 would she formalize an arrangement by which the townhouses would, upon her death, become Museum property.) Regardless, Johnson's initial studies were set aside the following year, and a new site, with a considerably larger addition, was under consideration. The new studies focused on the open space on Fifty-fourth Street, east of the sculpture garden and abutting the rear of Canada House at the southwest corner of Fifth Avenue and Fifty-fourth Street, which would dramatically increase the size of the Museum.[35] A proposal was unveiled two years later,[36] coinciding with the Museum's thirtieth anniversary and a major fund drive to raise the staggering sum of twenty-five million dollars, seven million of which was slated for a new building.[37] To demonstrate the serious lack of gallery space, Alfred Barr, then director of museum collections, mounted an exhibition titled *Toward the "New" Museum of Modern Art—A Bid for Space,* which opened on November 18, 1959, in the second-floor galleries. Paintings, drawings, prints, photographs, architectural drawings, and posters were hung salon-style, stacked one upon another, crowding the walls in a manner altogether antithetical to the Museum's installation philosophy (fig. 18). The exhibition remained on view throughout the capital campaign, and works of art were rotated from time to time. It was an effective means of persuading Museum audiences that without more gallery space they would continue to be denied the satisfaction of seeing the "invisible collection." A press release stated the sobering facts: Only twelve percent of the painting collection was on view at any one time; roughly a dozen drawings were usually shown; the thirty-five hundred objects in the Architecture and Design collection and fifty-five hundred prints in the Department of Photography normally were not shown at all.[38]

The Anniversary Campaign was terrifically successful, an effective combination of publications, exhibitions, auctions, and parties, all covered by the media. During the next several years, benefactors wrote checks amounting to millions of dollars, and a campaign committee mustered support from Museum members around the country. On February 16, 1963, the trustees announced the close of the fund drive. A year later, a new Museum of Modern Art opened in time for the 1964 New York World's Fair, but it looked nothing like the model Johnson had unveiled in 1959.[39]

That model of the proposed Fifty-fourth Street addition was first displayed in the Museum at the time of Barr's *Bid for Space.* The press release accompanying the unveiling stated:

The new wing, designed by Philip Johnson Associates, Architects, will be an 8 story building on a site approximately 113 feet by 100 feet. The five gallery floors will be completely

18. Installation view, *Toward the "New" Museum of Modern Art—A Bid for Space,* The Museum of Modern Art, New York, November 18, 1959. Installation design by Alfred Barr

19. Philip Johnson. Proposed East Wing on Fifty-fourth Street, The Museum of Modern Art, New York. Aeriel perspective looking southeast. ca. 1959. Pencil on vellum, 22 x 27¾" (56 x 70.5 cm). Philip Johnson archive (135.50), Department of Architecture and Design, The Museum of Modern Art, New York

free of columns, thus permitting maximum flexibility in installing works of art. This is accomplished by grouping all the services in a utility band on the south and east. Escalators as well as elevators will connect the gallery floors. A glass enclosed corridor will connect the new wing with the brick stair tower on the building at 11 West 53rd Street. The new wing will become the main entrance to the Museum and the entrance lobby will be shifted there from 53rd St.[40]

This was to be the "new" Museum of Modern Art. Not only would gallery space triple in area,[41] but the new building on Fifty-fourth Street would replace the Goodwin–Stone building as the primary entrance to the Museum. The old lobby on Fifty-third Street would be converted to gallery space. The prominence of the bold new proposal was reflected in the architecture, stylistically a departure from Johnson's earlier work. Rather than modeling the façade on the Miesian vocabulary of the Whitney Museum as rendered in a preliminary proposal[42] (fig. 19), thus creating nearly symmetrical wings at either end of the Garden, Johnson designed the two principal façades of the new addition—along Fifty-fourth Street and the Sculpture Garden—as tall arcades with slender stone pilasters, diamond-shaped in section and sheathed in stone to conceal the steel-and-reinforced-concrete structure[43] (fig. 20). At street level, an arcade eight bays in width, each bay measuring approximately twelve feet in width, shielded the transparent glass wall of the lobby (fig. 21). The façade of the upper gallery floors was a screen of blind bays, with inset marble panels thus preventing natural light from entering the galleries. Terminating each bay on the upper two office floors were rows of identical square windows with rounded corners—a further softening of the architect's earlier Miesian rectilinearity. A small rooftop glass pavilion with a cantilevered roof slab served as a guest house.

Johnson's design was both monumental and historicizing, the two chief tendencies that emerged in his work in the late 1950s. About his major institutional works of the period—the Amon Carter Museum of Western Art, Fort Worth (1958–61), the New York State Theater at Lincoln Center, New York (1958–64), and

Left:
20. Philip Johnson. Proposed East Wing on Fifty-fourth Street, The Museum of Modern Art, New York. Aerial perspective looking south. 1959. Drawing by Helmut Jacoby. (Whereabouts of original unknown)

Right:
21. Philip Johnson. Entrance to Proposed East Wing on Fifty-fourth Street, The Museum of Modern Art, New York. Model. 1959

the Sheldon Memorial Art Gallery at the University of Nebraska, Lincoln (1958–63; fig. 22)—Johnson proclaimed, "It seems I cannot but be Classically inspired; symmetry, order, clarity above all."[44] Historical references, more than Mies (his classical sense of order notwithstanding), were beginning to inform Johnson's designs.[45] A quest for monumental architecture was fulfilled by historical forms as well: arches and vaults inspired by the romantic classicism of nineteenth-century architects such as Karl Friedrich Schinkel and John Soane. Johnson explained this quintessentially formalist position in various talks and essays. In "Whither Away—Non-Miesian Directions," a seminal lecture of 1959, Johnson confessed, "We cannot not know history."[46] He cited the famous arcades of the Feldherrnhalle in Munich by Friedrich von Gärtner (1841–43) and the fourteenth-century Loggia dei Lanzi in Florence upon which the German monument was based,[47] making the observation that, for a building with basically one principal façade, such as a loggia or stoa, it did not seem to matter what was put behind the arcade. It could even be a glass box, a theater—or an art museum.

The relationship between the architectural symbolism of a museum and its functional role as a place to display art in flexible settings was a paramount concern to Johnson. How to reconcile these seemingly opposed agendas was, in his view, the modern architect's chief task. The flexibility of the loftlike interiors, with their column-free open plan, may accommodate the practical concerns of a museum director; as inspired architectural spaces, however, Johnson felt they leave one cold. What was needed was not only a greater hierarchy of rooms but also grander spaces. The Sheldon Memorial Art Gallery perhaps best exemplified the architect's ideas. A monumental central court, with a coffered ceiling in carved travertine and double staircases, was flanked by subsidiary galleries. The "Grand Salon" was clearly intended "to destroy museum fatigue at the same time giving a lift to the spirits."[48] He further outlined his position in an article published in *Museum News* shortly after designing the West Fifty-fourth Street addition:

Flexibility is the biggest bugaboo. It is a problem on which two of our leading museum men disagree completely: Alfred Barr and James Johnson Sweeney have fundamentally opposite opinions. The architect is bewildered. Mr. Barr feels the architect should provide the director with an anonymous loft building within which he can arrange the space best suited to the exhibit on hand. . . .[49]

Sweeney was director of the recently completed Solomon R. Guggenheim Museum, designed by Frank Lloyd Wright, with its extraordinary central rotunda enclosed by a spiraling ramp and crowned by a skylight.[50] "The great hall is a magnificent and . . . popular space," Johnson proclaimed of the Guggenheim rotunda, but, he noted, at the expense of virtually all other considerations: storage, lighting, flexibility. There were no pauses or vistas, and the exhibition spaces—narrow bays with slanted walls—were awkward.[51] He compared the Guggenheim's architecture to that of The Museum of Modern Art, which for Johnson lacked the critical third component of the Vitruvian trinity: It may have provided firmness and commodity but not delight:

The Museum of Modern Art, on the other extreme, works well over the years. It is the opposite of the Guggenheim. It has no central space, no way to tell where you are, on which floor, or even, in many installations, where you are on which floor. It is an efficient loft building without pretensions to interior architecture. On the other hand, by changing walls, great variety is maintained. . . . Could there have been just a little architecture, a little magnificence introduced into this efficient interior? For this lack I apologize to the architectural profession.[52]

With this dramatic apologia for the shortcomings of functionalist architecture, Johnson defined his own mission, as well as the client's, to create more meaningful architecture. This was particularly relevant for civic institutions, especially museums, which he reckoned "now are, or should be, considered as important as churches or city halls in our civic schemes."[53] Given the enormous cultural and social status the museum had assumed, Johnson admonished his colleagues: "[It] behooves you museum directors and us architects to spend much time and effort in finding a proper architectural expression for our new buildings, suitable to our times and fit to be monuments for times to come."[54] The responsibility he claimed was enormous: "Remember that civilizations are sometimes remembered only by their

22. Philip Johnson. Sheldon Memorial Art Gallery, University of Nebraska, Lincoln. 1963

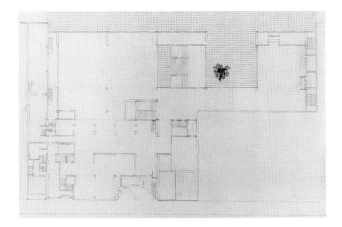 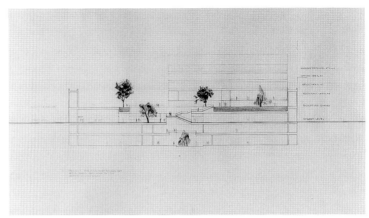

23.a–b. Arthur Drexler. Addition to The Museum of Modern Art, New York, Project. a) First-floor plan. ca. December 1960. Pencil on tracing paper, 18 5/8 x 23⅞" (47.2 x 60.5 cm); b) Section (east–west). December 1960. Print, 21½ x 33" (54.6 x 83.8 cm). Arthur Drexler archive, Department of Architecture and Design, The Museum of Modern Art, New York

buildings."[55] Historical precedent had become Johnson's chief inspiration, even for a museum devoted to modern art.[56]

Several months after Johnson's monumental proposal was unveiled, a significant gift to the Museum prompted a reconsideration of the plan. On March 8, 1960, the Museum announced Mrs. Prentice's conveyance of her two five-story brownstones on Fifty-third Street. Upon her death, the houses would become Museum property, but until that time, she would retain possession.[57] The intended gift offered the Museum greater freedom and flexibility in its planning, but at the time of the announcement it was unclear how this "invaluable advantage" would affect the plans.[58]

It is curious that an institution whose Department of Architecture and Design promoted competitions—for low-cost furniture, posters, textiles, and architecture—should not have considered a broader spectrum of ideas for its own home. There is little to suggest that anyone other than Johnson was ever considered to design the expansion. But by the end of 1960, Arthur Drexler, who had become director of Architecture and Design in 1956 at age thirty-one, prepared a series of alternative studies that bore no resemblance whatsoever to Johnson's proposals. Drexler, a member of the 30th Anniversary Drive Steering Committee, was generally regarded as a brilliant, self-made man. Although he had attended only one year of the architecture program at The Cooper Union for the Advancement of Art and Science, the changes in the program brought about by the Prentice bequest were something of a catalyst for Drexler to experiment with his own architectural ideas.[59] If the trustees supported his effort, there is no record.[60]

Over two hundred drawings and sketches for the project remain in the Drexler archive in the Department of Architecture and Design, many dating from December 1960 to January 1961, suggesting more than a little dissatisfaction with Johnson's 1959 project. Three main design ideas can be identified in Drexler's proposals, all of which are predicated on the idea of building on the large plot occupied by The Abby Aldrich Rockefeller Sculpture Garden. Treating the garden as a prime building site, Drexler explored a variety of terraced rooftop gardens. In one scheme the garden is raised to the second floor, with a new courtyard entrance on Fifty-fourth Street (figs. 23.a–b). After passing through the new lobby, visitors would proceed either directly ahead, to the old Fifty-third Street lobby-turned-gallery or to the sculpture garden and galleries above; or descend to large new galleries on two underground levels

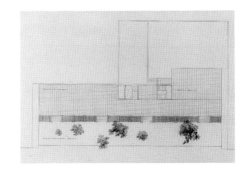

24. Arthur Drexler. Addition to The Museum of Modern Art, New York, Project. Upper-level plan of garden. December 1960. Pencil on tracing paper, 18⅝ x 23⅞" (47.2 x 60.5 cm). Arthur Drexler archive, Department of Architecture and Design, The Museum of Modern Art, New York

surrounding a central atrium with pool and trees. Another scheme plays with the idea of a promenade forming a linear division between a paved sculpture court and a promenade garden (fig. 24). A third scheme presents a four-story structure—a series of stacked, cantilevered parapets with outdoor terraces on each level, topped by a roof garden (figs. 25.a–b)—possibly inspired by Wright's Fallingwater (1934–37) and new Guggenheim Museum.[61] The profile of the balconies overlooking the street are varied in geometric configuration: Prows and indentations, intended solely for visual interest, obscure the continuity of the wall plane along the street. An aerial perspective illustrates the multilevel series of outdoor rooms that would result, yet the scheme nevertheless forsakes the unity and coherence of Johnson's walled paradise.

Perhaps the advantages to Drexler's schemes, in addition to maximizing the available site, were greater horizontal spaces and more direct physical connection with the existing Museum building. His proposals did not, however, convince the trustees to abandon Johnson's plans; one can well imagine that such a radical redesign of the garden alone would have curtailed further consideration of the schemes. (Ironically, the idea of maximizing the garden site by building galleries beneath it, and even raising the entire garden to the second story, would be proposed by Johnson less than a decade later; see pp. 93–98 below.)

In June 1962, Mrs. Prentice died at the age of ninety-one; her townhouses were demolished by the Museum the following January. With the site secure, Johnson and the Museum were anxious to break ground, and they acted quickly. Wilder Green, assistant director in the Department of Architecture and Design, was appointed liaison between the Museum and Johnson.[62] The monumental Fifty-fourth Street proposal was scrapped. In fact, even before Mrs. Prentice's death, the Museum had asked Johnson to rethink the initial 1956 study for an east wing on the site of the Prentice Houses. On May 25, 1962, he was authorized to proceed with working drawings for the East Wing.[63] Aware of the Museum's growing international stature, the trustees planned to inaugurate the new Museum in time for the 1964 World's Fair, an event of global significance.[64]

Four months later, on October 1, 1962, spectacular scale models of the new additions and the reconfigured lobby in the original building were unveiled at a press preview of the exhibition *The Museum of Modern Art Builds*[65] (fig. 1, p. 70). The models and plans illustrated three main elements to be constructed in two phases (fig. 26).

25.a–b. Arthur Drexler. Addition to The Museum of Modern Art, New York, Project. ca. December 1960–January 1961. a) Aerial perspective looking south from Fifty-fourth Street. Pencil and colored pencil on tracing paper, 18⅝ x 23⅞" (47.2 x 60.5 cm); b) Perspective view looking west on Fifty-fourth Street. Pencil on tracing paper, 18⅝ x 23⅞" (47.2 x 60.5 cm). Arthur Drexler archive, Department of Architecture and Design, The Museum of Modern Art, New York

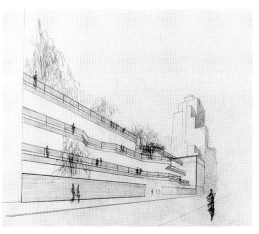

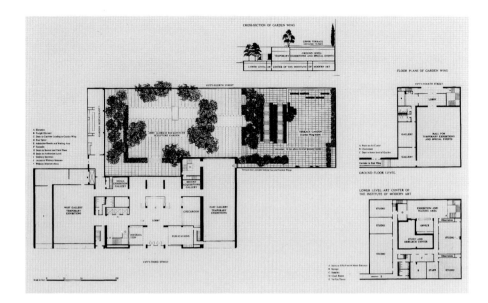

Left:
26. Philip C. Johnson Associates. The Museum of
Modern Art, New York. Ground-floor plan. October
1962

27. Philip C. Johnson Associates. The Abby Aldrich
Rockefeller Sculpture Garden, with Addition of
Roof Terrace and Stairs, The Museum of Modern Art,
New York. Aerial perspective. 1964. Drawing by
Helmut Jacoby. (Whereabouts of original unknown)

28. Philip C. Johnson Associates. The Abby Aldrich
Rockefeller Sculpture Garden with Addition of
Roof Terrace and Stairs, The Museum of Modern Art,
New York. View from west. 1964

The East Wing (on the site of the Prentice Houses) and a vastly reduced Garden Wing (on the Fifty-fourth Street site) were to be built immediately in the first phase along with the remodeled lobby. The proposed West Wing (replacing the Rogers Annex and two adjacent townhouses) was designated for a future second phase. A televised groundbreaking, aired live as a CBS Special Event, took place on November 25, 1962. Governor Nelson Rockefeller, accompanied by August Heckscher (consultant on the arts for the White House), René d'Harnoncourt, Alfred Barr, William Burden, and Philip Johnson, sunk their spades in the Fifty-fourth Street site of the new Garden Wing. The broadcast continued from the lobby, where Johnson discussed the exhibition of models. Although Johnson's designs would undergo some revisions, these models were a close approximation of the completed buildings.

The two-story Garden Wing fronting West Fifty-fourth Street housed the Art Center of the Institute of Modern Art, the Museum's affiliated school for eight hundred children and adults on the basement level, which moved from the Rogers Annex into more spacious quarters. At ground level was a large hall, sixty by seventy-five feet, for temporary exhibitions and special events. Its rooftop terrace (replaced in 1984 by the Members' Dining Room) provided a raised extension of the sculpture garden in the form of a belvedere,[66] linked to the garden by a grand staircase sheathed in the same gray-and-white Vermont marble as the garden plaza and oriented in a north-south direction (figs. 27, 28). While escalators may have been appropriate for interior galleries, Johnson labored over numerous studies for a garden staircase.[67] In one surviving drawing, a succession of stairs and landings, flanked by stepped waterfalls, is aligned on the long axis (fig. 29). Here, the axial symmetry of the addition and the asymmetry inherent in the earlier garden form an awkward marriage. As built, the gradual ascent of the monumental staircase, broken by periodic landings and a change in direction, created a rich spatial experience. In an essay on the "processional element in architecture," Johnson described the garden stairs:

We took space enough for STAIRS *in the old sense. We hope people will climb stairs, an experience lost in modern architecture, the ramps of the great Le Corbusier being the*

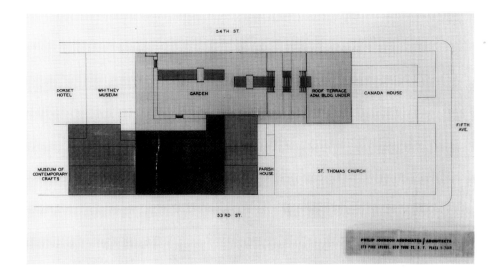

29. Philip C. Johnson Associates. Site Plan with Preliminary Study of Garden Stairs Roof Terrace, The Museum of Modern Art, New York. ca. 1962. Pen and ink and zipatone on coated linen, 25 x 32⅛" (63.5 x 81.5 cm). Philip Johnson archive (140.3), Department of Architecture and Design, The Museum of Modern Art, New York

noble exception. In our [the Museum's] garden about two domestic stories are climbed by many who would never go to the attic of a suburban house without complaining. It is the experience of the change of direction of what one sees as one rises. The speed of ascent (slow in the Museum stairs) is crucial. Time to look around, to feel the change that a rise gives. The curiosity of what is on top, the question: What will I see from up there? The comfort of a slow, obvious, and wide ascent. All of these considerations are more important than the "looks" of the stairway. Architecture is motion.[68]

Whereas in earlier studies for the East Wing Johnson had proposed relocating the lobby, in 1962, he completely redesigned the existing lobby of the Goodwin–Stone building to accommodate larger crowds, a bookstore and information center, and two small exhibition rooms. The original intimate lobby was approached from a corner entrance topped by an idiosyncratic curvilinear canopy (fig. 2, p. 71; figs. 30, 31). In redesigning and expanding the lobby Johnson created a stronger connection

Left:
30. Philip L. Goodwin and Edward D. Stone, Architects. Entrance Lobby, The Museum of Modern Art, New York. 1939

Right:
31. Philip L. Goodwin and Edward D. Stone, Architects. First Floor, The Museum of Modern Art, New York. Plan. 1939. Ink on linen, 20 x 27⅝" (51 x 70 cm). The Museum of Modern Art, New York

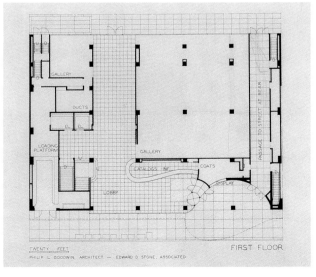

with the garden. The new entrance (with a more conventional rectangular canopy) was given a central location in axial alignment with the garden. A new garden wall of glass created an unobstructed view of the sculpture garden from Fifty-third Street as well as from any point in the lobby (figs. 32, 33). Up to that time, special exhibitions were often installed in the rear of the lobby, and the view to the garden was usually sealed off by temporary walls. The brilliant effect of the new axial alignment between lobby and garden was to bring the outdoors inside while drawing the visitor beyond the lobby to the garden. By virtue of a more visible connection, the popular sculpture garden assumed a more central focus in the overall plan: Museum buildings surrounded it on the east, south, and west. At the same time, the lobby walls were reclad in gray granite, a gesture toward a greater monumentality and chromatic harmony with the garden. Thus connected, the lobby and garden began to assume the character of a magnificent public space, which heretofore was lacking.

The galleries on the first three floors of the East Wing, built fifty feet wide and one hundred feet deep, were designed with clear spans. The open spaces were uninterrupted by interior supports to achieve the greatest freedom and flexibility for exhi-

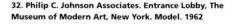

32. Philip C. Johnson Associates. Entrance Lobby, The Museum of Modern Art, New York. Model. 1962

33. Philip C. Johnson Associates. Entrance Lobby, The Museum of Modern Art, New York. 1964

34. Installation view, *Alberto Giacometti,* The Museum of Modern Art, New York, 1965. The installation, on the ground floor of the East Wing, was designed by Wilder Green.

bition installation—precisely the anonymous loftlike interiors Barr preferred (fig. 34). Floor levels and ceiling heights corresponded to those of the original building.

The steel-and-glass façade, which in the 1962 model suggested a design similar to the Rogers Annex, underwent numerous revisions. In his boldest scheme (fig. 35), Johnson took as his chief inspiration the original Goodwin–Stone building. Above the windowless galleries of the proposed East and West Wings, with their blind screens of stone panels set within a grid of mullions, the upper office floors are distinguished by deep-set balconies, echoing the original building's ribbon windows and upper terrace. The horizontality is underscored by massive trusses, expressive of the clear floor span inside. The West Wing is further articulated by what appears to be a stair tower, rendered in a fashion similar to the stair and exhaust towers of Louis I. Kahn's celebrated Richards Medical Research Building (1957–61) in Philadelphia.[69] The design did not appeal to d'Harnoncourt, who found it too formidable, and further studies were undertaken.[70]

As realized, the East Wing façade was treated more-or-less uniformly from top to bottom in black steel and glass, the dark wings forming a contrast to the white façade of the original Goodwin–Stone building (fig. 36). Taking its cue from the annex, the Miesian geometry was softened by curving the large floor-to-ceiling window frames in a manner similar to the upper rows of windows in Johnson's Fifty-fourth Street proposal of 1959. The black-steel curtain wall took on a lacier appearance, with deep mullions hinting at the elaborate tracery in the Gothic windows of St. Thomas' Church next door. (The similarity between the windows of the two buildings is even more apparent in a study where the large windows of the East Wing are subdivided vertically [fig. 37]. The additional mullion emphasizes the tall narrow proportion of the windows and adds to the sense of tracery.) The bronze-tinted glass gave a warm glow to the illuminated interiors, although some of the curators would have preferred natural light.[71] The overall effect of the richly detailed façade suggested the adjective frequently invoked in the 1950s and 1960s to describe Johnson's designs: "elegant."

If the interiors of the new galleries and Garden Wing required relatively little attention from the architect (Barr and d'Harnoncourt were much involved with the

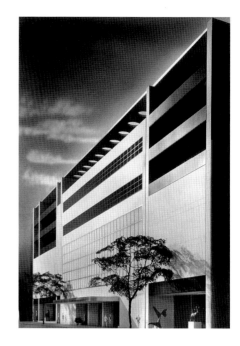

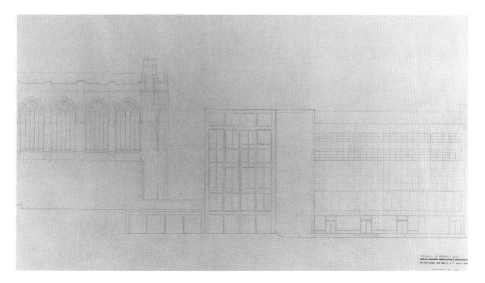

Top:
35. Philip C. Johnson Associates. Proposed East and West Wings, The Museum of Modern Art, New York. Model. ca. 1962

Above:
36. Philip C. Johnson Associates. East and West Wings, The Museum of Modern Art, New York. Perspective view. ca. 1962–63. Drawing by Helmut Jacoby. (Whereabouts of original unknown)

Left:
37. Philip C. Johnson Associates. Garden Elevation with Proposed East Wing and St. Thomas' Church, The Museum of Modern Art, New York. October 4, 1962. Pencil on tracing paper, 23⅜ x 45⅞" (59.3 x 116.5 cm). Philip Johnson archive (140.2), Department of Architecture and Design, The Museum of Modern Art, New York

38. Philip C. Johnson Associates. Founders' Room, East Wing, The Museum of Modern Art, New York. 1964

design of the galleries),[72] Johnson unleashed his flair for dramatic interiors in the Founders' Room, the Museum's principal entertainment room completed in September 1964 (figs. 38, 39). In a two-story space atop the East Wing (and adjacent to the adjoining trustee and meeting rooms) Johnson was permitted "to have his fling," as Wilder Green later recalled.[73] The program lent itself to Johnson's architectural wit—after all, it was not a gallery open to the public but rather the Museum's private entertainment room. The walls were covered from the black baseboard all the way to the cornice in light-gray, sound-absorbing, fireproof carpeting. Above the cornice a vaulted ceiling outlined with white-painted steel I-beams (the reverse of the black-steel façade) and ringed with bare light bulbs evoked a theatrical atmosphere. The mannerist sensibility in the combination of historical references and a corrupted Miesian vocabulary (I-beams painted white and applied to the interior walls) was observed by the architectural press. In an article titled "Camp Mies," the editors at *Progressive Architecture* clearly understood the humor:

Philip Johnson has designed another handsome, classic room in the Miesian idiom but sends it sky high. The joke may be sick architectural sacrilege, but it really gets off the ground because it is irresistibly funny. . . . The immediate effect is a combination of Mies, Gothic, and a carnival midway of the 90's and it comes out somewhat Turkish.[74]

But more extraordinary than the carpeted walls and vaulted ceiling was the treatment of the steel columns, which were mounted on the walls, stopping eighteen inches short of the floor—not unlike the applied I-beams on the Rogers Annex, which were mounted above the glass wall of the entrance canopy. Citing historic precedent, Johnson described his design as a modern manifestation of Goethe's observation that "the pilaster is a lie! One would answer him today—yes, but what a delightfully useful one."[75] Of course, Mies's I-beams applied to the building façades were also "a lie," in that they served no direct structural function but were symbolic of the structural I-beams concealed behind the façade. Nevertheless, the irony behind Johnson's gesture seems more akin to Pop art than to Mies's sober expression of the building's underlying structure. While it lasted, the Founders' Room provided a grand and appropriate setting for dinner parties and other special events.[76] (It is not surprising that on March 1, 1965, Johnson received the Elsie de Wolfe Award of the American Institute of Interior Designers and was recognized for his contributions to the "life, look, and enjoyment of New York City."[77])

On May 25, 1964, eighteen months after the groundbreaking, the new East Wing, Garden Wing, and redesigned lobby were opened to great acclaim. A series of exhibitions drawn from the Museum collections under the general title *Art in a Changing World 1884–1964,* filled the galleries. The "new" museum also contained the Edward Steichen Photography Center, the Philip Goodwin Galleries for Architecture and Design, and the Paul J. Sachs Gallery of Drawings and Prints—the first time in the Museum's history that permanent galleries were devoted to arts other than painting and sculpture. At a festive dinner in the Garden Wing, the First Lady, Mrs. Lyndon Baines Johnson, addressed the glittering crowd assembled on the new rooftop terrace. The other scheduled guest speaker was Paul Tillich, the eminent twentieth-century theologian who had fled Nazi Germany in 1933; as he was unable to attend, a colleague read his prepared speech.[78] One of the most influential aspects of Tillich's thought was his examination of the relationship between religion and culture in the modern world. His poignant address to the benefactors, artists, and other dignitaries that evening reflected upon his own experience as a refugee from Germany, and the significant role played by the Museum in extending hope for civilization: "This museum then appeared to us as an embodiment of honesty in creative expression, both in architecture and in the arts for which architecture gives the

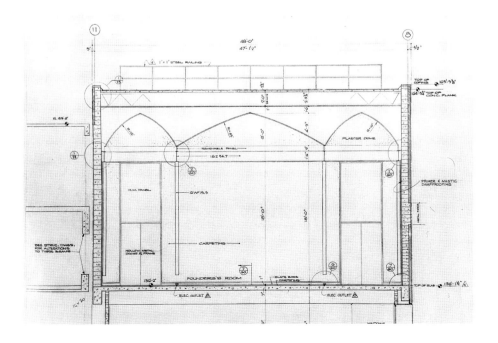

39. Philip C. Johnson Associates. Founders' Room, East Wing, The Museum of Modern Art, New York. Cross-section (detail). June 17, 1963, with later revisions. Pencil on coated linen, 36⅝ x 48" (93 x 122 cm). Philip Johnson archive (140.45), Department of Architecture and Design, The Museum of Modern Art, New York

space and the frame."[79] Assaying the unique power and meaning of the arts cloaked within the new "space and the frame," Tillich wrote:

The arts . . . open up a dimension of reality which is otherwise hidden, and they open up our own being for receiving this reality. Only the arts can do this; science, philosophy, moral action and religious devotion cannot. The artist brings to our senses and, through them to our whole being, something of the depth of our world and of ourselves, something of the mystery of being. When we are grasped by a work of art, things appear to us which were unknown before, possibilities of being, unthought of powers, hidden in the depth of life which take hold of us. They reach us through the language of art, a language different from that of our daily life, a language of symbols, however realistic the artistic style may be. This is true of all arts, and in a particular way of the arts of the eye, in the service of which this building has been renewed.[80]

The remarks contained in Tillich's address remain profoundly moving and idealistic, far removed from the cynicism and irony of the Pop art then emerging in 1964. By the end of the decade, the cultural climate had changed, and the impact would be felt by the Museum, even as it considered its next expansion project.

The critics were united in their enthusiasm and praise for the new Museum building. Ada Louise Huxtable, the *New York Times* critic, offered the most substantial and insightful review, remarking on the particular elements and the overall composition. Beginning with the East Wing, Huxtable observed:

Designed by Philip Johnson, an architect as poised and polished as the building, it is one of New York's most subtly effective structures, its refined simplicity quietly understanding the care of its detailing and the sensitivity of its relationships to older buildings and commercial and residential neighbors. It is successful not only as architecture, but also as cityscape, an area in which architects commit their most serious crimes. . . . The point is that the museum has not "modernized" itself in the conventional sense—one of the most atrocious of architectural practices—but shows a clear, consecutive, compatible sequence of evolving tastes within a period of dynamic architectural change. . . . It provides a lesson in proper relationships through scale and detail rather than through refacing the old and "frosting" the new with matching materials. Together, the three sections are a prime demonstration of how not to make buildings swear at each other or their surroundings.[81]

Sketching the Future: "The Most Spectacular Public Room of the Twentieth Century"[82]

The successful completion of the new East Wing and Garden Wing in 1964, which had more than doubled the gallery space and enlarged the sculpture garden by one third, was only the first phase of a two-part plan. The anticipated West Wing remained on paper. A set of drawings by Johnson dated March 8, 1966, illustrate a new eight-story wing to replace the Rogers Annex (no. 21), the old Theatre Guild Building, acquired in the early 1950s (nos. 23–25), and a townhouse at 27 West Fifty-third Street, donated by Wallace K. Harrison. The proposed wing, nearly twice the size of the East Wing, would provide additional galleries on several floors roughly eighty feet square, a new library and archives, and offices. But plans were delayed for a couple of years when the Museum took ownership of the Whitney Building in

June 1966.[83] Johnson transformed the Whitney into the Museum's Lillie P. Bliss International Study Center. The new center, which also provided additional storage, conservation, and library space, opened in May 1968. This project coincided with René d'Harnoncourt's retirement, which was announced in 1967. The design and construction of the West Wing would be the responsibility of d'Harnoncourt's successors.

To this end, on July 31, 1968, the Museum retained the consulting firm of Bowen, Gurin, Barnes & Roche to plan and conduct a survey of the Museum's fundraising potential in order to test the feasibility of a new fifty-million-dollar campaign.[84] As the survey was nearing completion, an imaginative new idea was proposed. Conceived by Richard H. Koch, the Museum's director of administration and counsel, the plan called for "financing—through $30 million in commercial loans—the construction of two buildings: a 41-story office building with the first 8 floors to be occupied by the Museum and a two-story garden building."[85] The report stated: "The rental income from commercial tenants would cover interest and amortization of the mortgage, taxes, and operating expenses of the office building; and, after the debt is retired in 25 years, it would make $2.7 million of gross annual income (subject to income taxes) available to the Museum."[86] The proposed tower would engulf the projected West Wing, two additional townhouses (not yet acquired), and the new International Study Center in the old Whitney building. Plans for the garden building called for "(1) raising the present garden by one floor and (2) building two floors beneath it . . . [to] provide the extensive additional gallery space that the Museum has long needed for both permanent and temporary exhibitions."[87] The overall plan was predicated on the concept of transferring the Museum's air rights—the undeveloped potential of the Museum's land holdings—to the new tower.

Based on an analysis of the survey, Bowen, Gurin recommended that the Museum's Planning Committee study the feasibility and desirability of the office tower and redefine the objectives of its campaign since the new idea was developed too late to be tested in the survey. The firm also suggested that the Planning Committee study the relevance of the Museum's policies and functions, and appoint a Community Relations Committee "to be more responsive to the current needs and aspirations of the total community"; such a position, it argued, "would strengthen the Museum's image and increase its prospects for financial support."[88]

The prospect of a commercial tower generating funds annually to support the nonprofit institution housed below it was particularly appealing. The financial situation at the Museum was strained. Although it had doubled in size in 1964, its operating costs had tripled.[89] The trustees recognized that it was growing increasingly unrealistic, and was potentially imprudent to rely on the resources of a few wealthy benefactors to keep the growing institution in the black. New sources of financial support were needed, and the Museum's air rights were a potential source that had yet to be tapped.

To study the idea of a tower above the Museum and galleries below a raised sculpture garden, the Museum once again turned to Johnson, who in 1967 had entered a partnership with John Burgee. Between the winter of 1968–69 and June 1970, Johnson and Burgee, Architects, produced a series of conceptual studies that focused on the massing, cost, and square footage of the tower and garden.[90] In their studies, the tower, ranging in height from twenty-eight to thirty-nine stories, was situated above the Goodwin–Stone building, with an entrance lobby west of the Museum, similar to the location of the Museum Tower entrance today. The idea of constructing galleries beneath the sculpture garden was explored in almost all the studies. (Some of the ideas were ultimately reflected in the 1984 addition designed by Cesar Pelli. Other concepts, had they been developed, would have altered radically the shape of the Museum and the sculpture garden.)

Not surprisingly, the question of altering the garden was the subject of much interest and debate. In an initial meeting with Mayor John V. Lindsay's Office of Midtown Planning and Development in June 1969, the city encouraged the Museum neither to alter the garden nor to demolish other recently completed additions.[91] In fact, city authorities questioned the wisdom of further expansion in midtown, and suggested that the Museum consider building in another borough, even in "ghetto" areas where land values were lower and the sites offered more flexibility. Why, they argued, should an institution invariably assume the greater costs of a midtown expansion; economically disadvantaged areas should also benefit from having major cultural institutions. Aside from zoning issues related to the tower, the city's reactions reflected wider cultural, social, and political changes of the late 1960s. In short, with no indication the plan would meet with the approval of the planning office, the Museum began to modify its proposal.

Shortly after the June meeting, Walter Bareiss, a trustee and member of the Museum's new Operating Committee (the triumvirate, with Wilder Green and Richard Koch, formed after Bates Lowry's brief tenure as director ended in May 1969), appointed an Ad Hoc Planning Committee to assist the trustees in defining their immediate and long-term goals.[92] Composed of staff members, the committee was chaired by Arthur Drexler, who was also asked to serve as liaison between the Museum and Johnson.[93] Drexler and his colleagues worked intensely on a "Report to the Trustees." By September 1969, the report was completed. Conceived to bring the Museum into the twenty-first century, the document also addressed the future of the sculpture garden and the changing relationship between the Museum, the artists it represented, and an increasingly diverse public. Johnson, Drexler, and the committee devised a plan to preserve the garden and transform it into a freely accessible public amenity—not only to satisfy the city's demands for a more community-friendly institution, but also to gain zoning variances and tax abatements necessary for the realization of the overall project.[94]

In light of Drexler's own 1960–61 proposals to build new galleries in place of the sculpture garden, one might have expected him to forsake the outdoor amenity willingly. But in the Ad Hoc Planning Committee's report, he acknowledged the significance of the garden:

The Sculpture Garden is our most valuable physical amenity. Because it is so popular our visitors have come to think of it as a public park. Some preliminary building studies have shown that new galleries at the required scale, together with a new entrance to the Museum, could be accommodated on the garden site. But the disappearance of the garden would provoke endless criticism; no less serious to the Museum would be the loss of an essential exhibition space. Other solutions are possible and there is no reason for us to lose the garden. We should in fact be striving to make it yield still greater advantages.[95]

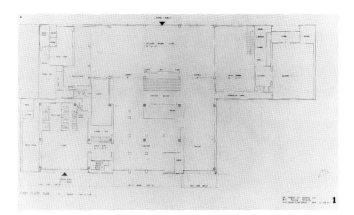

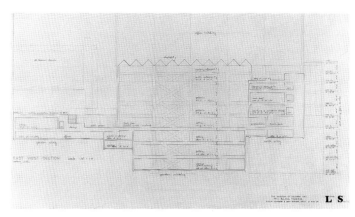

The new scheme hinged on the concept of enclosing the sculpture garden with a six-story glass atrium affording year-round use. While new galleries could be constructed beneath it, the garden would be preserved at street level as a free public plaza, becoming the new entrance to the Museum on Fifty-fourth Street (figs. 40, 41). Drexler's excitement over the new glass-covered court is evident in the report:

The entrance to the Museum is our first opportunity to prepare the public for the experience within. More than this: it is the link between the Museum and the city. *How we use it has great consequence, and the suggestions that follow would restore the exhilarating benefits of a truly public scale. . . .* It would serve not only as the entrance to the Museum but, symbolically, as a gesture of welcome to the community. . . . *Glass-walled and glass-roofed, the garden would be available at our discretion for both public and private events throughout the year. . . . The Museum's bookstore in the ideal arrangement would open directly into it; the Restaurant would overlook it from an upper floor. Nothing in the United States, or indeed the world, could be compared with it. MoMA's entrance—our link to the City—would be the most spectacular public room of the twentieth century.*[96]

On the one hand, the new public space was conceived to present the Museum "in a sympathetic relation to the community."[97] For the generous public amenity and gesture of welcome, the city was expected to grant concessions on zoning for the proposed tower. Moreover, the proposal also satisfied the architectural ambitions of both curator and architect. In an open confession of "museum envy," Drexler calculated that "if all the galleries in the Museum of Modern Art could be stacked in one large rectangle, they would fit into the main entrance hall of the Metropolitan Museum"[98]—a compelling image, no doubt meant to persuade the trustees to build something truly monumental.

Monumentality had great appeal for Johnson as well, and in comparison to the modest glass pavilion proposed for the garden in 1948, he now envisioned nothing less than a crystal palace: a steel-frame atrium with a transparent skin, flooded with natural light. Not only would the new design preserve the sculpture garden—Johnson's undisputed masterpiece—it would gain in prestige by becoming, at once, the main entrance to an internationally famous institution, a potential income-producer, and a year-round public amenity. The vaulted travertine ceilings typical of

Left:
40. Philip Johnson and John Burgee, Architects. Expansion Proposal, The Museum of Modern Art, New York. First-floor plan. August 27, 1969. Pencil and colored pencil on tracing paper, 17¾ x 36¾" (45 x 93.3 cm). Philip Johnson archive (165.17), Department of Architecture and Design, The Museum of Modern Art, New York

Right:
41. Philip Johnson and John Burgee, Architects. Expansion Proposal, The Museum of Modern Art, New York. Longitudinal section. August 27, 1969. Pencil and colored pencil on tracing paper, 17⅞ x 32⅛" (45.4 x 81.5 cm). Philip Johnson archive (165.20), Department of Architecture and Design, The Museum of Modern Art, New York

Johnson's grand salons of a few years earlier had been transformed by the "green-house aesthetic," as the architectural historian Helen Searing dubbed the phenomenon of glass-enclosed atriums, an increasingly popular trend for museums, hotels, and office buildings in the late 1960s.[99] One of the first was the atrium designed by Kevin Roche and John Dinkeloo and Associates for the Ford Foundation Headquarters Building (1963–67) in New York, cited by Drexler as an example of what was envisioned for the Museum.[100] (Roche and Dinkeloo would bring a similar aesthetic to The Metropolitan Museum of Art's American Wing, completed in 1980, which they had already begun planning in 1969.) Drexler found other examples to illustrate the concept as well, sending photographs of all-glass Japanese buildings to Operating Committee member Richard Koch (very likely the same buildings that later appeared in Drexler's 1979 exhibition *Transformations in Modern Architecture*).[101] Summerland Recreation Center (1966–67), a giant indoor tropical oasis near Tokyo, was such an example[102] (fig. 42).

While working on the Museum project, Johnson and Burgee were also designing the Crystal Court for the I.D.S. Center (fig. 43), a new office building in Minneapolis included in the 1970–71 Museum exhibition *Work in Progress: Architecture by Philip Johnson, Kevin Roche, Paul Rudolph,* and, later, in *Transformations.* The steel-and-glass pyramids of the Crystal Court roof peak at 121 feet, creating a heroically large central space that Johnson once described as "a town square that worked."[103] Pelli, while designing the Museum Tower and Garden Hall in 1979, would also praise the Crystal Court at I.D.S., not for its aesthetic qualities but rather for how well it functions as a social space:

This large hall is a very successful intensifier of urban life. And when one is there it is this intensity of life that is dominant and delightful. The building and its details are here very secondary. It is in the total experience that it became a great piece of architecture; in my own terms, his most successful.[104]

Left:
42. Ishimoto Architectural and Engineering Firm, Inc.: Kinji Fukuda, Project Architect; Minoru Murakami, Architect. Summerland Recreation Center, near Tokyo. 1966–67

Right:
43. Johnson and Burgee; Edward F. Baker Associates, Inc. Crystal Court, I.D.S. Center, Minneapolis. 1968–73

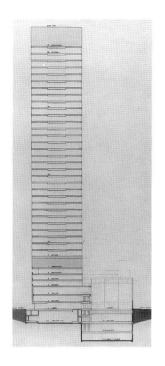

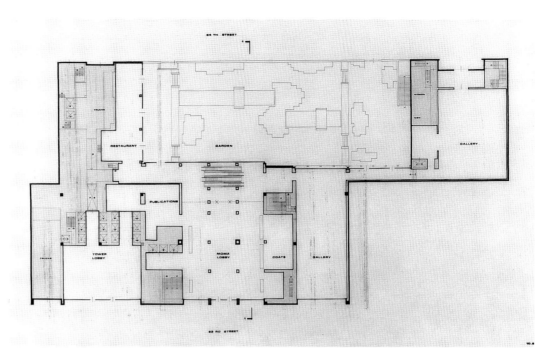

In the fall of 1969, shortly after the garden court was proposed, William S. Paley, president of the Museum, decided to scale back the scope of the feasibility studies to the three floors below the garden (one for mechanical services and two for galleries), while keeping open future options such as the tower and a new auditorium (figs. 44, 45). Perhaps foreseeing the legal complications in financing the tower, Paley placed a cap of ten million dollars on new construction without a tower. Several months later, in a presentation to the Museum's Steering Committee on April 21, 1970, Johnson recapitulated the various ideas under consideration and exhibited a model accompanied by professional renderings. The chief concepts were to elevate the garden to the second story, thereby freeing the ground it occupied for street-level galleries, beneath which a new underground level would be built (figs. 46–49). In its new, elevated position, The Abby Aldrich Rockefeller Sculpture Garden would be reproduced exactly.[105] The sublevel galleries, with twenty-foot ceiling heights, would be suitable for showing large-scale works of art. Principal circulation between floors would be through a dark-glass atrium, with escalators to handle the "endless, endless amounts of people without any possible clogging, as department stores do."[106] (As envisioned, it was not unlike the present Garden Hall designed by Pelli; see fig. 50, p. 100.) The 1964 Garden Wing would be transformed into a much-needed second auditorium with its own entrance on Fifty-fourth Street, facilitating access to screenings and other events when the Museum galleries were closed.[107]

During the presentation Johnson acknowledged some of the problems inherent in the schemes: the questionable wisdom of exhibiting art below potentially leaking garden pools, and the difficulty of reconciling floor levels between the various buildings and the elevated garden. But to him, these were details to be worked out in subsequent studies. His frustration at scaling back the project to a ten-million-dollar ceiling was graciously articulated. If an architect's responsibility is in part to lead a client, Johnson certainly met it, lobbying for (what Drexler called) "the

Left:
44. Philip Johnson and John Burgee, Architects. Expansion Proposal, The Museum of Modern Art, New York. Cross-section. October 20, 1969. Pencil with Letraline and Zipatone on vellum, 45 x 18" (114.3 x 45.7 cm). Philip Johnson archive (165.75), Department of Architecture and Design, The Museum of Modern Art, New York

Right:
45. Philip Johnson and John Burgee, Architects. Expansion Proposal, The Museum of Modern Art, New York. First-floor plan. October 29, 1969. Pencil with Letraline and Zipatone on vellum, 18¼ x 32" (46.3 x 81.2 cm). Philip Johnson archive (165.78), Department of Architecture and Design, The Museum of Modern Art, New York

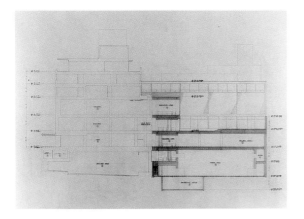

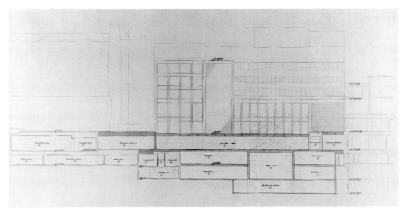

most spectacular public room of the twentieth century," and for the atrium with escalators to every floor, "which Bill Paley gave me strict instructions not to do."[108] In a pitch to the committee Johnson reminisced, "Wouldn't it be nice to go back to potted palms? Since the Plaza went, we've never had potted palms."[109] He then explained his rationale for a grander scheme: "[Because] it looks so awful to stop it where the budget says where to stop it. And I thought we'd better show it as if we had all the money in the world, and then we'd squeeze in afterwards the way we did in the last drive."[110]

Perhaps as a concession to the trustees' economic prudence, Johnson presented a modest final study for a four-story West Wing—the first three stories for galleries, the fourth for offices—in a set of drawings dated May 20, 1970. The schematic drawings were uninspired: The façade was treated simply and based on the restrained, Miesian vocabulary of the Whitney Museum. Construction cost was estimated at just under five million dollars.

Nothing was built at this time, but several years later the innovative financial, administrative, and zoning mechanisms were in place that would permit the creation of the Trust for Cultural Resources and the transfer of air rights to the commercial tower.[111] The process was engineered by Donald Elliott, chairman of the Planning Commission in the Lindsay Administration; Richard S. Weinstein, also a member of the Lindsay Planning Commission; and Koch.[112] Both Elliott and Weinstein had considerable experience with similar complex zoning and planning issues (by then already tested on other projects in the city). When it was time to engage an architect in the mid 1970s, Elliott was particularly concerned that, should the commission go to a Museum trustee (in addition to Johnson, other eminent trustee-architects were Edward Larrabee Barnes, Gordon Bunshaft, and Wallace K. Harrison), the deal would smack of impropriety and the appearance of a conflict of interest, a risk the Museum could not afford because of the public funds—real estate taxes—involved in financing the expansion.

The Trustee Building Committee on the Real Estate Development Project, chaired by Donald B. Marron, formed an Advisory Panel in the spring of 1976 to assist with the selection of an architect. The panel consisted of architects Barnes, Bunshaft, Ivan Chermayeff, Harrison, Johnson, and Drexler.[113] The committee interviewed three firms: Mitchell/Giurgola Associates, I. M. Pei and Partners, and Pelli, a partner in Gruen Associates who had just been appointed dean of the Yale

Left:
46. Philip Johnson and John Burgee, Architects. Expansion Proposal, The Museum of Modern Art, New York. Cross-section. April 10, 1970, with later revisions. Pencil and colored pencil with Letraset on mylar, 35⅝ x 48" (90.5 x 122 cm). Philip Johnson archive (165.164), Department of Architecture and Design, The Museum of Modern Art, New York

Right:
47. Philip Johnson and John Burgee, Architects. Expansion Proposal, The Museum of Modern Art, New York. Sectional elevation (longitudinal) through the garden. April 10, 1970, with later revisions. Pencil and colored pencil with Letraset on mylar, 35⅝ x 48" (90.5 x 122 cm). Philip Johnson archive (165.163), Department of Architecture and Design, The Museum of Modern Art, New York

Left:
**48. Philip Johnson and John Burgee, Architects.
Expansion Proposal, The Museum of Modern Art,
New York. Interior perspective, lower-level gallery.
1970. Drawing by Ronald Love. Pencil on tracing
paper, 15 x 28" (38.1 x 71.1 cm). The Museum of
Modern Art, New York. Gift of Philip Johnson
(69 ASC 75)**

Right:
**49. Philip Johnson and John Burgee, Architects. The
Abby Aldrich Rockefeller Sculpture Garden Elevated
to Second Story with Galleries Below, The Museum
of Modern Art, New York. Aerial perspective. 1970.
(Whereabouts of original unknown)**

School of Architecture. Angered and disappointed that he was no longer under consideration as architect of the Museum's largest expansion, for which he had already expended considerable effort, Johnson nevertheless supported the choice of Pelli, whose Pacific Design Center (1971) in Los Angeles had caught his eye.[114] Johnson thus relinquished the unofficial title he had held for nearly thirty years: the Museum's architect. Pelli's reputation for building on time within the constraints of a developer's lean budget (a reputation Johnson apparently did not enjoy[115]) while producing serious architecture helped him win the job.[116] In early 1977, Pelli was formally selected as architect of the new Museum expansion, and Johnson supported the decision. A new condominium tower, new West Wing galleries, and escalators gliding up and down within a glass-enclosed atrium proffering views of The Abby Aldrich Rockefeller Sculpture Garden opened in 1984—the culmination of planning begun more than twenty years earlier.

Throughout his professional career Johnson's involvement with The Museum of Modern Art—as curator, architect, trustee, and patron—has been virtually continuous. As architect, he gave physical shape to the Museum as it acquired new property and expanded over the course of three decades. As additions grew around the Goodwin–Stone building, he deftly maintained a consistent aesthetic sensibility. The underlying Miesian rigor, the cohesive vocabulary of materials, and a sense of scale relating part to whole provided an appropriate expression for a museum devoted to modern art. His architectural contributions to the Museum are but a small part of his *oeuvre*. Yet these commissions, the Rockefeller Guest House and the sculpture garden principal among them, are also among his most successful, and in the late 1940s and 1950s were seminal works in a nascent career. Of course, some of the ideas he explored for the expansions were of questionable merit. As his architectural career flourished, he more boldly expressed a desire that the Museum have generous and inspiring public spaces—grand architecture emblematic of the institution's increasing stature. An historicist architecture—for example, the 1959 proposal for the Fifty-fourth Street wing (unbuilt)—was one way of expressing these aims, but seems ill-matched to a museum devoted to modern art. Other ambitious ideas, such as enclosing the sculpture garden with a crystalline glass skin, however much they may enthrall with spectacle and structural heroics, would ultimately detract from what was already the Museum's most inspired and memorable space,

50. Cesar Pelli and Associates; Edward Durell Stone Associates; Gruen Associates, Architects. Garden Hall and Tower, The Museum of Modern Art, New York. Model. 1977–84

one gloriously affected by seasonal change: the garden. Nevertheless, Johnson's contagious joy and enthusiasm for art, design, and aesthetics is no less apparent in his architecture than in his writings and talks. In designing an art museum, one is reminded of the principal goal Johnson defined for himself: "to make the visitor happy, to put him in a receptive frame of mind while he is undergoing an emotional experience."[117] Reflecting upon his additions to The Museum of Modern Art, one concludes that Johnson succeeded admirably.

Notes

Readers of an earlier draft of this essay included Franz Schulze, Wilder Green, Richard Koch, Beatrice Kernan, Harriet Schoenholz Bee, and Terence Riley. I am indebted to them for their generous and wise comments. Many colleagues at the Museum also provided support. Rona Roob, Chief Archivist, and her assistants Leslie Heitzman and Michelle Elligott enthusiastically guided me through the extensive resources in their care. Meisha Hunter, a research assistant, was also very helpful in gathering information. Intern Elspeth Cowell expertly catalogued the nearly nine hundred drawings of the Museum by Johnson housed in the Department of Architecture and Design while I was preparing this article; our discussions about the drawings and her insights were engaging. Pierre Adler, senior cataloguer, kindly offered to photograph many of the drawings. Mikki Carpenter and Jeffrey Ryan, Department of Photographic Services and Permissions, assisted in locating archival photographs. Finally, I would like to acknowledge the editorial expertise of Barbara Ross.

Throughout these notes, *Philip Johnson archive* and *Arthur Drexler archive* indicate nonformalized collections of largely uncatalogued source material housed in the Department of Architecture and Design, The Museum of Modern Art, New York. The Museum of Modern Art Oral History Project, an extensive series of audiotaped interviews conducted by the oral historian Sharon Zane between 1991 and 1995, is cited herein as *MoMA Oral History Project.* Transcripts of all interviews are housed in The Museum of Modern Art Archives *(MoMA Archives).* All Museum of Modern Art press releases cited are located in the Department of Communications.

1.   Philip C. Johnson, "Letter to the Museum Director," *Museum News* 38 (1960), p. 22.

2.   For a history of the design of the Goodwin–Stone building, see Dominic Ricciotti, "The 1939 Building of the Museum of Modern Art: The Goodwin–Stone Collaboration," *The American Art Journal* 17, no. 3 (Summer 1985), pp. 50–76.

3.   For a cogent discussion of Johnson's early curatorial career, see Terence Riley, "Portrait of the Curator as a Young Man," pp. 34–69 of the present volume.

4.   *Mies van der Rohe* opened at the Museum September 16, 1947, closing on November 23.

5.   The extensive use of glass in a residence was foreshadowed in the first of Johnson's architectural designs to be exhibited at the Museum, a model house in *Tomorrow's Small House,* held May 28 to September 30, 1945.

6.   Proposal in Photo File, Department of Architecture and Design, The Museum of Modern Art, New York.

7.   Philip C. Johnson, *Mies van der Rohe* (New York: The Museum of Modern Art, 1947), p. 109.

8.   Ibid., p. 197.

9.   Drawings for the model illustrating the addition are dated August 1946. See also "Building Postponement," *The Museum of Modern Art Bulletin* 15 (Fall 1947), p. 20; and Russell Lynes, *Good Old Modern: An Intimate Portrait of The Museum of Modern Art* (New York: Atheneum, 1973), pp. 391–92. Earlier, in spring 1943, Goodwin had proposed an addition, with a west building and a large east building housing television studios and an auditorium. In this proposal the length of the garden corresponded to the length of the Goodwin–Stone building.

10.   Lynes, *Good Old Modern,* pp. 391–92.

11.   In an interview with the author, October 10, 1995, Johnson did not recall the reason it was not built.

12.   Ibid.

13.   See *The Museum of Modern Art Bulletin* 21 (Winter 1953–54), p. 18.

14.   Drawings for the Guest House are in the collection of the Department of Architecture and Design, The Museum of Modern Art. At the time, Johnson did not yet have an architecture license, and was thus associated with C. Frederick Genz, and later Landis Gores. On some drawings the project is called "O'Hare House," a code name for the Rockefeller Guest House used during the permitting and construction phases.

15.   Most of the furniture was also designed by Johnson.

16.   Philip Johnson in an interview with the author, October 10, 1995.

17.   Robert A. M. Stern, Thomas Mellins, and David Fishman: *New York 1960* (New York: The Monacelli Press, 1995), pp. 305–06.

18.   For an extended discussion of this topic, see Mirka Beneš, "A Modern Classic: The Abby Aldrich Rockefeller Sculpture Garden," in the present volume.

19.   Unidentified press clipping [1954]. Johnson Archive, The Museum of Modern Art Library.

20.   The house was purchased by Mr. and Mrs. Robert Leonhardt, former clients of Johnson. In 1972, Johnson lived there as a tenant.

21.   For this project Johnson was associated with Landis Gores and Marios A. Contopoulos, Architect. The Rogers Annex was demolished in 1979–80 to make way for the Museum Tower.

22.   The house was purchased from Mabelle R. Shoemaker in April 1946; see reference in MoMA Archives: Public Information Scrapbook Index, p. 66 (General N).

23.   Memorandum, Ione Ulrich to René d'Harnoncourt, March 15, 1949: "Total of 14,500 sq ft (six floors plus smaller 7th floor). Priority list: classroom space (4200 sq ft), storage (2000 sq ft), Architecture depart. office (400 sq ft, since Philip is using space in the Painting and Sculpture Department), and additional library stacks (600 sq ft)." MoMA Archives: D'Harnoncourt Papers, file 403.

24.   Philip Johnson Oral History (1991); transcript, p. 137. MoMA Archives: MoMA Oral History Project.

25.   In 1959, Johnson nearly repeated the scheme in his design for Asia House, at 112 East Sixty-fourth Street in New York: a seven-story building with a Miesian curtain wall of steel and glass, sandwiched between existing rowhouses.

26.   Johnson Oral History (1991), p. 138.

27.   "The Year's Work: The Projects," *Interiors* 112 (August 1952), pp. 68–69. Johnson donated the tapestry (Untitled, 1939) to the Museum in 1968.

28.   Johnson probably also influenced the design of the north façade. Among the drawings in the Philip Johnson archive in the Department of Architecture and Design are a study and two axonometrics relating to this façade.

29.   In an early agreement between the two museums, The Museum of Modern Art exercised control of the design of the garden façade. See "Draft of Agreement b/w Whitney Museum and MoMA," May 7, 1949. MoMA Archives: René d'Harnoncourt Papers, file 402. In the Johnson archive in the Department of Architecture and Design there are thirty-nine drawings, most of them façade studies and several axonometrics to study the overall massing of both museums; the earliest drawings date from 1949. Johnson was associated with Landis Gores for this project.

30.   The titles are taken from two Museum pamphlets: *Toward the "New" Museum of Modern Art* (1959) and *A Problem Created by Success* (March 1961), both published for the 30th Anniversary Drive Steering Committee.

31.   "Annual Report of The Museum of Modern Art," June 30, 1955. The Museum of Modern Art Library.

32.   Memorandum, d'Harnoncourt to Burden, October 6, 1955. MoMA Archives: D'Harnoncourt Papers, file 346.

33.   Memorandum, Burden to d'Harnoncourt, October 31, 1955. MoMA Archives: D'Harnoncourt Papers, file 347.

34.   See drawings 125.1–6 and 125.10–11, Johnson archive, Department of Architecture and Design.

35.   Letter, Burden to Johnson, September 5, 1957. MoMA Archives: D'Harnoncourt Papers, file 343. The letter begins: "Dear Phil: Many thanks for your note together with the floor plan of the proposed extension to the Museum. I have discussed it with Nelson [Rockefeller] who is definitely interested."

36.   In the interim, a fire had devastated the Museum's second-floor galleries, and Johnson was involved in planning the addition of a fire-stair tower, altering the original building to meet current fire codes, and making minor interior alterations to the adjacent mansion at 23–25 West Fifty-third Street, which housed Museum offices beginning in 1958.

37.   The drive was announced at a dinner held, appropriately, at the recently completed Four Seasons restaurant, designed by Johnson for Mies's Seagram Building (1958) at 375 Park Avenue. Museum of Modern Art press release no. 104, November 17, 1959.

In April 1960, a closed-circuit coast-to-coast televised auction at Parke-Bernet Galleries enabled collectors nationwide to bid for paintings and sculptures donated by private collectors, artists, and dealers, to support the anniversary fund; see Museum of

Modern Art press release no. 43, April 23, 1960. In a release of May 2, the results of the sale were announced: $871,850.

38.   Museum of Modern Art press release no. 104, November 17, 1959.

39.   "Final Report of the 30th Anniversary Drive: Chronological Resume," March 14, 1963, p. 1. MoMA Archives: Reports and Pamphlets, Box 2/14. Johnson was listed as a contributor in the $100,000–$999,999 donor category.

40.   Museum of Modern Art press release no. 104, November 17, 1959.

41.   Ibid. "The 'new' Museum of Modern Art will have 43,000 square feet of exhibition space instead of 12,000 and 11,000 square feet for accessible storage instead of about 4,500."

42.   This preliminary illustration appeared on the cover of "Confidential Report to the Trustees from the Committee on the 30th Anniversary Museum of Modern Art" (1959). MoMA Archives: D'Harnoncourt Papers, file 494.

43.   The diamond-shaped column, of concrete or stone, was used in numerous contemporary projects by Johnson, including the Sheldon Memorial Art Gallery at the University of Nebraska, Lincoln (completed 1963); the Pavilion in New Canaan (1962); preliminary studies for Asia House, New York (1958); and the New York State Theater at Lincoln Center (1964).

44.   Philip Johnson, "Johnson," *Perspecta* 7 (1961), p. 3.

45.   If the proposed Museum addition presented a stylistic departure from the more orthodox modernism of the earlier buildings, to which there was only a tenuous physical connection, it was perhaps a modern evocation of its neighbor across the street: the University Club, an Italian Renaissance stone palazzo with arched windows built in 1899 by McKim, Mead and White.

46.   Philip Johnson, speech delivered at Yale University, New Haven, Connecticut, February 5, 1959; published in Vincent Scully, Peter Eisenman, and Robert A. M. Stern, *Philip Johnson: Writings* (New York: Oxford University Press, 1979), pp. 226–40.

47.   Ibid., p. 236.

48.   Johnson, "Johnson," p. 5.

49.   Philip C. Johnson, "Letter to the Museum Director," *Museum News* 38 (1960), p. 23.

50.   Sweeney became director of the Guggenheim Museum in 1952. In 1945–46, he served briefly as director of The Museum of Modern Art's Department of Painting and Sculpture.

51.   Johnson, "Letter to the Museum Director," p. 25.

52.   Ibid.

53.   Ibid., p. 22.

54.   Ibid., p. 25.

55.   Ibid., p. 22.

56.   For a discussion of Johnson's work in the late 1950s, see William H. Jordy, "The Mies-less Johnson," *Architectural Forum* 111 (September 1959), pp. 115–23; and Franz Schulze, *Philip Johnson: Life and Work* (New York: Alfred A. Knopf, 1994), pp. 228–72.

57.   Museum of Modern Art press release no. 21, March 8, 1960; and no. 8, January 24, 1963.

58.   Museum of Modern Art press release no. 21, March 8, 1960.

59.   Drexler had designed an apartment interior for Mrs. Bliss Parkinson (completed 1958) as well as the Chase Water Garden (1960; not built); he would later collaborate with Justin Henshell, AIA, on the design of the Chase Manhattan Bank Money Museum at Rockefeller Center (1961–63).

60.   According to Wilder Green, David Rockefeller probably saw Drexler's schemes; he has suggested that, as a result, this may be the reason Rockefeller commissioned Drexler to design the Money Museum at Rockefeller Center. Green in an interview with the author, August 10, 1995.

According to his colleague Mildred Constantine, who was assistant curator (1949–52) and associate curator (1952–67) in the Department of Architecture and Design, Drexler lobbied d'Harnoncourt assiduously. See Mildred Constantine Oral History (1991); transcript, p. 119. MoMA Archives: MoMA Oral History Project.

61.   In his later exhibition, *Transformations in Modern Architecture* (1979), Drexler included a category called "Elements: Parapets" that began with Fallingwater, the residence Wright designed for Edgar J. Kaufmann in Mill Run, Pennsylvania.

62.   An architect, Green was well-suited for the position in temperament. He had also worked as an architect in Johnson's studio in the 1950s.

63.   Letter, Green to Johnson, May 25, 1962. MoMA Archives: Wilder Green Papers, 1960–65, "1964 Expansion, The Museum of Modern Art Phase I (General) Building Program: Philip Johnson Correspondence."

64.   There was a conscious recognition that the Museum had an international significance and therefore the expansion must be completed in time for the fair. See, for example, the letter from d'Harnoncourt to Mrs. John D. Rockefeller 3rd, November 10, 1960. MoMA Archives: D'Harnoncourt Papers, file 377. According to the "Final Report of the 30th Anniversary Drive: Chronological Resume" (1963), coordinating the construction schedule with the fair had been announced on February 7, 1961; see p. 3.

65.   Museum of Modern Art press release no. 114, October 1, 1962.

66.   Robert Zion and Harold Breen served as landscape architects for the garden extension.

67.   Green once recalled Johnson and d'Harnoncourt—himself something of an architect manqué—making numerous studies for the stairs. See Wilder Green Oral History (1991); transcript, pp. 73–74. MoMA Archives: MoMA Oral History Project.

68.   Philip Johnson, "Whence and Whither: The Processional Element in Architecture," *Perspecta* 9/10 (1965), p. 171.

69.   The Richards Medical Research Building was presented in an exhibition organized by Wilder Green at the Museum in 1961. Green, who was par-

ticularly interested in Kahn's work at the time, recalls working with Johnson on this scheme; he also recalls that he and Drexler had hoped Kahn would be considered for the commission to design the East Wing. Green in an interview with the author, May 23, 1996.

70.   See Green Oral History (1991), pp. 72–73. About this scheme, Green recalled, "I think René felt it was too plain. He kept saying how it didn't relate to the existing structures and didn't have any texture. . . . I don't remember his exact language, but, obviously, the kind of direct structural aesthetic did not sit with him comfortably. The façade design went through scheme after scheme."

71.   Barr was particularly concerned about the effect of the bronze-colored glass (Parallel-O-Bronze, Libbey-Owens-Ford Glass Co.) on Monet's paintings. See, for example, the memorandum from Barr to Green, March 27, 1964. MoMA Archives: D'Harnoncourt Papers, file 458.

72.   Green in an interview with the author, August 10, 1995.

73.   Ibid.

74.   "Camp Mies," *Progressive Architecture* 68 (December 1967), p. 128.

75.   Johnson, "Johnson," pp. 3–5.

76.   In 1984, the Founders' Room was rebuilt to house the Museum Library stacks.

77.   *Interiors* 124 (March 1965), p. 10.

78.   Tillich was president and his friend Alfred Barr vice-president of an organization called the Foundation for the Arts, Religion and Culture. See Minutes of the Organizational Board Meeting, May 10, 1962. MoMA Archives: Alfred H. Barr, Jr., Papers, "Foundation for the Arts, Religion and Culture (ARC), Series A: Correspondence 1962–1975." An undated typescript concerning the purposes of the organization states its aim "to initiate and foster collaboration between religion and the arts in contemporary life." Tillich had previously presented a lecture ("Ultimate Reality and Art") at the Museum on February 17, 1959, sponsored by the Junior Council.

79.   Address by Dr. Paul Tillich on the occasion of the opening of the new galleries and sculpture garden of The Museum of Modern Art, May 25, 1964; unpaginated. MoMA Archives: Opening, 1964.

80.   Ibid.

81.   Ada Louise Huxtable, ". . . And It's Big and Beautiful," *The New York Times,* May 31, 1964, sect. 2, p. 15.

82.   Ad Hoc Planning Committee, The Museum of Modern Art, New York, "Report to the Trustees," September 1969, p. 14. MoMA Archives: Reports and Pamphlets, Box 2/14.

83.   In 1963, the Whitney Museum took title of its new Madison Avenue site, and under terms of the contract with The Museum of Modern Art had to deliver its present building to the Museum by June 14, 1966. See memorandum, Koch to Building Committee, July 8, 1963. MoMA Archives: Expansion, Subgroup B, "1964 Expansion," Box 1, file "Building Program: Minutes of Meetings."

84. "Report of a Feasibility Survey for the Museum of Modern Art prepared by Bowen, Gurin, Barnes & Roche, Inc." (December 1968); unpaginated. MoMA Archives: The Museum of Modern Art: Reports and Pamphlets, 1950's 1960's and 1970's; Box 5/14.

85. Ibid. In his oral history, Koch recalled that in the late 1960s, he and Tom Lowry, an architect who had worked for Johnson and then came independently to the Museum staff, conceived the idea of coupling the expansion with a commercial development utilizing the air rights. See Richard Koch Oral History (1991); transcript, p. 148. MoMA Archives: MoMA Oral History Project.

86. "Report of a Feasibility Survey for the Museum of Modern Art prepared by Bowen, Gurin, Barnes & Roche, Inc." (December 1968), op cit.

87. Ibid.

88. Ibid.

89. Lynes, *Good Old Modern,* p. 408.

90. Nearly one hundred seventy drawings in the Johnson archive in the Department of Architecture and Design illustrate the various ideas. A model (whereabouts unknown) also accompanied a recorded presentation by Johnson to the Museum in April 1970, when many of the concepts were discussed.

91. Minutes of a meeting held June 17, 1969; prepared by William G. Bardel, Deputy Director Office of Midtown Planning and Development, Office of the Mayor. Arthur Drexler archive, Department of Architecture and Design. Among those representing the Museum at the meeting were Johnson, Burgee, and Paley.

92. Memorandum, Walter Bareiss to Museum staff, June 27, 1969. Drexler archive, Department of Architecture and Design: "A. Drexler—MoMA Planning Committee."

93. See letter, Drexler to Green, undated [ca. August 1969]. Drexler archive, Department of Architecture and Design.

94. See, for example, the memorandum from Koch to Bareiss, July 29, 1969, with copies to Drexler and Green. Drexler archive, Department of Architecture and Design: "A. Drexler—MoMA Planning Committee."

95. Ad Hoc Planning Committee, "Report to the Trustees" (1969), p. 14.

96. Ibid., pp. 12–14. Also, in a letter to Green, who was vacationing in the southwest (ca. August 1969),

Drexler related his reactions to Johnson's sketches: "Philip has already shown to Walter and myself a first sketch plan and section of this scheme; my immediate reaction is that it is almost good enough to start building tomorrow. It looks very promising indeed, but I am sure we are going to hear that it costs much, much more than has been so far anticipated. In any case, more detailed studies are due either late this week or early next." Drexler archive, Department of Architecture and Design: "A. Drexler—MoMA Planning Committee."

97. Memorandum, Drexler to Bareiss, July 22, 1969. Drexler archive, Department of Architecture and Design: "A. Drexler—MoMA Planning Committee."

98. "The total volume of our galleries is 706,902 cubic feet; the total volume of the Metropolitan's entrance hall is 1,133,472 cubic feet." Ad Hoc Planning Committee, "Report to the Trustees" (1969), pp. 12–13. Copies of sectional drawings of the Metropolitan Museum's entrance hall are found in the Drexler archive, Department of Architecture and Design.

99. Helen Searing, *New American Art Museums* (New York: Whitney Museum of American Art in association with the University of California Press, Berkeley, Los Angeles, and London, 1982), pp. 61–65.

100. Drexler cited the Ford Foundation Building as an example; see memorandum, Drexler to Bareiss, July 22, 1969. Drexler archive, Department of Architecture and Design: "A. Drexler—Memos to Mr. Bareiss."

101. Memorandum, Drexler to Koch, November 12, 1969. Drexler archive, Department of Architecture and Design: "A. Drexler—MoMA Planning Committee."

102. This was fig. 174 in *Transformations in Modern Architecture.* Drexler also included the Nagashima Tropical Garden, Mie Prefecture, Japan (1967–68), designed by Takenaka Komuten Co. Ltd. Design Dept. and Takao Kohira; see fig. 173, *Transformations.*

103. *Philip Johnson, Architect: The First Forty Years* (New York: The Municipal Art Society, 1983), unpaginated.

104. Cesar Pelli, "A Few Words on Philip Johnson's Buildings," in *Philip Johnson* (Tokyo: A+U Publishing, 1979), p. 84.

105. Johnson, recognizing the popularity of the

garden among city officials and the Museum's patrons, knew that it would have been too controversial to consider a more radical alteration. He remarked of the final proposal: "That's a good deal for public consumption" (Philip Johnson, "Model to Museum," presentation to The Museum of Modern Art Steering Committee, April 21, 1970; audiotape). MoMA Archives: Sound Recordings (70.35).

106. Ibid.

107. In other studies from this period, the 1964 Garden Wing was reconsidered as a new gallery wing several stories tall.

108. Johnson, "Model to Museum" (1970), op. cit.

109. Ibid. Here Johnson was referring to the famous Palm Court in New York's Plaza Hotel, built in 1907. According to Stern et al., in *New York 1960,* the Palm Court's Tiffany stained-glass ceiling, through which light had filtered from an open courtyard above, was replaced by a vaguely Dorothy Draperesque dropped ceiling in 1955, and the palms removed; see p. 1123.

110. Ibid.

111. See the oral histories of Donald Elliott (1994) and Richard Weinstein (1994) in The Museum of Modern Art Archives for a chronicle of these events.

112. Both Elliott and Weinstein were founding members of the Urban Design Group, established by Lindsay in 1967 to help revitalize the Planning Commission.

113. Minutes of the meeting of the Board of Trustees of The Museum of Modern Art, April 21, 1976. MoMA Archives: Board of Trustee Minutes, V.39.

114. In a 1991 interview, Johnson recalled, "Since no trustee could be architect of the museum, I suggested Pelli" (Johnson Oral History [1991], p. 169). See also, Cesar Pelli Oral History (1991); transcript, p. 14. MoMA Archives: MoMA Oral History Project.

Johnson's support of Pelli is recorded in the minutes of the meeting of the Board of Trustees of The Museum of Modern Art, New York, November 10, 1976. MoMA Archives: Board of Trustee Minutes, V.40.

115. Elliott Oral History (1994), p. 19.

116. Pelli Oral History (1991), p. 14.

117. Philip C. Johnson, "Letter to the Museum Director," *Museum News* 38 (1960), p. 22.

1. Philip Johnson. The Abby Aldrich Rockefeller Sculpture Garden, The Museum of Modern Art, New York. View to northeast. 1950–53

A Modern Classic:
The Abby Aldrich Rockefeller
Sculpture Garden

Mirka Beneš

The sculpture garden designed by Philip Johnson in 1950–52 behind The Museum of Modern Art in New York has long been recognized as a significant achievement in urban garden design after World War II[1] (fig. 1). Its evocative powers stem from the architect's conceptual and synthetic approach to the garden's design, to which he gave a character of urbane formality. From the beginning, the public appreciated the multivalent aspects of this character, which signified the melding of urban space for public gathering and of garden space for both public edification and private contemplation.[2] The sculpture garden employed a particularly architectural and urban vocabulary:

The space is rectangular, bounded on the west by the high blank walls of the Museum restaurant and the Whitney Museum, on the south by the windowed walls of the Museum proper, and on Fifty-fourth Street by a high wall with two wide wooden gates. These gates would be justified if only because they form a visual break in the mottled-gray expanse of variegated brick, the same in color if not in bond as the northernmost three panels of the Whitney Museum. Two rectangular watercourses (no falls or water lilies) parallel the street wall, and a central white marble plaza, sunk below the level of the Museum and restaurant terraces, forms a solid oblong, bordered on three sides by a green embankment of myrtle. At either end of this plaza are irregular geometric patches of green. The one to the west is the base for a clump of lovely tall white birches; directly in front of the Museum are two irregularly formed weeping beeches, while on the right is a group of Japan cedars, and there is even, further to the rear, a tree of heaven.[3]

Conceived in the midst of contemporary debate on how to renew the city center, the new garden was recognized by critics as continuing "the pattern of formality" within the "stylized life of a big city," and its spaces were heralded as the "Museum's marble *piazze.*"[4] The Italian word *piazza,* or *piazze* in the plural, used by most critics to describe the garden, emphasized its urban character (fig. 2). At the same time, these architectural components were juxtaposed with plantings—designed by Johnson in collaboration with the landscape architect James Fanning[5]—and rectangular

2. The Abby Aldrich Rockefeller Sculpture Garden, view to north and northwest steps, 1964

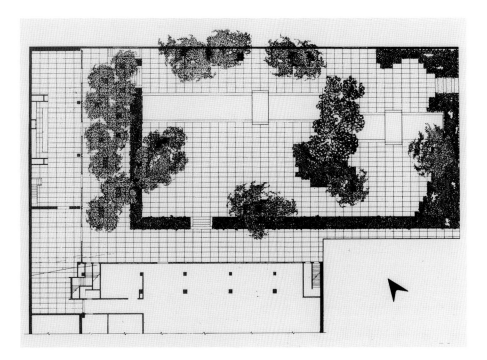

pools in a configuration that was simultaneously abstract—modernist—and legible in terms of the great traditions of garden design. Two marble slabs crossed the formal canals as bridges. Small groves of trees defined four open spaces for the display of sculpture and the circulation of the public, who entered the principal space directly from the Museum's ground floor (figs. 3, 4). Johnson's sculpture garden cannot be understood without taking into account his own broad concerns in the design fields in the early 1950s: the architecture of Ludwig Mies van der Rohe; art and its installation; ideas about civic spaces and urban culture; modern classicism in architecture; modernist landscape architecture, including its translation of traditional Japanese gardens into modern terms; and historical precedents.

The Sculpture Gardens at The Museum of Modern Art, 1939 to 1950

Johnson's design had been preceded on the same site by a sculpture garden designed by the Museum's founding director, Alfred H. Barr, Jr., and its curator of architecture, John McAndrew, and built in 1939 (fig. 5). This sculpture garden was truly a first. Today, when we think of the complex of buildings and grounds that make up a museum of modern art, we take the outdoor sculpture garden or court as a given. However, many of the most well-known models—the Kröller-Müller Museum in Otterlo, The Netherlands (completed 1961),[6] Storm King Art Center, Mountainville, New York (1960), the Frida Schiff Warburg Sculpture Garden, Brooklyn, New York (1966), and the sculpture garden at Jersusalem, designed by Isamu Noguchi (1966), among many others in the United States and Europe—are essentially open-air parks, not gardens bounded by walls. As The Abby Aldrich Rockefeller Sculpture Garden eclipsed the garden of 1939 in public memory, the press in 1953 rushed to claim it as "the first garden in America designed for the exhibition of modern sculpture."[7]

From the evidence uncovered so far, The Museum of Modern Art's sculpture garden of 1939 appears to have been the first attempt anywhere to build a sculpture

Left:
3. Philip Johnson. The Abby Aldrich Rockefeller Sculpture Garden, The Museum of Modern Art, New York. Plan. 1950–53

Right:
4. The Abby Aldrich Rockefeller Sculpture Garden, view to southwest, 1964

garden according to modernist principles of garden and architectural design.[8] Before that, modern sculptors had created outdoor settings for their sculptures around their studios (for example Rodin and Maillol had done so, and Carl Milles had built himself a grand garden to display his sculptures at his island estate at Lidingö, Sweden). But none of these were museum gardens open to the public in an institutional setting, and Milles's garden, built in 1906–29 for himself and not for a public, was traditional in its terraced forms, even if constructed using a modern stylistic vocabulary of European architecture of the 1910s.[9] An innovative exception, although it was not a sculpture garden proper, was Milles's work at the Cranbrook Academy of Art in Bloomfield Hills, Michigan, from 1931 to 1951. There Milles made a contribution to the use of open-air sculpture in a landscaped setting, following the lead of Eliel Saarinen, the Academy's architect and first director, who had fostered the integration of sculptural work in the buildings he designed in 1926–27. As Diana Balmori has recently shown, Milles's fountains and sculptures were "unifying pieces between the architecture and the landscape."[10]

Until European modernism in the 1920s, the public in Europe and America identified garden settings for sculpture with historical gardens, such as the Villa d'Este at Tivoli, Versailles, and nineteenth-century public gardens lined with busts and statues of famous citizens. The use of the garden as an outdoor gallery for sculpture had origins in Greek and Roman antiquity (we need think only of Hadrian's Villa), and in the Renaissance and Baroque periods the ancient model was the springboard for many Italian sculpture gardens, particularly in Rome, where the collecting of large ancient sculptures was a programmatic motivation for the design of garden spaces, thus extending indoor galleries and curiosity cabinets to the outdoors.[11] In the historicist architectural culture of the nineteenth century, sculpture

5. John McAndrew and Alfred H. Barr, Jr.
The Museum of Modern Art Sculpture Garden.
View to southeast. 1939

was used in gardens as it had been in the Renaissance, namely, as figurative works of art that carried iconographical associations related to the functions and programs of the garden. From classical antiquity to modernism, in fact, sculptures in gardens had one major aspect in common—they were *fixed* elements. Even at the Versailles of Louis XIV, where every few decades major changes in the iconographical program required changes of statuary, once the statues were created, they were fixed in place.

All this changed in the nineteenth century. New conceptions of the art object and of its potential for diverse settings developed, as sculpture and painting were placed on temporary exhibition in different public venues. With modernism, the garden not only maintained its traditional structural function as a container for sculptures on fixed pedestals, it also was called upon to serve as an additional space for temporary exhibitions, much like an indoor museum or salon. The application of the modernist style to garden design began in Europe in the 1920s and in the United States in the 1930s, but the co-opting of the garden as a space for changing exhibitions of sculpture was first observed at The Museum of Modern Art.

From 1937 to 1939, when plans were first made for a sculpture garden at the Museum, until 1950, when Johnson received his own commission, many proposals and revisions for the garden were made by a number of individuals who were closely tied to the founding of the Museum and to the patronage and practice of modernist architecture in the United States. They were curators at the Museum and architects and landscape architects in top practices and graduate teaching centers. They all knew each other and they included Barr, McAndrew, Joseph Hudnut, Alice Carson, Philip L. Goodwin, Edward Durell Stone, Christopher Tunnard—and Philip Johnson. Their ongoing debates about what a modern sculpture garden should be are recorded in their correspondence, in committee minutes, and in publications on art and garden design, and form one of the primary frameworks in which Johnson's designs at The Museum of Modern Art must be considered.

Founded in 1929, the Museum was housed in a suite in the Heckscher Building at 730 Fifth Avenue until 1932, when it occupied a townhouse at 11 West Fifty-third Street that had been leased to it by John D. Rockefeller, Jr., the husband of founding trustee Abby Aldrich Rockefeller. Plans were made starting in 1936 to construct a new, modern building on the West Fifty-third Street site and on adjacent properties also owned by the Rockefellers.[12] Goodwin and Stone were selected as the architects. One of Goodwin's proposed designs for the new building, dated June 1936, shows trees rising behind it, implying some sort of garden.[13] Dominic Ricciotti, who has analyzed the projects for the Museum building, attributes ideas for a permanent walled sculpture garden to Stone, who since 1936 had been involved in the design of gardens for private homes.[14]

During construction in 1937, Mr. Rockefeller, at his wife's behest, donated land behind the building to be used "as a garden for the exhibition of sculpture."[15] It is not known what Mrs. Rockefeller had in mind at that time, in stylistic terms; the model includes a grass court with two parallel rows of trees—a "surrogate" for the plantings that would ultimately be designed (fig. 6). Such an issue, however, was taken up in several meetings by the Museum Garden Committee, formed sometime in 1938. The Committee consisted of Mrs. Robert H. Fife; Mrs. Stanley Resor, a trustee and a patron of Ludwig Mies van der Rohe; and, ex officio at the Museum, Barr, McAndrew, and Goodwin, who was also a trustee; the committee was chaired

Mrs. Rockefeller, who had been working for over a decade on her Seal Harbor garden in Maine with the noted landscape architect Beatrix Farrand.[16] Additional support for the idea of a sculpture garden must have been provided by the important donations Mrs. Rockefeller planned for the Museum in 1939: a collection of thirty-six modern sculptures, "including six Despiaus, four Kolbes, seven Lachaises, two Lehmbrucks, four Maillols, Matisse's *La Serpentine,* Modigliani's *Head* (stone), and a Zorach." Also in 1939, a Barlach, Despiau's *Assia,* and Lehmbruck's *Kneeling Woman* were purchased by the Museum.[17]

The Garden Commitee met on December 3, 1938, and January 1, 1939. In the first meeting, the Committee considered the budget and whether the garden would be a temporary installation, coinciding with the New York World's Fair in 1939, or permanent. McAndrew felt that constructing a temporary garden would be an unnecessary added expense if a permanent garden would ultimately be built. The Committee wanted the garden to be protected from Fifty-fourth Street by walls, considered "essential as backgrounds," yet they should not be "too strong in character." Goodwin proposed that "it would be more desirable to treat the area very simply as a courtyard, with temporary partitions, for sculpture," as it was uncertain what buildings would go up on either side of the garden plot. The Committee ultimately decided on a more relaxed approach: the garden would be as "elastic" as possible, serving primarily as an outdoor sculpture *gallery* rather than as a *garden* ("garden and planting should be considered as a background for sculpture") and the possibility of building a pavilion for sculpture should also be considered. As for the plantings, there was some debate. Mrs. Resor took a Miesian courtyard-house approach; she did not want any plantings at all, and preferred the concept of an area "more in the nature of a courtyard, in which preferably a single piece of sculpture, and at most only a few pieces, could advantageously be exhibited." Others on the Committee wanted to find out what plants could best withstand urban smog, stating: "One [species of] tree was better than no tree at all."[18]

In its second meeting, the Committee was joined by Joseph Hudnut, dean of the Graduate School of Design at Harvard University. Hudnut had a particular interest in modern sculpture and its display. He had written a book on the subject in 1929, in which he pronounced in favor of figurative sculpture and of "no difference between architecture and sculpture"; the conceptual models for modern sculpture should be those of ancient Greece—for example, those on the temple pediments at Olympia, whose "structure and disposition, their intention, is as architectonic as the peristyle beneath." In sum, Hudnut argued, "There is no great sculpture that is not Hellenic,"[19] and extolled "the new classicism" of Adolf Hildebrandt, Charles Despiau, and, especially, Aristide Maillol.[20]

Hudnut had museum architecture and exhibition installation on his mind, as he had just been asked to be the adviser to the Committee on the Smithsonian Gallery of Art, proposed for the Mall in Washington, D.C., for which a major competition ran from January to April 1939.[21] In late 1938, he had helped devise the program brief for the Smithsonian competition, which stated:

The functional elements shall include enclosed or semi-enclosed areas adapted to the exhibition of sculpture and other works of art, some of these objects being free-standing and some to be provided with backgrounds varying in character. It is essential that works of

6. Philip L. Goodwin and Edward Durell Stone. The Museum of Modern Art, New York. Model, rear view. 1937–39

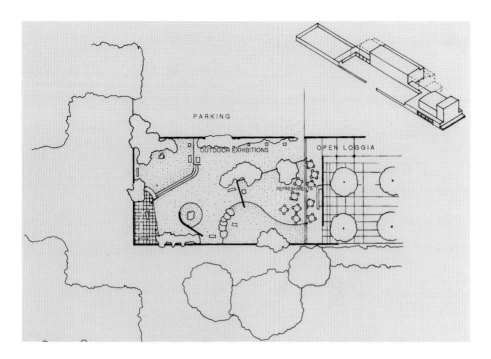

7. Edward Durell Stone. Sculpture Garden for Outdoor Exhibitions, Smithsonian Gallery of Art Competition, Washington, D.C. Plan, second-stage entry.
Spring 1939. Redrawn to scale 1": 40' with small
axonometric drawing by Eric Kramer, Department of
Landscape Architecture, Graduate School of Design,
Harvard University, Cambridge, Massachusetts, 1996

*sculpture should be exhibited, so far as practicable, isolated from one another since they
are so often disparate in style and scale. . . . It is hoped that the participants will provide*
some garden treatment *for enclosed or partly enclosed areas which will not require
extensive upkeep and which will be interesting in the winter as well as in the summer.*[22]

When the Smithsonian competition results were announced on June 29, 1939,
Eliel and Eero Saarinen won first prize, and Philip L. Goodwin and Edward Durell
Stone, who had competed independently, each won a third prize. The scheme by the
Saarinens foresaw a massive, marble-sheathed building in the modern style (a design
praised for its "classicism" by Hudnut), overlooking a great paved terrace that broke
in a curvilinear edge along a vast reflecting pool; in the proposal, several monumental sculptures were placed along the marble wall of the building and in the pool.
While Paul Cret, also a finalist, placed sculptures in huge greenery-covered niches
along the flank of his proposed building—obtaining an effect nearly identical to that
of the massive Renaissance garden niches at the Villa Madama in Rome—Goodwin
included in his scheme no less than two "sculpture gardens," one with a rectangular
pool, but these were simply courtyards with isolated trees. In contrast, the modernist
building complex envisioned by Stone included a garden for "Outdoor Exhibitions"
attached to an "Open Loggia"[23] (fig. 7). This garden was partly paved, partly graveled,
and was subdivided by steps, screens, and freestanding walls on the diagonal, forming enclosures for sculptures; on one side of the garden was an open-air dining area.
In plan it is remarkably similar to the sculpture garden that McAndrew and Barr
would devise for the Museum in late April 1939 (figs. 8, 9) and that Goodwin would
revise in 1942, and to one that Goodwin and the British landscape architect Christopher Tunnard would propose jointly in 1946–47 (see p. 119). Although the Smithsonian Gallery was never realized, Stone's project did not, apparently, go unnoticed
at the Modern.

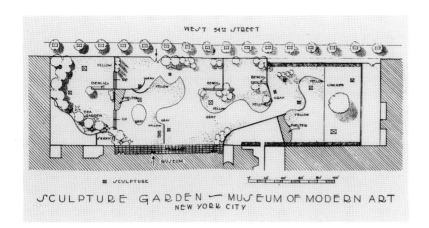

Left:
8. John McAndrew and Alfred H. Barr, Jr. The Museum of Modern Art Sculpture Garden. Ground plan. 1939

Right:
9. John McAndrew and Alfred H. Barr, Jr. The Museum of Modern Art Sculpture Garden. View to northeast. 1939

The Garden Committee continued to debate the issue of the plantings, and, rather than calling for a permanent planting design, recommended a temporary solution of renting boxed plants and erecting some freestanding walls as backgrounds for sculpture. Hudnut, however, wanted the design to be carried out by professionals, by architects rather than landscapers, "as he did not believe that there were landscape architects qualified to handle the problem."[24] (Hudnut's attitude toward landscape architects and their involvement with modern sculpture would change soon enough, as later that year he was so impressed with the work of Tunnard that he convinced him to abandon England for a permanent teaching post at Harvard.) With the Smithsonian competition in mind, Hudnut called for a closed competition for the Museum garden, to be held among four or five selected architects working in collaboration with landscape architects, each to provide a model. The competition would be for the purpose of identifying a theoretical design for the plot only, with no assurances that the winner would carry out the commission. Goodwin, however, opposed the idea of staging a competition, unless the definite use of the outdoor space had been decided upon. The Committee agreed, postponing any competition until the fall of 1939, after the opening of the new building.[25]

A competition for the Museum sculpture garden was, in fact, never held. Two weeks before the opening of the Goodwin–Stone building in May 1939, restrictions placed on additional Fifty-fourth Street frontage promised to the Museum by John D. Rockefeller, Jr., were lifted, extending the original garden plot to approximately 100 by 400 feet.[26] Within those two weeks, Barr and McAndrew would design and install the first sculpture garden for an urban museum of modern art. (Barr and his colleagues obviously had planned on there being an outdoor exhibition for the opening of the new building. On January 27, 1939, Barr wrote to the sculptor Mary Callery in New York: "As you may not have heard of this sculpture show, I will say that it may occupy a space at the rear of the museum equivalent to about fourteen ordinary 25 ft. building lots facing 54th street, within a stone's throw of Fifth Ave. and will we believe be the most remarkable exhibition of sculpture so far held in New York."[27] A month later, he cabled Callery in Paris: "Outdoor sculpture exhibition opens with new building May 1st. . . . Please inform Picasso."[28])

The new Museum building was a landmark in the adoption and transformation of European modernism by American architects.[29] The sculpture garden, although temporary, was as well. The Garden Committee had clearly touched on some of the key issues, both practical and theoretical, but it was left to McAndrew and Barr to determine what a sculpture garden for a museum of modern art should look like. Many years later, Elizabeth Mock Kassler, who in 1939 was a curator in the Department of Architecture and Industrial Art, traced the sculpture garden's development in the 1940s and 1950s, and stated that McAndrew and Barr had had no built modern precedents to go by.[30]

These two curators (McAndrew, who held a degree in architecture from Harvard, was the principal designer) made an important contribution to that start, even though it was not a very good design in spatial terms. They seem to have taken the approach advocated by the Garden Committee in the previous year, veering toward Mrs. Resor's wish for a minimalist, Miesian approach in their design of an enclosed garden with walls.[31] In it they installed over a third of the sixty modern sculptures included in the inaugural exhibition *Art in Our Time: Tenth Anniversary Exhibition* (see p. 115). Along the street and as spatial dividers within the garden they erected lightweight walls of plywood and wood basketry, some curvilinear, some rectilinear in shape, thereby creating a series of outdoor rooms in which the sculptures and slender trees were placed. For the spatial configurations of sculptures, plantings and backgrounds, they drew upon the work of Mies, whom Barr had tried to bring to MoMA as its architect in 1936. In particular, they referred to the asymmetrical composition of Mies's Barcelona Pavilion of 1929, the Tugendhat House, and the courtyard houses of the 1930s (see, for example, fig. 10). They seem to have translated Mies's use of marble panels (or silk scrims, as in his work with Lilly Reich) as spatial dividers into light screens of wood, along the lines of those used by Alvar Aalto for the façades of the Villa Mairea and his large curvilinear wall display at the 1937 Paris Exposition of modern industrial design. In sum, it was as though Jean Arp had designed the ground planes and Aalto the vertical panels and

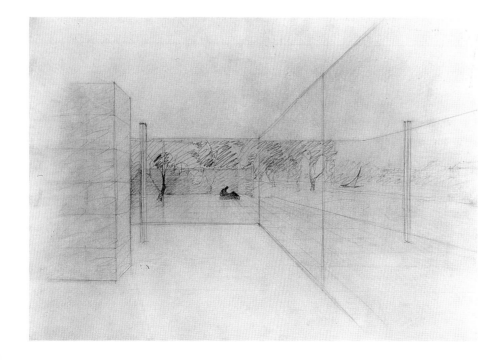

10. Ludwig Mies van der Rohe. Living Room of the Hubbe House, Magdeburg. Perspective view. 1935. Mies van der Rohe Archive, The Museum of Modern Art, New York

curving ground forms, with Mies informing the selection and placement of the (primarily figurative) sculptures.[32]

Aalto's work had great appeal for contemporary landscape architects from the mid-1930s on as his work became known outside Finland. Fletcher Steele in New England and Thomas Church in California were strongly taken with his wood basketry fences, vertical boarding, and curvilinear walls[33] (fig. 11). Earlier in 1939, Aalto's work had been presented in New York, at the World's Fair, with a long, sinuous wall of wood slats that dominated the interior of his Finnish Pavilion.

In addition to Aalto's influence, the idea to use wood screens in a modern garden—in some ways a necessity for McAndrew and Barr, given the limitations of time—could also have been justified by a look at recent publications of the work of contemporaries, such as Heinrich Tessenow and the noted German garden designer Leberecht Migge, both of whom incorporated wood screens in numerous garden designs.[34]

McAndrew and Barr also must have looked at contemporary publications on modern gardens, as they were clearly eager to provide the new building with a garden in the modernist style. In addition to Aalto's organic forms, landscape architects such as Roberto Burle Marx set examples of the use of free-flowing forms, which the curators took up in the contrasting yellow-and-gray free-form pebbled areas on the ground of their sculpture garden[35] (fig. 12).

However, owing to limits on time, the lack of topographical features, and the fact that McAndrew and Barr were curators and not professional landscape designers, their garden had little to do with the spatial and volumetric articulation seen in most contemporary modern gardens of noted design, where permanent terraces and walls articulated topography, (such as gardens by Le Corbusier and Jean Forestier in France, and by Jean Canneel-Claes in Belgium [fig. 13]). In assessing the Museum garden, however, it must be remembered that the primary goal of McAndrew and Barr was museological.

Barr and McAndrew followed the latest curatorial trends, which advocated placing modern sculptures outdoors in nature, as well as isolating them in individual settings.[36] The idea of exhibiting contemporary sculpture outdoors—and not, as

Left:
11. Thomas Church. Rear Garden of the Kirkham House, San Francisco. 1948

Right:
12. Roberto Burle Marx. Roof Garden of the Ministry of Education and Public Health, Rio de Janeiro, Brazil. 1937–39. Le Corbusier, architect

13. Jean Canneel-Claes. Garden of a Small Country House, Valley of the Dendre River, Belgium. 1935

a rule, as an integral part of a garden's design—was a novelty in the early 1930s, both in Europe and the United States. European museum curators, especially in Germany, as well as sculptors themselves advocated the museological turn toward the outdoors by citing the precedent of the ancient Greeks in placing sculpture outdoors. And modernist architects ranging from Mies and Le Corbusier to Paul Nelson made a point of including isolated sculptures in their work.[37]

The exhibition technique used in their indoor galleries was the point of departure for the arrangements of sculptures and backgrounds in the garden. In particular, they referred to the long narrow sculpture gallery on the second floor of the new Museum, which had been designed specifically for this purpose (figs. 14, 15). As this technique is precisely the one that Johnson would later use in the sculpture garden of 1953, we will consider it in some detail. The walls of the sculpture gallery of 1939 were painted white or a neutral light color, and the space was divided by curtains and movable panels into asymmetrical spatial units, which changed with different installations. A key difference with the painting galleries was that in the sculpture gallery the artworks themselves were used as significant spatial divisions and that curtains and flexible panels were more frequently used as colored contrasts to create sculpture-specific backgrounds.[38] All these additional means controlled and affected the visitor's path and experience of the works much more than in the painting galleries.

In reviewing the new building, critics were quick to notice not only the flexible use of open galleries with temporary divisions, seen as a radical innovation in American museum design, but especially "all of the galleries given over to sculpture, [which] offer valuable lessons in exhibition technique."[39] These innovations had in fact come from the German museums. For more than a decade, German curators and artists such as László Moholy-Nagy had been translating the new design principles of abstract art into three-dimensional exhibition installations of modern art.

Left:
14. Installation view, *Art in Our Time: Tenth Anniversary Exhibition,* The Museum of Modern Art, New York, May 10–September 30, 1939

Right:
15. Installation view, *Art in Our Time: Tenth Anniversary Exhibition,* The Museum of Modern Art, New York, May 10–September 30, 1939

In 1925, the director of the Hannover Museum, Alexander Dorner revised the galleries there using this approach, and in 1927 he commissioned from El Lissitzky a version of *The Abstract Cabinet* (1919). El Lissitzky used curtains, abstract sculptures (with mirrors to reflect their volumes) and constructions, and curvilinear metal and glass panels, in order to energize the psychological reactions of visitors and to channel their spatial movements. Other artists adopted the same approach in totally designed exhibition environments, for example Moholy-Nagy at the Werkbund Exhibition in Paris and the Moholy Room in Hannover, both of 1930.[40]

In 1938, the artist Herbert Bayer, a former teacher at the Bauhaus and designer of the Werkbund Exhibition of 1930, brought the new approach to exhibition design directly to the Modern, for which he designed the exhibition *Bauhaus 1919–28* in 1938. Dorner described the installation as follows: "In order to establish a smooth flow of the public, all exhibits were placed so as to create a sequence and continuity. This was accomplished by painting the floor with directional shapes, lines and footprints. . . . The power of abstract composition was set to work at floors and walls."[41]

Bayer's innovative approach, described by him in the article "Fundamentals of Exhibition Design" (1936) and displayed at the Museum two years later, was a key source of inspiration for McAndrew and Barr in the conceptualization of their sculpture garden as an outdoor gallery. Their yellow-and-gray ground plan and curvilinear basketry walls adhered to Bayer's dictum that the ground plan "and the direction of the viewer must become one."[42] Bayer also thought that "contents" and "container" of display should be inseparable: "What the modern displayer introduces as a new way of exhibiting is of course inseparable from a new content to be exhibited."[43]

Barr's and McAndrew's interpretation involved the organic forms and biomorphic lines that were ubiquitous in much design of the 1930s, from Surrealist art to interiors. In 1953, Johnson would offer yet another formal interpretation of Bayer's exhibition philosophy. He would take Bayer's conception of the unity of form and contents of the display, and interpret both in architectonic terms that had a classical reference: there would be an architectural "container" for sculptures (the sunken garden and its walls) that had an architectural, if not a classical, structure, like the works of Maillol, Kolbe, and Despiau, and the structured volumes of Renoir's and Duchamp-Villon's pieces. Johnson's position would be akin to and echo that of his former teacher and dean at Harvard, Joseph Hudnut, with whom he studied in 1938–43. In his 1929 book *Modern Sculpture,* Hudnut had pronounced: "The important characteristic of modern sculpture is the return to the classic principle: the conception of sculpture and architecture as essentially identical arts," and "Sculpture attains its greatest significance and its greatest power in the presence of an architecture that imposes its firm and lucid relationships upon it."[44]

Even years later, Barr would continue to underscore the organic character of his and McAndrew's design. In 1948, when Goodwin told him he thought the sculptures chosen for the garden "too mechanistic," Barr responded that only a few were (the Duchamp-Villon and the Calder), and defended the garden's overall design:

Our original plan for the garden was of course just as anti-mechanistic as possible. We laid it out in free curves inspired by Arp, partly by English garden tradition with screens as background for the sculpture and as much informal planting as we could afford. . . . The garden was designed to contrast with the severe rectangular layout of the rear facade of the Museum, not to mention the severe rectangular layout of the surrounding New York City.[45]

Hudnut's view that modern sculptural display required an architectonic, classic condition would not materialize at MoMA until Johnson's sculpture garden in 1953. The power of Johnson's design had to do with the fact that he did take on "the severe rectangular layout" both of the Museum's rear facade and of the surrounding city.

The first sculpture garden at MoMA was a curatorial and a social success. Barr and the curators saw the garden as part and parcel of their development of the Museum's collection. When he presented his annual report in 1941, Barr noted: "Though this is not generally known, we already have the most comprehensive and important collection of modern sculpture in the world. There are many serious omissions which we should correct, particularly in view of the fact that we have an outdoor garden which is in almost continuous need of more good large pieces."[46]

In his history of the Museum, written on the occasion of its tenth anniversary, Museum President A. Conger Goodyear, also reported that, as the collection "stood on its tenth birthday, it was particularly strong in sculpture."[47] Emphasizing the public response to the sculpture garden in the new museum, he also cited a *New Yorker* article by Lewis Mumford of June 3, 1939, in which Mumford had written:

Dramatically there are two specially rewarding spots in the building. One is on the ground floor, where, as one turns a corner to go into the exhibition halls, one immediately beholds a wide expanse of garden [fig. 16]. *Here the sense of air space and light is in absolute contrast to the marmorial bleakness affected by most museums. . . . The other spot that gives one a sharp pleasure is the main stairs as they mount upward against a stunning frieze of statuesque green plants.*[48]

Between the sculpture garden of 1939 and that of 1953, several additions were made

Left:
16. John McAndrew and Alfred H. Barr, Jr. The Museum of Modern Art Sculpture Garden. View to northeast from within the Museum. 1939

Right:
17. Christopher Tunnard. Garden Terrace of the Serge Chermayeff House, Halland, Sussex, England. 1936–37

to the original garden and its program, and in the years 1946–49, several completely new designs were submitted to the Museum's board for review. None of these projects was realized, but they obviously were proposed right under Johnson's eyes, as he was part of the Museum's curatorial staff, from 1945 to 1949 when he was officially named to head the newly formed Department of Architecture and Design.

In 1942, when the Museum first considered new plans for the sculpture garden, the trustees and curators looked at proposals by Goodwin and Tunnard, who was then teaching at Harvard University's Graduate School of Design.[49] No records of Tunnard's proposals have yet come to light; however, as a landscape architect concerned with modern art and, particularly, with the use of modern sculpture in the garden, he was a most appropriate candidate for the project. Tunnard had come from England in 1939, at Hudnut's behest, to teach at Harvard; he was already a designer with an international reputation. In 1938, he had published the first major treatise in English on gardens and modernism, *Gardens in the Modern Landscape,* in which he advocated placing modern sculptures in modern design contexts. He illustrated his point with Gabriel Guevrékian's use of a "focal sculpture by Lipchitz" at the Noailles garden, Hyères, in southern France, and with his own use of a Henry Moore sculpture at the Serge Chermayeff estate at Halland, Sussex (1934–37; fig. 17), and at his garden of St. Ann's Hill, Chertsey, England (1934–37).[50] Even as he was being approached by MoMA for its garden, Tunnard continued his polemical writings on modern landscape architecture, stating in an article of January 1942: "Our gardens desperately need ideas. The first of these ideas must be the understanding that modern landscape design is inseparable from the spirit, technique, and development of modern architecture." For Tunnard, one of the key factors in creating a modern landscape architecture was "the introduction of modern sculptural art into the garden. This is as organic in its way as the decoration of the wall, because modern sculptors design for the outdoors rather than for museums and galleries. Their scale is the scale of the open landscape."[51]

In the end, the curators and trustees chose Goodwin's proposal: The center of the original garden was replaced by a restaurant garden with a formal grove of plane trees, surrounded by tables, chairs, and stands for food and drink.[52] A restaurant pavilion anchored the garden's west end (fig. 18). A letter from Goodwin to Barr, dated April 1942, discussed the possible colors for the new asphalt ground for the garden: Should it be black, pink, red, green, gray, or blue? Barr responded to Goodwin in the same month, saying that he preferred sand or gray. They finally chose "Jersey red (brown gravel)" for the western area of the garden adjacent to the stone terrace, below the steps, continuing up them, and west; two other spaces around the food pavilion were to be "cowbay gravel (yellow)." The colored organicist composition of the original garden floor continued to reign in Goodwin's revision of it. In the decade after 1942, the restaurant garden functioned as a gathering place, although Barr abhorred the sight of people eating in the sculpture garden; to disguise this "horrendous sight," he proposed putting in tall trees between the restaurant section and the rest of the garden.[53] Others found it highly agreeable; for example, Alicia Legg, who later joined the Museum's curatorial staff, remarked: "That's when I was an art student and used to hang out there, at least in the early 40's, and it was a very informal, gravel around the trees that had a plot around them. There was a kind of stand, like a bar, that served tea, and umbrellas and chairs and tables. . . . It was just very pleasant, and of course no one expected much more."[54]

In 1946, needing more space for exhibitions and the public, the trustees commissioned Goodwin to design a new museum wing, to be "in the same architectural style as the existing building," along the west flank of the garden. A model was published in early 1946 and the project in April 1947.[55] The new wing was to be accompanied by an entirely new design for the sculpture garden by Tunnard, who had left Harvard in 1945 to teach city planning at Yale[56] (fig. 19). Tunnard's proposal envisioned the sculpture garden still bounded by a wall on Fifty-fourth Street, but with new contents and divisions. His project contained hedges on the diagonal with tree masses in counterpoint, subdivisions varying in texture from Aalto-like wooden paling to stone walls and low brick borders, and walkways, many of which were also on the diagonal. The main concept was to create complex, interlocking spaces with

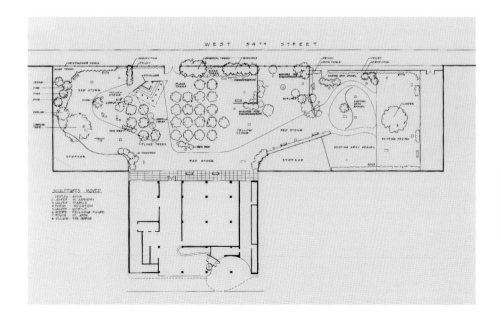

18. Philip L. Goodwin. Sculpture Garden, The Museum of Modern Art, New York. Plan. 1942. Redrawn to scale 1":40', by Jane Shoplick, Department of Landscape Architecture, Graduate School of Design, Harvard University, Cambridge, Massachusetts, 1990

19. Philip L. Goodwin and Christopher Tunnard.
Proposed New Wing and Sculpture Garden for The
Museum of Modern Art, New York. Model and
photomontage. 1946–47

these elements.[57] In effect, Tunnard's project was in the same mold as the original
sculpture garden of 1939—a container of dispersed elements—but informed by the
expanded modernist vocabulary of garden design in the intervening years.[58] A good
deal of that vocabulary had been evolved by his former students at the Harvard
School of Design, James Rose, Garrett Eckbo (fig. 20), and Daniel Kiley, who studied there between 1937 and 1943.

The interest of Tunnard's proposal lies not so much in his garden's design,
which was based on his work of the mid-1930s, but in his use of sculptures that could
be associated iconographically with traditional garden *sculpture,* an approach that
contrasts strongly with the neutral one taken by Barr and McAndrew in their garden
of 1939. His perspective drawing shows that his formal approach to the sculptures followed theirs, namely, the isolation of each piece in an individual setting. The sculptures he illustrated were a Wilhelm Lehmbruck, *Standing Youth* (1913), and Gaston
Lachaise's *Floating Figure* (1927; cast 1935), two of the most well-known figurative
pieces in the Museum's collection.[59] To incorporate them in his drawing, Tunnard
borrowed Mies's technique of photocollage for visualizing sculptures in an architectural project. He placed a photocollage of the Lachaise bronze "on a pedestal in the
pool among the fountain jets."[60] He thus took a sculpture that until then had been
exhibited at the Museum as part of abstract spatial compositions and made it into a
traditional piece of garden sculpture, like the many figures found in Renaissance garden fountains. (Johnson and René d'Harnoncourt, appointed director of the
Museum in 1949, would use the same representational approach with garden sculpture,
placing statues with aquatic associations—for example Maillol's *The River* [begun

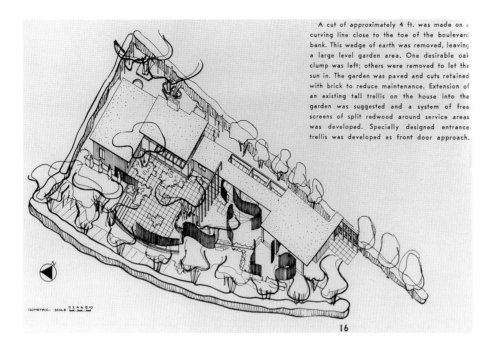

A cut of approximately 4 ft. was made on a curving line close to the toe of the boulevard bank. This wedge of earth was removed, leaving a large level garden area. One desirable oak clump was left; others were removed to let the sun in. The garden was paved and cuts retained with brick to reduce maintenance. Extension of an existing tall trellis on the house into the garden was suggested and a system of free screens of split redwood around service areas was developed. Specially designed entrance trellis was developed as front door approach.

20. Garrett Eckbo. Garden in Oakland, California. 1941

1938–43; completed 1943] and Renoir's *The Washerwoman* [1917]—alongside one of the two pools in the reconfigured garden of 1953 [see fig. 1].)

This project of Tunnard's was not accepted by the trustees, nor were several other projects—one by Johnson, dated 1948, and another by McAndrew of ca. 1946–49, years during which the trustees were deliberating over what form the new sculpture garden should take. Johnson's project was drawn up two years after his return to the Museum and hard on the heels of his triumphant *Mies van der Rohe* exhibition of 1947. The project is known from a brief description and two photographs, a plan and a perspective view, attributed in captions to Johnson and titled "The House of Glass."[61] It is a highly Miesian "glass house," proposed just when Mies's Farnsworth House had been designed and presented in his exhibition and when Johnson had arrived at the final design for his own Glass House in New Canaan, for which groundbreaking took place in March 1948.[62] Nothing is shown of the original garden, which presumably was to be cleared away and its space paved. The project description states:

The Museum of Modern Art proposes to erect in its sculpture garden a permanent building to be called "The House of Glass." Present plans call for a rectangular "prism"' raised above the garden on steel columns. Its entire walls are to be of plate glass, and its floors and stairs will be of rough plate glass. A series of freestanding walls made of sheets of translucent plate glass will surround the building site and an entrance from 54th Street will consist of tempered glass doors. . . . The building as it is projected, will have the appearance of a huge crystal floating above the Museum's garden space in the center of Manhattan. . . . [It] will be the first building of its kind in the world.[63]

In the perspective view (see p. 72), drawn in taut outlines, this glass house is sited on the eastern half of the original garden (one hundred feet in length), between

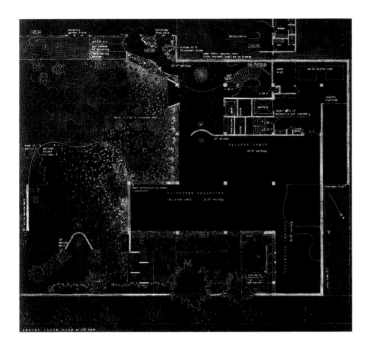

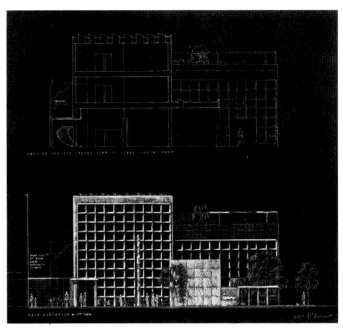

the newly proposed East Wing and the original south-lying Museum building on Fifty-third Street; the Rockefeller townhouses on Fifty-fourth Street appear at left. The intended function of the raised glass house is clearly visible through its transparent walls; large panels subdivide the space into gallery and exhibition spaces. The glass container is elevated on piers and a podium above a gridded ground plane—the floor of a sculpture garden in which one sees the profiles of three figurative sculptures. Two trees are depicted in this garden court, which is entirely enclosed by glass walls of above-human height. To the right in this view, a tall glass panel stands in isolation as a spatial divider, a transparent one, through which a tree is viewed. The visible garden elements are minimal—two trees and some climbing plants on the glass walls—and the sculptures few in number, very much in the style of Mies in his courtyard houses of the 1930s.[64]

While Johnson was proposing a Miesian glass house as a "revision" of the sculpture garden, McAndrew—who had left his curatorial post in 1941 to become director of the Wellesley College Art Museum—also submitted to the Museum proposals for a new West Wing and alterations to the garden that he had helped design.[65] Three unpublished drawings in colored chalk on blueprint, undated but signed by McAndrew, record this project[66] (figs. 21–23). McAndrew's proposal included a revision of the western end of the original garden of 1939 and its restaurant successor. He intended to connect the indoor and outdoor displays of sculpture by extending a ground-floor sculpture gallery into the garden as a glassed-in wing, with views onto sculptures set in greenery, white marble walls, straight and alcove-like, and a pool with "removable background for sculpture." There was also to be a garden terrace on the third floor and outdoor lighting.

Several formal aspects of McAndrew's proposal suggest that it might have been more at home in the urban centers of Latin America. The façades, with their *brise-soleil*, were clearly inspired by Lucio Costa and Oscar Niemeyer's Brazilian Pavilion

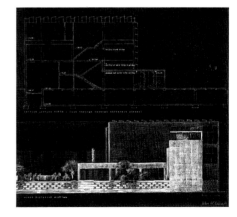

at the New York World's Fair of 1939, and by Le Corbusier's Ministry of Education and Public Health, built in Rio de Janeiro in 1936–45.[67] The influence of Burle Marx, whose free-form garden, designed for the ministry in 1936–38, had been one of the sources for the ground plan of the original Museum garden, can be seen in McAndrew's proposal for the east garden elevation. This shows the access to the revised sculpture garden from the ground-floor sculpture galleries, and in front of it stands a large totem pole covered with greenery and flowers, very much like the columnar floral arrangements favored by Burle Marx in his gardens.[68] The *brise-soleil,* the totemic column at the front entrance, and the large bricks of the garden wall along Fifty-fourth Street, which look as if crafted by hand, give McAndrew's project a character very different from the formal and elegant building materials used in mid-town Manhattan and particularly in the projects built there by the Rockefeller family. In contrast to McAndrew, Johnson would use such materials in his Abby Aldrich Rockefeller Sculpture Garden—marble paving, fine gray bricks, and polished bronze railings, leading a critic to state in 1953 that the garden "is of an elegance, and luxury, and refinement that we don't associate with museum grounds or with public parks."[69]

As McAndrew's project was not accepted, in September 1949 Tunnard re-entered the fray of competing proposals with a project that was decidedly classical in its modernist architectural language[70] (figs. 24–28). Severe lines were provided by paving, low-sitting walls, and concrete curbs that surrounded rectangular enclosures of wall and hedge, in which sculptures were sited in focal points. There was an overall gravity, classical composition, and elegant serenity, which had not been hallmarks of Tunnard's approach to garden design in the late 1930s and 1940s, especially in his joint project with Goodwin of 1946–47 for the Museum sculpture garden. Gone were the hedges and wood screens on the diagonal, the fragmented patches of paving and planted ground cover, which had been inspired by French modernist landscape architects. Instead, order, clarity, and serenity reigned. In plan, the new garden looked like an abstract painting, a De Stijl composition of tree groves, a long

24. Christopher Tunnard. Garden for The Museum of Modern Art, New York, Project. Perspective view, facing north. September 19, 1949. Gouache on composition board, 20 x 30" (50.8 x 76.2 cm). Department of Architecture and Design, The Museum of Modern Art, New York

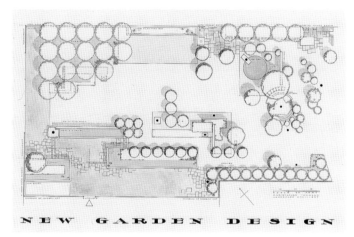

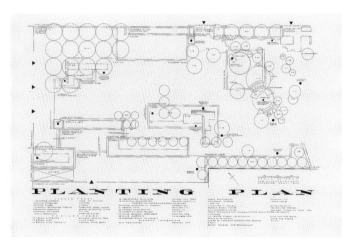

pool with jets, and formal flowerbeds, all of which emphasized rectangles and lines parallel to those of the Museum itself.

Tunnard presented his project in three colored gouache views, in which the ground is painted gray and ochre (the Planting Plan [fig. 27] identifies it as gravel), the low planting boxes and stone edges are ochre-pink, the paving a gray wash, the lawns pale green, and the pool and jets cerulean blue. Light and dark greens color the varied trees, birches in the far ground, planted on the lawn and off it, cryptomeria, one on the lawn, one off, plane trees, weeping willows, an oak, and a tree of Heaven. (Many of these species would be used by Johnson and Fanning in the garden of 1953.) Tunnard's Planting Plan provided for the rich coloration of seasonal floral change, with hyacinths and tulips in the spring, pelagonia and petunias in summer, and chrysanthemums in the fall.

In the perspective drawing (fig. 26), a man stands watching a small boy feeding pigeons; in the background, along Fifty-fourth Street, a high wall of gray brick rises, cut by a wall-high egress to the street; to the rear, the struggling figure of Maillol's bronze *River* is frozen in place over the edge of a circular pool with a very tall jet, the kind that André Le Nôtre made in the seventeenth century for the great basins of the Tuileries gardens, Chantilly, and Versailles. The thirteen sculptures, according to the

Clockwise from top left:
25. Christopher Tunnard. Garden for The Museum of Modern Art, New York, Project. Perspective view, facing east. September 19, 1949. Gouache on composition board, 20 x 30" (50.8 x 76.2 cm). Department of Architecture and Design, The Museum of Modern Art, New York

26. Christopher Tunnard. Garden for The Museum of Modern Art, New York, Project. Perspective view, facing northeast. September 19, 1949. Gouache on composition board, 20 x 30" (50.8 x 76.2 cm). Department of Architecture and Design, The Museum of Modern Art, New York

27. Christopher Tunnard. Garden for The Museum of Modern Art, New York, Project. Planting plan. September 19, 1949. Gouache on composition board, 20 x 30" (50.8 x 76.2 cm). Department of Architecture and Design, The Museum of Modern Art, New York

28. Christopher Tunnard. Garden for The Museum of Modern Art, New York, Project. Plan. September 19, 1949. Gouache on composition board, 20 x 30" (50.8 x 76.2 cm). Department of Architecture and Design, The Museum of Modern Art, New York

Planting Plan, are fewer than the twenty originally set up in the garden in 1939, and several, such as the Maillol, Bernard Reder's *Torso,* Moore's *Family,* and Lipchitz's *Figure,* would be part of the sculpture garden of 1953. With fewer sculptures, Tunnard's design has the character of a public *garden,* in which people can stroll and sculptures are placed in relation to the garden's design, as in traditional public gardens in Europe.

Overall, Tunnard's garden project evokes urbanity (even the cobbles are a material of streets), a certain grandeur, and the materials and style of French classical gardens, and it has something in common with the work that his former student, Daniel Kiley, was doing in the late 1940s, also inspired by the formal tradition of Le Nôtre.[71]

The cultural climate that seems to have inspired Tunnard's new classicism had been fed in part by the Museum itself, where in the spring of 1948 Philip Johnson had held a symposium on "What Is Happening to Modern Architecture?" Tunnard, Barr, the architectural historian Peter Blake (then a curator in Johnson's department), Marcel Breuer, Walter Gropius, McAndrew, and others took part.[72] Tunnard advocated a "middle ground" between the hard-edged modernism of European architects, such as Mies and Gropius, and the use of natural materials, primarily wood and stone, by Breuer and architects of what Barr derisively called "'wooden domestic buildings [of] the International Cottage Style.'"[73] And this compromise is precisely what Tunnard offered in his garden project of 1949: classical composition, but with flagstone paving, cobbles, and textured wall surfaces.

While the trustees and curatorial staff reviewed the projects for the new sculpture garden in 1946–49, the Museum had an opportunity to become an arbiter in the stylistic debates in the field of modern landscape architecture. In 1946, it nearly took on the publication of the seminal treatise "Landscape for Living" by the landscape architect Garrett Eckbo; having contacted William A.M. Burden, who then chaired the Committee on the Museum's Collections, Eckbo wrote in June 1946 to Monroe Wheeler, the Museum's director of publications, "with regard to a possible book on modern developments and a new approach to the theory and practice of landscape design."[74] Eckbo had studied landscape architecture at Harvard in 1936–38, where he had begun his prolific writings and had been a great admirer of Tunnard's work. Responding to Eckbo in July 1946, Wheeler answered:

[It] would be very appropriate for the Museum to publish such a book provided it took into account all the significant new work in this field. I have read your magazine articles and I feel that you could write an excellent book on this subject. Would it be possible for you to prepare an outline of what you think the book might include so that I could present it to our Architecture Committee for their consideration? [75]

Eckbo planned to do the outline, as his letter to Wheeler of September 1946 states,[76] but there is no record of it in the Museum's files.[77] What the Eckbo proposal shows, however, is that the Museum was interested in taking a leading position in the field of modern landscape architecture.

None of the several projects by Tunnard and McAndrew was accepted by the trustees, although Tunnard's scheme of September 1949 came close, in terms of urbanity, elegance, and classicism—not to mention the tall, gray street-wall, and specific tree species and sculptures—to Johnson's design. Perhaps by this time, certain plantings and sculptures were part of a definite program envisioned by the trustees. Tunnard may also have been inspired by the Miesian classicism of Johnson and others. However, by the end of 1949, when d'Harnoncourt was appointed director of the Museum, the trustees had turned to Johnson for a new design.

The Abby Aldrich Rockefeller Sculpture Garden

Johnson had been curator of architecture from 1932 to 1934, and became departmental director in 1949, when he succeeded Elizabeth B. Mock.[78] It was thus as a member of the Museum's curatorial staff that he designed the new sculpture garden. It was to be named after Abby Aldrich Rockefeller, who had died in 1948. It was Mrs. Rockefeller who, as a Museum trustee in 1937, had secured the donation of the land for the original garden of 1939.

The commission for the new sculpture garden appears to have been awarded in conjunction with that of the new annex and West Wing that Johnson would design for the Museum as well. These new additions were most likely planned together around 1949–50.[79] It was early in 1950 that Johnson produced a model of the proposed sculpture garden for the trustees (fig. 29). Construction of the seven-story annex, adjacent to the original Goodwin–Stone building on West Fifty-third Street, began in the summer of 1950. Work on the garden started in the spring of 1952 and was completed in April 1953[80] (figs. 30, 31). In 1954, the annex was extended by the new Whitney Museum wing, also designed by Johnson, along the western boundary of the original garden, extending to Fifty-fourth Street; the ground floor of this wing housed the Modern's restaurant, opening onto Johnson's paved new sculpture garden terrace, and Whitney offices above.[81] (In 1961, the Whitney Museum acquired its present site on Madison Avenue, and the entire West Wing was taken over by the Modern the following year.)

The site that Johnson had to work with was shorter on both the east and west than the original garden, and was bordered on the south and west by the existing

29. Philip Johnson. The Abby Aldrich Rockefeller Sculpture Garden, The Museum of Modern Art, New York. Model. 1950–53

and planned Museum wings. In contrast to the 400-by-100-foot site available to McAndrew and Barr in 1939, Johnson's garden site now measured 175 by 100 feet. However, the fundamental architectural program for an outdoor sculpture garden remained unchanged, and the interim proposals by Tunnard and McAndrew had given Johnson much to think about.

The model that Johnson presented in 1950 shows the garden essentially as it would be built; as in the House of Glass project drawings of 1948, however, few sculptures are indicated.[82] There were only two significant differences between the model and the final design. First, the three boulders seen in the model, used to anchor the composition near its center, would be replaced by a clump of eight Japanese cedars; second, the vertical retaining walls of the *L*-shaped terrace would be replaced by sloping earth embankments, planted with ivy and myrtle. The boulders and the unembanked terrace, from which the visitor descended to the garden court, suggest that Johnson was interested in motifs associated with the traditional Japanese house, with its cantilevered porches providing views of a lower garden that often features isolated boulders set into a level plane of smaller stones and plantings. His subtle use of these motifs will be examined below in the context of the design's other historical and modern sources.

The architectural programs for the projected annex and sculpture garden were published in *Interiors* Magazine in August 1950, while the annex was being built. Here, Johnson provided a concise statement of his conceptual and spatial organization of the garden; the emphasis was clearly on the opportunities that the new design allowed for the display of sculpture: "All these measures [the wall on the street, water-channels, bridges] will provide four different areas and backgrounds in which to display various kinds of sculptures. There will be an open central plaza for monumental works, a long narrow plaza, a small square and a large square"[83] (fig. 32). While Andrew C. Ritchie, the director of the Department of Painting and Sculpture, made preparations in 1951–52 for *Sculpture of the Twentieth Century,* the exhibition that would inaugurate both the garden and the new indoor galleries, the

Left:
30. The Abby Aldrich Rockefeller Sculpture Garden under construction, summer 1952

Right:
31. The Abby Aldrich Rockefeller Sculpture Garden, view from atop the Whitney Museum northeast to Fifty-fourth Street, June 1953

Museum's curators hotly debated whether the proposed new garden was better than the old one. The formality and the pavement in Johnson's design irked some. ("The whole city is paved!" complained Curator of Collections Dorothy C. Miller.[84]) In general, however, the Museum viewed its new sculpture garden as a stunning new public attraction, and as early as June 1952 drew up plans for publicizing it.[85]

When it was completed, the 1953 garden was paved almost entirely in unpolished slabs of gray Vermont marble, and bounded by buildings on three sides and by a high gray-brick wall along Fifty-fourth Street. In contrast to the temporary and somewhat diffuse quality of the original garden and the later proposals by Tunnard and McAndrew, Johnson's design is compact, highly unified, and permanent. Most of the garden is sunk two feet below the narrow terrace that frames it on the west and south. The idea of a sunken garden appealed immediately to the public imagination, and the press picked up on it right away, referring repeatedly to "the Museum of Modern Art's new sunken garden (most of it four feet below street level)."[86] The quality of the garden as a sunken courtyard may have evoked enchanting historical associations with ancient Babylonian and classical gardens. Johnson today, as in 1955, says that he used "the idea of [a] sunken area" as a formal device by which the apparent size of the garden would be increased.[87]

The compact proportions and the all-encompassing view afforded by the raised terrace, combined with the marble grid of the garden floor, made this an urban space in the long tradition derived from Renaissance piazzas. The first reactions of the press, echoed time and again, focused on the refined materials, the unexpected presence of water channels and garden plantings in an urban museum's backyard, and the almost classical grandeur of a distinctly modern—and public—space:

Here it is, all paved in grey marble, with stone steps, terraces, trees, flowers, and even those promised canals of shallow water disappearing in an approximation of nature

32. The Abby Aldrich Rockefeller Sculpture Garden, view from the garden terrace north to Fifty-fourth Street, June 1953

beneath the pine trees only to reappear in the distance at the far end of the garden, for all the world as though we were still living in the seventeenth century with Louis XIV on the throne . . . the effects achieved by this machineage [design] are more than a little princely.[88]

The origins of such a "princely" public setting surely lay in the grand European capitals (the new Museum café on the ground floor of the Whitney building was in fact praised for its "continental" air[89]). Johnson himself declared just before the opening in April 1953: "My conception was a piazza. . . . I have always loved the square of St. Mark's, in Venice."[90] From the start, the uses of the sculpture garden have echoed this urban conception. Out in the garden, the public gathers to walk and look at the sculptures, to eat at tables on the western end of the terrace, to read or converse with each other, and to seek respite in the open air from the intensive study of art works inside the Museum building. The design of the garden as a paved container of immobile sculptures and moving people allows for a concentrated grouping of the public in a small urban space.

The "sunken" garden is cut along its length by two parallel, shallow water channels (just 16 inches deep), offset like long slipped rectangles. The disjunction in the course of these two channels, which are bridged by identical marble slabs, is both marked and masked from the south by the focus of the entire composition, namely a grove of eight massive Japanese cedars, called cryptomerias, rising thirty feet tall.[91] The floor of the garden is not fully paved. Here and there, particularly along the edges of the garden and its more open end on the east, the earth is revealed, planted with ground covers. From these green patches rise other groves of slender trees with relatively thin foliage.

The original plantings included ten low European hornbeams on the west, two plane trees on the north, a copse of European birches some twenty feet in height, two Hankow willows, two weeping beeches in the central areas, and the clump of eight Japanese cedars at the junction of the two canals; then to the east, silver birch, ailanthus, and bushes of azalea, greenbrier, and honeysuckle, among others. The ground covers ranged from creeping roses and myrtle to evergreen pachysandra and winter jasmine. Fanning, who provided the list of plantings, noted that their careful selection replaced a dense overgrowth of plane and linden trees, which had been planted in 1942.[92] The patches of ground cover—"pseudo-accidental planting areas," as Johnson called them—set up a delightful tension between the spontaneous vegetal growth and the "strong paving lines to give order."[93]

The sculpture garden was enclosed along the street by a fourteen-foot-high gray-brick wall pierced by a gate with an open grille; the garden was left somewhat open to the east, with three large marble pavers providing a path through the planted ground cover.[94] The pavers are a motif that Johnson had previously used in designing the atrium of his Rockefeller Guest House (1950; see p. 75), where they are stepping stones across a reflecting pool. In both designs, the pavers evoke in modern form the stepping stones of historical Japanese gardens; this aspect was recognized publicly, for example, when the Guest House, along with other work by Johnson, was published in Clay Lancaster's *The Japanese Influence in America* (1965).[95]

While Johnson started from the same broad range of sources in contemporary design available to Barr and McAndrew eleven years earlier, he came up with a very different formal solution to the task of designing a sculpture garden. Yet the funda-

33. The Abby Aldrich Rockefeller Sculpture Garden, view from within the Museum north to Fifty-fourth Street, 1964

mental principles that the two curators had contributed in 1939 can still be found in his design. In addition to the notion of exhibiting modern sculpture outdoors in a modern garden, these were: the placing of sculptures in isolated settings, as Mies had used them; the concept of a formally arranged garden where the public had ample room to circulate; and the notion of a fluid spatial continuity between indoors and out, which was a key premise of much modernist design. In the 1939 building, "the ground floor was a unity of galleries and garden," because "virtually the entire rear wall was glass from floor to ceiling to unite the interior with the garden," as John Coolidge recalled.[96] This was also a key to Johnson's design (fig. 33), and it remained so until 1984, when the escalators were installed at the rear of the main lobby, partially blocking the view out to the garden (see p. 100).

Johnson also retained two other aspects of the original design, although the addition of the restaurant in 1942 had already altered the central area considerably. These were the large open plaza to which the public acceded directly from the entrance floor of the Museum and the grove of trees to the right of the central axis. In both the gardens, of 1939 and 1953, a grove on this spot functioned as a compositional anchor for the garden as a whole (the grove had been left untouched in the restaurant garden of 1942). In the original design, the grove screened a bench opposite the doors onto the garden; in Johnson's design, it masked the disjunction between the pools.

Johnson described the garden as "really a sort of outdoor room."[97] Part of the sculpture garden's evocative character was inherent in the overlapping aspects of private and public in the commission itself. The Modern was a public museum, but from the start it was given a "conceptual resemblance to a city residence,"[98] and, as noted above, its ground-floor access to the sculpture garden emulated the direct indoor-outdoor connections of residences. Nearly every article on the new sculpture court in 1953 called it an "outdoor room" or "an outdoor living room," echoing Johnson's own definition;[99] indeed, the marble paving resembles the floor of a grand interior hall.

The sculptures that were placed on the paved surfaces of the new garden in 1953 were relatively few, about a dozen, and they were carefully chosen for their formal-spatial effects and, in several instances, for their iconographical associations. The original installation was made for the exhibition *Sculpture of the Twentieth Century,* which occupied both the sculpture garden and several interior galleries. Apart from the four bronze *Backs* (1908–ca. 1931) by Henri Matisse, which were affixed to the high brick wall along Fifty-fourth Street, only half of the works—five or six—would continue to occupy roughly the same locations. The rest would rotate with other works in the Museum's collection or be replaced by temporary exhibition pieces. In the public's mind, the half-dozen set pieces would become permanently associated with the sculpture garden, and in this way, part of its formal configuration.[100]

The initial arrangement of the sculptures appears to have been done by John-son himself, working with d'Harnoncourt.[101] However, Ritchie selected the works for the exhibition (those placed indoors as well as those installed in the garden) in advance, working from 1951 to 1953 to secure loans of the works or to acquire them for the collection. He went on "an exhausting tour" of Europe in 1951, visiting sculp-tors as well as dealers. In a letter of September 26 posted from Milan, he wrote:

First, I saw Moore in England and got his agreement on the best pieces to represent him. . . . I also saw a good deal of the work of the younger English sculptors, much of it very promising indeed. . . . In Paris saw Giacometti and have the promise of a new double figure. . . . Spent a good deal of time with [the dealer Daniel-Henry] Kahnweiler going over his stock. The most important news from him is that he, and presumably Curt V[alentin] in association, are buying a number of the finest Picasso sculptures, besides the Man with Lamb, *already offered to us. We can have anything we want, including the* Man with the Lamb (sic) *for exhibition. This means, fortunately, we don't have to deal directly with Picasso who, as you know, might have proved difficult to say the least. I did not see Brancusi. . . .Today I spent with Marini, Manzù and Toninelli. Marini has a magnificent new horse in process, somewhat larger than anything heretofore and archi-tecturally very impressive. We will have the first showing of the bronze in New York.*[102]

The sculptures chosen for the garden were quite homogeneous: most were fig-urative, representational works, recently created and acquired between 1948 and 1953, and cast in either bronze or lead to withstand harsh weather.[103] Compared with the crowding that occurred in later years, a lot of open space surrounded the sculp-tures installed in 1953, so that they could be seen well by the public and so that the garden could continue to be the site of openings and parties.[104] The pavement served as an orienting grid along which the rectangular or square sculptural pedestals were aligned, but the overall arrangement was decisively asymmetrical: the works on their pedestals were placed in counterpoint to other sculptures and the backgrounds of plantings and walls. Unlike historical garden displays, none of the works were paired. Seven of the sculptures stood on the north side of the garden, arrayed within their own outdoor "gallery," and the balance positioned on the much larger south side closer to the Museum.[105] The visitor could observe the garden through the floor-to-ceiling glass wall of the ground floor, and then exit through the garden doors to stand on the narrow south terrace.

Reconstructed in plan, the original configuration of sculpture-pedestals and garden spaces recalls the abstract geometrical paintings of Piet Mondrian and Theo van Doesburg. Johnson, like many exhibition designers, translated abstract artistic forms into three-dimensional installations. In his 1947 exhibition of work by Mies, Johnson himself described the plan of Mies's Brick Country House project (1924) as "closely resembling the orthogonal patterns of a van Doesburg painting."[106] Several sculptures in the 1953 garden were placed so that their forms echoed the architectonic structure of their surroundings. An example is Lachaise's *Floating Figure*, which was placed on a high pedestal next to the northwest stairs leading from the garden to the terrace: it is a directional statue, pointing both upward and to the left, and its dynamic, stepped profile echoed the form of the steps nearby.

Many of the representational sculptures, however, were placed in ways that also denied a perception of the garden as only an abstract formal composition. These works were specifically selected for their representational character and their iconographical associations with gardens, water, and piazzas. For example, Maillol's *River*, which was modeled on the classical nymphs representing the rivers of France on the Parterre d'Eau at the Château of Versailles, and Renoir's *Washerwoman* were sited on opposite sides of the longer pool (see fig. 1). (Even when these sculptures were moved for different spatial effects, they were placed near the water or in it.) Marini's seven-foot-high bronze *Horse* (1951), temporarily on loan for the exhibition of 1953, recalled Renaissance equestrian statues set up in Italian piazzas with gridded pavements. Although this modern one is riderless, it rears up in front of the dark mass of cryptomerias. Picasso's *Shepherd (Man) Holding a Lamb* is a pastoral piece, suitable for a garden; over seven feet in height, it stood alone in the midst of the central court.[107] His bronze *She-Goat* of 1950, acquired by the Museum in 1959 and immediately placed in the garden is similarly pastoral. Efforts were clearly made by Ritchie, Johnson, and d'Harnoncourt to select sculptures with thematic associations apt for the garden, and their approach was followed at first.[108] But when modern sculpture became increasingly abstract and larger in scale, the pieces acquired by the Museum no longer fit the garden in this way. In effect, once the scale and the forms of the sculptures outgrew the conceptual and physical boundaries of Johnson's original design, the composition of the sculpture garden would be radically altered.

The installation of 1953 emphasized the individuality of each sculpture and its specific environment—all had different heights, shapes, pedestals, and backgrounds. Johnson and d'Harnoncourt paid careful attention to the colors, materials, and textures of the sculptures and their surroundings, and to effects of light and shadow. For example, Reder's 1938 *Torso* of pale limestone was set against the deep green of the cryptomeria grove that masked the juncture of the pools. The dark-gray lead *River* by Maillol was placed on the dove-gray marble floor, adjacent to the steely surface of the longer pool, thus forming a chromatic "bridge" between pavement and water. As the sun moved during the day, sculptures passed from sunlight to shadow and back into the light, and appeared alternately as light-colored bodies in open space or as dark silhouettes against their sunlit backgrounds of gray-brick wall or marble pavement.

In 1955, Johnson summarized his compositional moves in the garden's design, half of which had to do with the creation of spaces to enhance the viewing of the sculptures: "1) A study in forced circulation: pedestrians must turn and walk, and walk and turn in order to view sculpture from different angles. Means: steps, bridges, planting beds; 2) the creation of four areas, merging but distinct, each a different size for different effects as background for different scales of sculptural art; and 3) Breaking up backgrounds to isolate pieces of sculpture so that each can be viewed separately."[109]

What were the conceptual bases and artistic principles of Johnson's design of the configuration of sculptures and backgrounds in the garden of 1953? And how was his approach related to those taken by the curators who set up exhibitions of sculpture and rearranged pieces in the permanent galleries inside the museum building?[110] According to the late John Coolidge, a curator himself and a friend and colleague of many curators at the Museum from the 1930s on, Johnson, "worked with his gut." That's the way he has worked with his sculptures in his own gallery in New Canaan, Connecticut. That is, you could try a given piece in a half dozen different places—but you see how and where it looks well."[111] Ever since the start of his career, Johnson has collected art and designed spaces for its exhibition, including in his own houses. As a Museum curator in 1932–34, he had rapidly gained fame for being in the forefront of exhibition design and installation technique.[112] At the time he designed the Museum sculpture garden in 1950–52, he was completing the Richard C. Davis House in Wayzata, Minnesota, the design of which centered on the display of the clients' large art collection.[113]

Within his broad concerns with modern art, Johnson has always had a particular interest in sculpture.[114] His approach to the display of the individual work, which emphasized its isolation and its use of a sculpture-specific background, echoed one that he himself had advocated in the 1930s and that was used by McAndrew and Barr in the 1939 garden. In *The International Style* (1932) Johnson had written that, just as "was true of the best Greek sculpture . . . it is particularly important today that sculpture should be isolated."[115] Just like the curators, who continued to experiment with indoor exhibition techniques and were experimenting with bringing modern sculptures out-of-doors, Johnson's approach in the Museum garden of 1953 was to re-create the indoor sculpture galleries in outdoor terms. He described his sculpture garden as a "roofless room, with four subrooms formed by the planting and the canals, to provide four space backgrounds for the sculpture,"[116] and he compared it to the interior of his Glass House.[117]

How clearly he conceived of these four garden "subrooms" as sculpture galleries taken outdoors and arranged according to the latest curatorial techniques can be seen by the example of the long, narrow "subroom" in the garden's northwest-quadrant (see pp. 104–106). Johnson gave this area the elongated shape and roughly the same proportions of the gallery that had been specifically designed for sculpture in the Goodwin-Stone building of 1939.[118] And he used the sculptures—Lachaise's *Floating Figure,* Maillol's *The River,* Moore's *Double Figure,* Renoir's *Washerwoman,* and Epstein's *Madonna*[119]—as elements in the spatial composition of this long corridor. A major aspect of these innovations in the sculpture gallery of 1939 was the way in which the route and experience of the visitor among the sculptures were controlled. John Coolidge emphasized that entrances and spatial divisions were carefully designed in order to encourage the visitors to confront the sculptures in a planned sequence.[120] This approach to controlling sequence was continued in later exhibitions at the Modern and elsewhere and it is exactly the one Johnson used in his design of the sculpture garden.[121]

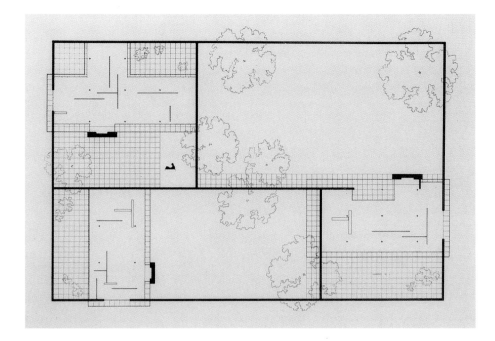

34. Ludwig Mies van der Rohe. Group of Three Court Houses. Plan. 1938. Mies van der Rohe Archive, The Museum of Modern Art, New York

"Classical" Harmony within an Eclectic Modern Design

In the early 1950s, civic spaces and classicist tendencies—and the Japanese house and garden—were part of the contemporary architectural debate; exposure to landscape design was part of Johnson's academic professional training at Harvard's Graduate School of Design in 1940–43; and modern art and architecture, particularly the buildings of Mies van der Rohe, were among Johnson's longstanding concerns.

Johnson had admired Mies since their first meeting in 1930.[122] Like Mies, he had always been involved with modern art and art installations, and he shared with Mies the notion that sculpture, as in ancient Greece, should be displayed discretely, in the round. For his sculpture garden Johnson chose the model of Mies's garden spaces in his courtyard houses. Many of Mies's projects were for dense urban sites; only a few involved suburban landscapes. Their language was also urban, with high enclosed walls for privacy and paved courtyards[123] (fig. 34).

At first glance, one might indeed say that Johnson's sculpture garden is a Miesian residential courtyard. But I will argue here that a difference of approach, namely to what a garden was, distinguished Mies's houses and Johnson's garden, which at first appear similar in their design vocabulary (for the parts invented by Mies and used by Johnson). Apart from Johnson's unique commission for the Museum garden, neither architect received specific commissions for gardens alone (separate from houses). In contrast to Johnson, Mies was not concerned with conceptualizing the garden as a primary object of design. It is doubtful that he would have been interested in building a garden alone without a house, such as the Museum garden (despite the façades of the surrounding buildings). We shall first look at the similarities and then at the differences in the two architects' approaches to the design concept of the garden.

Many formal motifs in the Museum garden derive from Mies's houses, from the country houses of the early 1920s to the Farnsworth House in Plano, Illinois

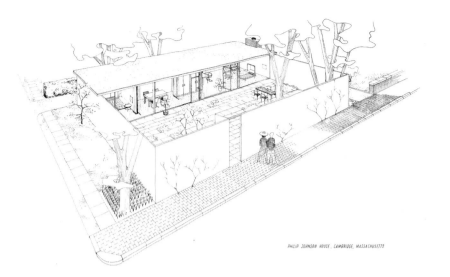

PHILIP JOHNSON HOUSE, CAMBRIDGE, MASSACHUSETTS

35. Philip Johnson. 9 Ash Street, Cambridge, Massachusetts. Perspective view. 1941–42. The Museum of Modern Art, New York

36. Philip Johnson. 9 Ash Street, Cambridge, Massachusetts. View to garden court from living area. 1941–42. The Museum of Modern Art, New York

(1946–51). From the Barcelona Pavilion of 1929 and the courtyard houses come the gridded marble pavement (made even more current for Johnson, when it was used by Canneel-Claes in his gardens of the late 1930s and the 1940s), the simple stairs that constitute the approach to or from a terrace, the use of asymmetry in the design of the garden court, the containing walls, the predominance of pavement over plantings, and the use of well-placed sculptures. Even certain details recall Mies's work: for example, the steps used by Johnson for the bridges over the water channels bring to mind those of the Farnsworth House. However, there are significant differences between Johnson's and Mies's approaches to designing a garden. Already in his own houses Johnson had relinquished strict adherence to Mies's approach to design, first in the one of 1942–43 in Cambridge, Massachusetts (figs. 35, 36), and then in the Glass House in New Canaan, Connecticut (1949). A brief comparison of the two architects' approaches can help to clarify this point.

Mies was not a garden or landscape architect, but he did design several garden spaces early in his career (for the Perls House [1911] and the Werner House [1913], both in Berlin-Zehlendorf; and projects for his own house at Werder [1914]), and the courts with trees and sculpture that he projected or built for several of his houses and courtyard houses of the 1930s can properly be called gardens—for example, the Gericke House, Berlin, Project (1932), and the Wolf House, Guben (1925–27), an extant drawing of which shows a richer version of the sunken garden (replete with planting beds, a large tree, proliferating ground cover, and a bench) than the bare space built in brick and known from photographs.[124] In the two versions of his project of 1914 for his own house at Werder, there are avenues, massive tree gardens (*bosquets*) laid out in geometric order, grand staircases, sunken gardens, and indicated in writing on one of the two versions, a sunken *Rosengarten* (fig. 37).[125] The magnificent profusion of *bosquets* in the Werder project does not reappear in Mies's later designs, where gardens are conceptualized as enclosed (or partially so) courtyards, paved and with very few plantings; the courts usually are bounded by high walls and the plantings are limited to a few trees and ground covers.

Although he designed his houses and the Museum garden using a Miesian vocabulary, Johnson configured its elements very differently. Whereas Mies started from abstract spatial compositions in which house and garden terraces (or courts) interlock in ways derived from De Stijl work, Johnson started instead from a representational tradition of architecture, namely, from classical configurations of house, garden, and courtyard. To these he then applied a Miesian language of modernism. This is already the case with his house in Cambridge, conceived as a traditional walled-in garden in which the dwelling lies at the back of a rectangular court enclosed by high walls.[126] As for the Glass House, even if it is a glass container, it has the axial symmetry and overall form of a house in the Western classical idiom. It does not interlock with outdoor spaces as did Mies's courtyard houses and the Farnsworth House, with its overhanging roof; rather, it sits on a low brick "podium" in the middle of a grassy terrace.[127]

Johnson did not redo Mies in the Museum sculpture garden, just as he had not redone the glass containers of Mies's Museum for a Small City (1942; fig. 38) and Farnsworth House in his own Glass House. In all of Mies's projects involving garden courts or elements of garden design to about 1940, the treatment of architecture as an abstract spatial composition largely erased recognition of traditional typologies.[128] Johnson approached the project of devising a sculpture garden in terms that

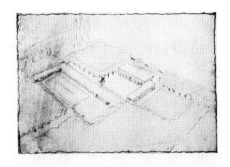

37. Ludwig Mies van der Rohe. Two Versions of a House for the Architect, Werder, Germany, Project. 1914. Mies van der Rohe Archive, The Museum of Modern Art, New York

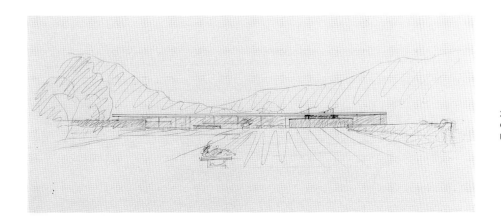

38. Ludwig Mies van der Rohe. Museum for a Small City, Project. Perspective view. 1942. Mies van der Rohe Archive, The Museum of Modern Art, New York

engaged certain key traditional concerns and modes of representation belonging to the practice of landscape architecture. Thus, aided by the site itself, he designed his sculpture garden at the Modern as a bounded garden, connected visually to the Museum building but not interlocking spatially with it. Also, like a traditional garden, Johnson's contains stairs, sloped embankments, streams, bridges, terraces for viewing paved garden spaces, and groves of trees. Although he configured these representational elements rather abstractly, together they are clearly legible in terms of a tradition of garden design, now formulated in modernist terms.

The different compositional uses of sculpture by Mies and Johnson also underline my point. In many of his courtyard houses and in the Barcelona Pavilion, Mies used reclining or standing statues as elements of planar and spatial composition the same way he used planes of glass and marble based on De Stijl spatial concepts. However, the uniqueness of the Miesian configuration, namely the importance given equally to sculptures and architectural elements, was only partially taken over by Johnson. In Mies's works, the sculptures are given specific architectural compositional roles, and to remove a statue from Mies's courtyards would destroy the compositional balance. Not so with Johnson's sculpture garden, which does not depend compositionally on the presence of sculpture, as seen in his model of 1950. Sculptures in his garden can play important compositional roles, but they do not have intrinsic ones.

Mies's Museum for a Small City project was a catalyst for Johnson's thinking about the relationships between his several larger concerns, including the importance of designed civic spaces. Mies published the project in 1943, illustrating it with an exquisite exterior perspective view, a plan, and two photocollages for the display of art. He provided a brief:

The first problem is to establish the museum as a center for the enjoyment, not the interment of art. In this project the barrier between the art work and the living community is erased by a garden approach for the display of sculpture. *Interior sculptures enjoy an equal spatial freedom, because the open plan permits them to be seen against the surrounding hills. The architectural space becomes a defining rather than a confining space.*[129]

After the Museum garden of 1939, this project, which was never built, was the only other elaborated scheme for the display of sculpture on terraces surrounding an urban museum of modern art.[130] It was therefore more important as a conceptual source for Johnson's garden than Mies's courtyard houses. It was designed for a museum; it was urban; it included a great paved plaza, and it posited the museum as a civic space for the "living community." In it, Mies used "a garden approach for the display of sculpture"; "the living community" of visitors would be able to walk around sculpture both indoors and outdoors on the paved plaza, just as they would later in Johnson's MoMA garden. There was a remarkable indoor-outdoor connection, in that building and surrounding landscape were conceived as one great composition providing backdrops for the sculptures. In this project, Mies articulated the notions of garden and garden pool more fully than ever before.[131] And he brought the concerns of his courtyard-house studies into contemporary discourse on civic spaces by presenting his indoor-outdoor museum as a kind of civic center for modern culture, set in the landscape like a classical temple complex on built-up terraces.[132]

By the early 1940s, there was much interest in the related issues of classicism and humanism, civic spaces, monumentality, and public art. The debates on these continued through the 1950s.[133] It is clear that Johnson designed his sculpture garden as a paved urban court in the context of these debates. In a 1943 symposium on aesthetic questions and the city, the Swiss art historian Sigfried Giedion first addressed "The Need for a New Monumentality."[134] In 1949, when the eighth International Congress for Modern Architecture (CIAM) met in Hoddeston, England, its theme was "The Heart of the City: Towards the Humanisation of Urban Life." The introductory statement called for a process of "recentralization" through "the creation of new Cores," and illustrated the idea with Rockefeller Plaza in New York City. The discussion then focused on the Italian piazza and other communal gathering places. In his contribution, "Sculpture and the Core of the City," James Johnson Sweeney stated that "if 'the Core' is to function spiritually as a Core, human attention must be brought to focus there as intensely as possible; and sculpture by its very nature is a most efficacious means to this end."[135] Two years later, clearly continuing the spirit of the eighth CIAM, Johnson chaired a symposium at the Museum on "how to combine architecture, painting, and sculpture" in civic centers.[136]

Giedion continued to be a prominent voice for these concerns, for example in an article of 1952 on the Italian Renaissance piazza. His and Johnson's affinities for this classical, humanist, and collective type of design as a model for contemporary work surfaced when Johnson showed Giedion his model for the Museum garden. Reportedly, Giedion exclaimed: "At last, a piazza in New York!"[137] Indeed, the sculpture court at MoMA was recognized early on by visitors as an urban space and called a piazza, although it is closed off from the street and small in scale.[138] Conceptually, the sculpture court at MoMA was a small-scale descendant of the Lower Plaza at Rockefeller Center.[139]

Classicism (or more accurately, neoclassicism) was an important component among Johnson's broad concerns in design in the early 1950s,[140] and it appears, clothed in the language of modern garden design, in the Museum sculpture garden. Johnson's colleague Henry-Russell Hitchcock (with whom he wrote *The International Style*) was perhaps the first to recognize this component in several of Johnson's earliest houses. Hitchcock wrote in 1955: "Philip Johnson's classicist leanings . . . occasionally produce coincidental resemblances to classical prototypes, even without conscious imitation. Thus the Rockefeller [Guest] House . . . shares an almost identical planning discipline with the House of Pansa, in Pompeii." Similarly, Hitchcock qualified Johnson's Richard Hodgson House (1950–51; designed with Landis Gores) in New Canaan as "almost ancient Roman in its planning concept."[141]

The study of history and an affinity for classical and neoclassical forms had always been part of Johnson's culture: witness his writings on Karl Friedrich Schinkel and his use of Palladian plans in his houses of the early 1950s (for example, the Hodgson House, which reinterprets the distribution of rooms in the Villa Poiana at Poiana Maggiore and several related plans by Palladio). The Modern's sculpture garden has some elements in common with the ancient Roman townhouse garden as a type: both have formal compositions of canals, bridges, and low terraces built to look down upon the garden, and are contained within high walls. As one among many examples, the garden of the House of Loreius Tiburtinus in Pompeii bears interesting comparison, particularly the narrow terrace and level slab bridges in its outdoor triclinium.[142]

But the classicism that the Museum sculpture garden embodies is really that of a type, the paved Mediterranean garden since Roman antiquity. Thus, in a general but evocative way, Johnson's sculpture garden and many similar paved and enclosed modern gardens designed in the 1950s and 1960s, such as the McIntyre garden, Hillsborough, California (1959–61), by Lawrence Halprin, find a place in a long tradition that includes the garden courts of Hadrian's villa at Tivoli and the Alhambra palaces at Granada. In all of these gardens, the juxtaposition of paved or marble surfaces with reflecting pools constitutes the dominant feature.

Johnson's particular professional training in design and his subsequent experience in designing houses and their gardens (1949–53) enabled him to make use of the contemporary formal language of modernist landscape architecture in the MoMA sculpture garden. By 1953, that language rested on a highly articulated forty-year-old tradition, which he had absorbed at Harvard. At that time, the university offered a singularly comprehensive synthesis of the field, based on a very professional tradition in the teaching of landscape architecture since 1900.[143] In 1936, to encourage collaboration between the disciplines, Dean Hudnut brought together the three departments of architecture, landscape architecture, and planning. Walter Gropius and Marcel Breuer joined the faculty in 1937, Tunnard in 1939. The next fifteen years saw the flourishing of an academic and eclectic version of modernism.[144] Johnson was Tunnard's student, along with Lawrence Halprin and Edward Larrabee Barnes. Foremost among their predecessors were also Rose, Eckbo, and Kiley, who began to publish their new work and ideas around 1936–37, notably in architectural magazines such as *Architectural Record, Pencil Points,* and, beginning in early 1940s, *Arts + Architecture.*

This training changed the position that Johnson had held while he and Hitchcock were writing *The International Style* in 1932. At that time, both felt that there was no place for the garden in modernist design.[145] Following Le Corbusier's view of a "Virgilian dream" in houses like the Villa Savoye of 1928–30,[146] they advocated two approaches to landscape: one, in which gardens "may often be treated as part of architecture," simply as "outdoor living rooms," extensions of the building through pergolas or hedges; the second, in which landscape, preferably "untouched nature," should be used as a uniform, natural [neutral] background for modern architecture.[147] Hitchcock, the architect Richard Neutra, and presumably Johnson, too, continued to hold this position around 1937.[148]

But then came the training at Harvard, where Hudnut strongly supported the cause of modernist garden design as a way of reinvigorating the professional landscape design tradition. In an article of 1940, Hudnut, an architect and a planner, directly attacked the claims that Hitchcock and Neutra had made in 1937. He was against "those architects who propose the abandonment of all attempts at garden form in the landscape setting of the modern house"; he declared that modern gardens should derive a "wide vocabulary of forms" from "the uses of contemporary life," and not be left as an accessory; "gardens like houses, are built of space."[149]

Hudnut's thinking, Tunnard's teaching, and Eckbo's, Kiley's and Rose's deployment of new spatial qualities and design vocabularies in their student projects for modernist gardens provided Johnson with elements for the design language he would develop over the next decade. As his subsequent design work revealed, the architectural and formal versions of modernist gardens must have been most interesting to

39. Le Corbusier and Jean Forestier. Garden Terrace of the Villa Church, Ville d'Avray, France. 1927–29

him. Johnson's Museum garden is an heir to the work of designers such as Jean Forestier, Le Corbusier, Gabriel Guevrékian, Mies (in his courtyard houses), Burle Marx, and the Belgian Jean Canneel-Claes.[150]

For entire garden designs or for parts of them, most of these designers used the jardin dallé (the paved garden) with its evocation of Mediterranean vernacular forms and gridded pavements, for example, Le Corbusier and Forestier in the Villa Church at Ville d'Avray (1927–29; fig. 39).[151] Around 1937, Fletcher Steele and Thomas Church, followed by Eckbo, Kiley, and Rose, and later Lawrence Halprin, began to apply their principles to garden design in the United States. Their plantings, placed among or alongside paved areas, ranged from formal and miniaturized reconstructions of French seventeenth-century parterres to drifts of native grasses and wildflowers with regionalist associations in the manner of Gertrude Jekyll and Burle Marx.[152] In its variations from classicist to regionalist, the paved garden was still a powerful formula in the 1950s.

Rose, who had left Harvard in 1939 but returned in 1941–43 to complete his degree (as Johnson's classmate), published a remarkable project in 1939 (figs. 40, 41) that may directly have inspired Johnson's thinking. It was a highly articulated and successful integration of Miesian and Constructivist compositional principles into the recent traditions of landscape design, including paved and biomorphic forms. Rose described the project as "sculpture in plant materials; not in the ordinary sense of an object to be looked at, but the constructivist type of sculpture which is large enough and perforated to permit circulation."[153] Rose's innovations in spatial and volumetric composition with plant forms in this and other projects, as well as his emphasis on sculpture and on facilitating circulation, formed a significant precedent that Johnson and Fanning could use for the division and interlocking of spaces by groves and small screens of trees in the Museum garden of 1939.[154]

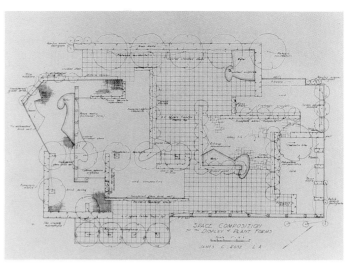

By the time he received the commission for the Museum garden, Johnson commanded a vocabulary of modernist garden design, and he knew where to look for recent developments.[155] Synthesizing an array of techniques, Johnson took the Miesian garden court, he articulated in it the approach of Canneel-Claes to reflecting pools, water jets, pavement, and plantings, as in the latter's country house garden of 1945 (fig. 42), as well as his own understanding of complex architectural modernist garden spaces, inspired by the spatial use of plantings devised by Rose in 1939–40. For certain details, such as the relationship between planted sloping embankments and sets of stairs, he found configurations that ultimately stem from modern German garden design of around 1900 (fig. 43), but that were then taken over by American and French designers, particularly the modernists.

Johnson's built works from 1942 to 1953 had all been houses that involved particular attention to landscape and garden elements. His first project, and his thesis

Left:
40. James C. Rose. "Space Composition for the Display of Plant Forms." Model for a Garden. 1939. Reproduced in *Pencil Points* **(April 1939), p. 226**

Right:
41. James C. Rose. "Space Composition for the Display of Plant Forms." Plan. 1939. Reproduced in *Pencil Points* **(April 1939), p. 227**

42. Jean Canneel-Claes. Garden of a Country House, Haecht, Belgium. 1945

for his architectural degree at Harvard in 1942–43, was his own house at 9 Ash Street in Cambridge, Massachusetts. It was a transformation, more representational in its approach than Mies's, of a basic Miesian courtyard house of the 1930s. Indoor-outdoor connections were emphasized by the simple juxtaposition and separation of house and garden court through a glass wall; the garden pavement with its unaligned slabs, which speak of American regionalist styles and the teachings of Breuer at Harvard, breaks to meet planted ground covers and pre-existing trees on the site. This abutment of pavement and plantings was an approach favored by Canneel-Claes in the 1930s and 1940s, and may have had its origins in the contemporary study of traditional Japanese garden design.[156] The regular slabs, the "pseudo-accidental planting areas" (to quote Johnson again), the limited use and delicate forms of the trees, and the high enclosing walls are already in place here as Johnson's basic design language for a garden. They would all reappear, although more richly orchestrated, in the Museum sculpture garden of 1953.[157]

In each subsequent project leading up to the design of the Museum garden, Johnson put in place the results of a deeper understanding of modern architectural garden forms. Mies's use of gridded terraces, a reflecting pool, and two enclosed courts with trees in his Museum for a Small City project appears reinterpreted at smaller scale in Johnson's garden courts for the Rockefeller Guest House, and the Hodgson and the Davis Houses.[158] These works and the Museum sculpture garden also had in common a subtle interpretation of elements taken from traditional Japanese gardens. Other modernists were doing the same in these years. Such elements were especially pronounced in the model Johnson made in 1950, including the artfully placed boulders, the slab bridges over the pools, and the raised *L*-shaped terrace with its straight drop, from which stairs descended into the garden's sunken court. Traditional Japanese houses are surrounded by verandas or porches that overlook enclosed gardens and pools (fig. 44). The model reveals that Johnson had considered making a composition of big stone boulders the focal point of the sculpture court. Over twenty years later he described this composition of boulders with reference to historical Japanese garden design: "I'd really wanted a single huge boulder, twelve or fourteen feet high, to serve as [an] orientation point amid the greenery. So that you'd know where you were as you revolved about it. . . . Then I tried three boulders, still very Japanese, but that also was too expensive and anyway I didn't like it."[159]

43. Leberecht Migge. Designs for Garden Stairs. ca. 1910–13

44. Kare-sansui Garden of Honpa Hongan-ji, Kyoto.
ca. 1555–1623

The references to Japan that Johnson emphasized in his model reflect the particular interest that the Japanese aesthetic held for modern architects and landscape architects in general, and for Johnson in particular, throughout the 1940s and 1950s.[160] The approach to gardening in Japan and the use of sliding screens, porches, and terraces to connect houses with gardens were particularly meaningful to modernists. Tunnard and Rose, among others, looked to the Japanese use of plantings, stones, and water for inspiration in designing modern gardens.[161]

The Japanese garden was the subject of particular interest at The Museum of Modern Art in the early 1950s. Arthur Drexler, the Museum's curator of architecture, was preparing a major exhibition, *The Architecture of Japan,* which would open in 1955, and the Museum had commissioned a traditional wood-frame Japanese house, to be made in Nagoya, Japan, for reassemblage and exhibition in New York beginning in 1954.[162] The Japanese Exhibition House was erected at full scale in the open space to the east of the garden's central court: it had an *L*-shaped porch overlooking a pool and a garden with large boulders. As a scheme, Johnson's original model for the Museum sculpture garden was not unlike it and was probably inspired by its type.[163]

Mumford rapturously described the Japanese Exhibition House and its garden, designed "to be seen from the porch," as "a fine example of the Japanese faculty for creating a miniature world, almost overpowering in its variety of form"— words that could be applied to Johnson's model for the sculpture garden as well.[164] By eliminating the boulders and the vertical, unbanked edges of the porch in his final design, Johnson abandoned a direct evocation of the Japanese garden for a more allusive one, inscribed mainly in the *L*-shaped terrace and isolated plantings within a level field of stone.

Armed with his professional foundation, Johnson began his career as an architect. He returned to his longstanding interest in Mies, but, significantly, he gave equal weight to many sources, both historical and modern. Louis Martin has noted that Johnson's decision to be simultaneously a continuing disciple of Mies and a student of Gropius (at Harvard) was a "strategic" one, related to his ambition to become a major figure in the new American architecture to come after World War II.[165] Writing of that strategy, Hitchcock noted that, although Johnson's monograph on Mies in 1947 made him "in some sense an official spokesman for Mies," Johnson was catholic in his tastes: "Johnson actually knows and admires the work of the other leaders [Wright and Le Corbusier] as intimately as that of Mies."[166] The Glass House in New Canaan was the first major accomplishment in this synthesis; as Franz Schulze has recently pointed out, Johnson immediately situated his use of a wide range of sources for the House, when he published it himself in September 1950.[167] Johnson's ability to put together this range of eclectic formal choices and to present them in a resolved and compelling design to the American public, in an age of postwar confidence, lies at the heart of his architecture, including the Museum sculpture garden. While Mies's work is timeless and placeless and he resolves his sources into abstract forms, Johnson's conveys a sense of being grounded in a particular time and place, victorious America after World War II. Johnson's close juxtaposition of different borrowings from history, resolved within a modernist shell that was far more representational than the work of Mies, brings a sense of contemporaneity to the project.

Since 1953, the garden itself has remained basically unchanged, although several additions have altered both views of and access to it. In 1962–64, a broad garden terrace, or raised plaza, was built on the empty plot to the east of the sculpture garden (fig. 45).[168] Designed by Johnson, the new terrace, at fourteen feet in height, towered above the earlier grade, which lay below like a broad marble plain. From that plain visitors ascended to the terrace by a multileval transverse stairway. The terrace addition, which increased the area of the original garden by one third, was augmented by a handsome new planting plan for both garden levels, designed by the landscape consultants Zion and Breen.[169]

In 1982–84, the high terrace and staircase were removed, and the sculpture garden of 1953 was surrounded by additional constructions designed by Cesar Pelli and Associates. The clear boundaries once afforded by the garden's enclosing walls were compromised by the construction of a new glass cage containing the escalator—it was now less a sunken garden than a paved courtyard extending north to the wall fronting Fifty-fourth Street and east and west to terraces.[170] The south terrace was enclosed, effectively becoming an extension of the central lobby exhibition space.

The Abby Aldrich Rockefeller Sculpture Garden remains, however, perhaps Johnson's most lasting achievement. The power of Johnson's original design resided in its exquisite proportions and refined materials, its conceptually cohesive formulation, and especially its ambiguous, and hence evocative, character. While his conception was a piazza, he stated that it still would clearly be a garden, with a variety of trees. The design mingled different categories, the typologies and functions of the public urban plaza and those of the private modern garden. It thus maintained a tension between its garden character and its urban character. The latter enabled it to stand out as a strong design in respect to its urban surroundings, while the former provided the public the sense of enclosure and respite offered by the garden of a private home.

45. Philip Johnson. The Abby Aldrich Rockefeller Sculpture Garden, The Museum of Modern Art, New York, with Addition of Roof Terrace and Stairs. Model. 1964

Notes

This article was begun in the fall of 1991, and revised in 1993 and again in 1996. I wish to thank the late John Coolidge (d. 1995), Neil Levine, Peter Nisbet, Laurie Olin, and Peter Reed, Associate Curator in the Department of Architecture and Design at The Museum of Modern Art, for enjoyable conversations with me on the topic. Mr. Reed, in particular, was most generous in sharing several archival documents and making them accessible to me, while we prepared companion articles. I also thank John Dixon Hunt, Philip Johnson, Sarah Ksiazek, Francesco Passanti, Franz Schulze, and Marc Treib for kindly reading an early draft of this essay and making helpful comments—Professors Schulze and Treib, especially, for their meticulous and insightful readings, and Mr. Johnson for so kindly talking with me about his garden designs for the Museum and his interest in landscape architecture. Louis Martin and Laurie Olin graciously shared with me their unpublished papers, of 1986 and 1991, respectively, on the Museum garden by Johnson. My thanks also go to Rona Roob, Chief Archivist of The Museum of Modern Art; to Meisha Hunter and Maura Reilly, research assistants at the Museum, for their extensive help in my archival research; to Alexia Hughes, Department of the Registrar; to Mikki Carpenter and Karin Jansen, Department of Photographic Services; and to Linda Pollak for her collegiality in selecting photographs at the Museum in 1994, as well as for insightful exchanges on the topic.

Throughout these Notes, *MoMA Archives* designates The Museum of Modern Art Archives, New York.

1. For Johnson's sculpture garden of 1953, see John M. Jacobus, Jr., *Philip Johnson* (New York: Braziller, 1962), pp. 27–28; Elizabeth B. Kassler [née Mock], *Modern Gardens and the Landscape,* rev. ed. (New York: The Museum of Modern Art, 1984), pp. 58–59; Kassler, "The Sculpture Garden," *MoMA: A Publication for Members of The Museum of Modern Art,* no. 4 (Summer 1975), Special Issue, pp. 3–4; Sidney Lawrence and George Foy, *Music in Stone: Great Sculpture Gardens of the World* (New York: Scala, 1984), pp. 90–93; Louis Martin, "From the Courthouses to the Garden of the MoMA," unpublished paper, Massachusetts Institute of Technology, Cambridge, Mass., December 1986; Laurie Olin, unpublished paper on The Museum of Modern Art sculpture garden, October 1991; and Franz Schulze, *Philip Johnson: Life and Work* (New York: Alfred A. Knopf, 1994), pp. 207–10. Significant reconstructions of the garden's history are in Kassler's brief but well-documented history, "The Sculpture Garden," and Martin's paper, which focuses on Johnson's architecture and its relation to Mies's work.

2. Public reception of the garden is documented in numerous press clippings in The Museum of Modern Art Archives, Philip C. Johnson Papers, II.15. Contemporary architectural criticism includes: "New Sculpture Garden," *Interiors* III (July 1952), p.

14; "The Museum's Marble Piazze," *Interiors* 112 (June 1953), pp. 98–99; Otis Gage, "Modern Backyard," *Arts Digest* 27 (June 1953), p. 4; "Museum Garden Is an Outdoor Living Room for Sculpture Display," *Architectural Forum* 99 (July 1953), pp. 136–37; Lewis Mumford, "Windows and Gardens," *The New Yorker* 29 (October 2, 1954), pp. 130–31; and Henry-Russell Hitchcock, "Philip Johnson," *Architectural Review* 117 (April 1955), p. 245. Gage's is an interesting, lone dissenting opinion among the general applause.

3. Mumford, "Windows and Gardens," p. 130.

4. Gage, "Modern Backyard," p. 4; "The Museum's Marble Piazze," pp. 136–37.

5. Both Fanning and Johnson had practices in New Canaan, Connecticut. Johnson acknowledged Fanning's role in the design of the Museum garden as follows: "James Fanning, landscape architect, for collaboration in the first designs for The Abby Aldrich Rockefeller Sculpture Garden, The Museum of Modern Art" (Philip Johnson, *Philip Johnson: Architecture 1949–1965,* Introduction by Henry-Russell Hitchcock [New York: Holt, Rinehart, 1966], p. 6). Fanning, while giving a tour of the sculpture garden to an interviewer from *The New Yorker* in the week before the grand opening, remarked, "Philip and I picked out the trees. We did a lot of nursery crawling" (*The New Yorker,* April 25, 1953, p. 25 [clipping]). MoMA Archives: Johnson Papers, II.15.

The name of James Fanning is listed as Gardening Consultant in *House & Garden* in 1970 and 1979, when he contributed short "Gardener's Notes." I thank Virginia P. Purviance for bringing this to my attention.

6. It was only in 1950–51 that sculptures for the Kröller-Müller Museum were acquired with the intention of creating a sculpture park. Construction of that park began in 1954 and was completed only in 1961, long after The Museum of Modern Art had become renowned for its sculpture garden of 1939 and nearly a decade after the opening of The Abby Aldrich Rockefeller Sculpture Garden in 1953. See Mirka Beneš, "Inventing a Modern Sculpture Garden in 1939 at the Museum of Modern Art, New York," *Landscape Journal* 13, no. 1 (February 1994), p. 8. Earlier written proposals had been made in 1918 and 1923 for a sculpture garden at the new Kröller-Müller Museum; these were never built, and no visual documentation of them survives. In 1918 and 1923, first a "Statues and flower garden" and then a "Sculpture Park" were proposed, the latter ultimately realized as a nature reserve for Dutch flora and fauna. Plans in 1938 to extend the sculpture hall into an outdoor sculpture park, begun that year by Henry Van de Velde, were not realized until 1954. On these projects, see *Kröller-Müller: The First Hundred Years,* with essays by R. W. D. Oxenaar et al. (Haarlem, The Netherlands: Enschede, 1989), pp. 19–21, 36, 52–53, 88, 94, 97, 108.

7. Associated Press Newsfeatures, April 29, 1953 (clipping). MoMA Archives: Johnson Papers, II.15.

8. See Beneš, "Inventing a Modern Sculpture Garden in 1939 at the Museum of Modern Art, New

York," pp. 1–20; see especially p. 1 and fn. 2 for modernism as applied to landscape architecture. For an extensive listing of the general literature, see Edward H. Teague, *Sculpture Gardens: A Bibliography of Periodical Literature* (Monticello, Ill.: Vance Bibliographies, 1985). For an interpretative view, see Marc Treib, "Sculpture and Gardens: A Historical Overview," *Design Quarterly* 141 (1988), pp. 44–58.

9. For sculptors' private gardens, see Madison Cox, *Artists' Gardens: From Claude Monet to Jennifer Bartlett* (New York: Harry N. Abrams, 1993). For Milles, see M. P. Verneuil, "Les Jardins de Lidingö," in Verneuil, *Carl Millès: Sculpteur suédois* (Paris and Brussels: Les Editions van Oest, 1929), pp. 93–112; and Treib, "Sculpture and Gardens," p. 54. Millès's approach, described by Verneuil (p. 98), is the same taken earlier by Rodin and Maillol: *"En créant ses jardins, Millès se donnait la possibilité de montrer enfin de la sculpture dans le milieu qui lui est propre; de la mêler à la nature, de l'éclairer au soleil, de la faire participer à un ensemble, à la vie. Architectures, bassins, masses de verdure et d'arbres sont le cadre naturel d'une statue, d'une fontaine, d'un groupe. . . ."* ("In creating his gardens, Millès at last realized the possibility of showing sculpture in the appropriate surroundings; from the variety of nature, of sunlight, he created a unity, like life. Buildings, ponds, masses of greenery and trees become a nature frame for a statue, a fountain, a grouping").

10. See the excellent analysis by Diana Balmori, "Cranbrook: The Invisible Landscape," *Journal of the Society of Architectural Historians* 53, no. 1 (March 1994), pp. 50–51.

11. In these gardens, both classical sculpture and exotic plant species were considered part of the collections; see John Dixon Hunt, "Curiosities to adorn Cabinets and Gardens,'" in Oliver Impey and Arthur MacGregor, eds., *The Origins of Museums: The Cabinet of Curiosities in Sixteenth- and Seventeenth-century Europe* (Oxford: Oxford University Press, 1985), pp. 193–203.

An extensive literature exists on the use of sculpture in gardens. For overviews of the sculpture garden as a type, see H. A. Caparn, "Garden Architecture and Sculpture," *Architecture,* 39 (February 1919), pp. 34–38; Elisabeth B. MacDougall, "Introduction," in *Music in Stone,* pp. 8–19; and Treib, "Sculpture and Gardens," pp. 44–58. The narrative and political functions that sculpture had in Ancien Régime gardens and parks became pedagogical ones as well in the new public parks of the nineteenth century. Perhaps the first well-known public garden for sculptural display was that designed for the Musée d'Antiquités et Monuments Français, begun by Alexandre Lenoir in 1791–96 in the former convent of the Petits Augustins in Paris; a painting of this garden, by Hubert Robert, is reproduced in Jean de Cayeux, *Hubert Robert et les Jardins* (Paris: Hersher, 1987), p. 126.

12. See Rona Roob, "1936: The Museum Selects an Architect: Excerpts from the Barr Papers of The Museum of Modern Art," *Archives of American Art Journal* 23, no. 1 (1983), pp. 22–30; and Dominic Ric-

ciotti, "The 1939 Building of the Museum of Modern Art: The Goodwin–Stone Collaboration," *The American Art Journal* 17 (Summer 1985), pp. 50–76.

13. Ricciotti, "The 1939 Building," p. 63; and fig. 14, p. 64. "In one [scheme a] . . . narrow court at the rear of the main block is the first suggestion of what would later become the Sculpture Garden" (p. 63). The drawing is in pencil on tracing paper.

14. See Ricciotti, p. 66 and fig. 19, for a project dated August 5, 1936, in which there is a "prominent, walled garden. Running along 53rd Street, the garden would have terminated at the proposed Rockefeller Center extension, thereby bringing its openness into the confines of the Museum—an intelligent, highly urbanistic means of joining the two projects. That Stone may be credited with this design is supported by his related efforts contemporary with it. In early 1936 he planned his first enclosed garden, of which he later became so fond, for the winter home of Mr. and Mrs. Henry Luce outside Charleston, South Carolina. (Such gardens were traditional there and in many parts of the South, where Stone was born)." For the Luce garden, Ricciotti refers to Edward Durell Stone, *The Evolution of an Architect* (New York: Horizon Press, 1962), pp. 48–53.

15. *New York Herald Tribune,* June 18, 1937 (clipping); a photograph of the model is reproduced. MoMA Archives: A. Conger Goodyear Papers, V.39.

16. In 1926–28, Mrs. Rockefeller had asked Beatrix Farrand to design the main garden in the woods near the family home at Seal Harbor, Maine, and she worked on the garden herself until her death in 1948. Her original intention had been to have a sculpture garden for her collection of Chinese and Korean statues. See Patrick Chassé, *The Abby Aldrich Rockefeller Garden: A Visitor's Guide* (copyright David and Peggy Rockefeller, 1990).

17. The lists of sculptures are from Alfred H. Barr, Jr., *Painting and Sculpture in The Museum of Modern Art, 1929–1967* (New York: The Museum of Modern Art, 1977), pp. 626–27.

18. All quotations this paragraph, Minutes of the Temporary Garden Committee Meeting, December 3, 1938. MoMA Archives: Committee Minutes, Box 1. There was also a discussion of models of the proposed sculpture garden, with a note to obtain estimates on the relative costs of the two models exhibited, but no visual records of the models are attached.

19. Joseph Hudnut, *Modern Sculpture* (New York: W. W. Norton, 1929), pp. 3, 10, 41. The book was based on a series of lectures given by Hudnut at the New York Public Library in the winter of 1929. Hudnut was a professor of architecture at Columbia University beginning in 1926, and dean of the School of Architecture from 1933 to 1935; from 1935 to 1953, he was dean of the Graduate School of Design at Harvard University.

20. Ibid., pp. 38, 44, 60–61.

21. Hudnut was asked ca. May 1, 1938, "either to be chairman of the jury or to help prepare the competition program." He responded on May 9 that he was "'greatly interested in the project.'" Travis C. McDonald, Jr. "Smithsonian Institution: Competi-

tion for a Gallery of Art, January 1939–June 1939," p. 182; for the competition, see pp. 177–95.

22. *A National Competition to Select an Architect for the Proposed Smithsonian Gallery of Art, Washington, D.C.* (Washington, D.C.: Smithsonian Institution, 1939), p. 16.

23. Hudnut is cited in *Modernism in America, 1937–1941, A Catalog and Exhibition of Four Architectural Competitions: Wheaton College, Goucher College, College of William and Mary, Smithsonian Institution*, ed. James D. Kornwolf (Williamsburg, Va.: Joseph and Margaret Muscarelle Museum of Art, 1985), p. 194, where the entries are discussed extensively. Newly discovered drawings by the finalists in the Smithsonian competition were published by Mina Marefat in "When Modern Was a Cause: The 1939 Smithsonian Art Gallery Competition," *Competitions* I (Fall 1991), pp. 36–49, where the sculpture gardens can be seen in the plans submitted by Goodwin (p. 44) and Stone (p. 49).

24. Notes of the Informal Meeting of the Garden Committee, January 1, 1939. MoMA Archives: Committee Minutes, Box 1.

25. Ibid. The Committee also urged using the plot to set up the Jacobs house by Frank Lloyd Wright during the 1939 World's Fair in New York, charging admission to cover the cost of the house and possibly costs of the garden later on.

26. The first donation of land, by Mr. Rockefeller in 1937, was 75 feet wide (along the rear of the new building) and 100 feet deep, up to West Fifty-fourth Street; the new donation, in May 1939, of 400 feet by the same depth of 100 feet, provided an oblong site transversal to the new building. Johnson's sculpture garden would later be placed in the center of this site. See Beneš, "Inventing a Modern Sculpture Garden."

27. Letter, Barr to Callery, January 27, 1939. Exhibition #85, *Art in Our Time*, Department of the Registrar, The Museum of Modern Art, New York.

28. Cable, Barr to Callery, February 28, 1939.

29. See Paul J. Sachs, "The Museum of Modern Art, New York," typescript, ca. 1936. Fine Arts Library, Harvard University, Cambridge, Massachusetts.

30. Kassler, in writing "if any public or semipublic garden had been designed for the enjoyment of modern sculpture, they [Barr and McAndrew] had not heard of it, and they knew little or nothing about the handful of modern gardens of any kind that then existed" ("Sculpture Garden," p. 1), makes an overstatement about the two curators' lack of knowledge of modern garden design. They were aware of Roberto Burle Marx's work.

31. See also the unidentified clipping, dated December 25, 1938, in MoMA Archives: Goodyear Papers, V.39: "The rear plot . . . will be made into a garden spot for walks and exhibition of sculptures. It will be walled in and will only have a gate for egress for emergencies."

32. For the sculpture garden of 1939, see Alice Morgan Carson, "A Garden Gallery of the Museum of Modern Art," *Bulletin of The Garden Club of America,* Series 7, No. 4 (July 1939), pp. 72–75 (plan,

pp. 74–75); and Robert A.M. Stern et al., *New York 1930: Architecture and Urbanism Between the Two World Wars* (New York: Rizzoli, 1987), 142–43.

33. After the visit to Aalto in Finland in 1937, Church's wife, Betsy, became Aalto's commercial representative in San Francisco; Church, meanwhile, adopted Aalto's free-form wood walls in stone garden walls and curvilinear ground plans in work from 1939 on; see David C. Streatfield, "Thomas Church and the California Garden, 1929–1950," in *Festschrift: A Collection of Essays on Architectural History* (Salem, Ore., 1978), pp. 70–71. My thanks to Marc Treib for indicating that Church was Aalto's representative.

McAndrew was particularly involved with Aalto's work at the time, as he had just organized an exhibition of the architect's work at The Museum of Modern Art (*Alvar Aalto: Architecture and Furniture*, Exh. #75, March 15–April 18, 1938).

34. See, for example, Leberecht Migge, *Gartenkultur des XX. Jahrhunderts* (Jena, 1913).

35. Such connoisseurs or professionals, if they had not been to the actual sites, could have seen a répertoire of modern works in design journals and in books, for example, André Lurçat, *Terrasses et Jardins* (Paris: C. Moreau, 1931), which featured works by French designers but also by Mies; and Christopher Tunnard, *Gardens in the Modern Landscape* (1938), 2nd rev. ed. (London: The Architectural Press, 1948).

36. An architect who specialized in museum design and who contacted the Museum in 1939 to "study the gallery divisions," was Clarence S. Stein; see A. Conger Goodyear, *The Museum of Modern Art: The First Ten Years* (New York: The Museum of Modern Art, 1943), p. 128. Stein advocated the use of outdoor garden courtyards in "The Art Museum of Tomorrow," *Architectural Record* 67 (January 1930), pp. 5–12. He illustrated garden courts (p. 6) and wished "to give all visitors to the museum an opportunity from time to time to glimpse gardens and outdoor vistas. Nothing causes so-called museum fatigue so much as miles of rooms filled with inanimate objects and allowing no sight of living nature" (p. 5). Further, the interior exhibitions and the gardens should be in the same style: "These gardens not only complete the background for the works of the same period and place, but at the same time give that pleasant relaxation which a visitor to a museum so much needs" (p. 7).

37. In the late 1920s and throughout the 1930s, both Mies and Le Corbusier incorporated individual sculptures in the design of their houses and villas. See, for example, the latter's Villa De Mandrot, where two modern sculptures, one by Lipchitz, were sited outdoors on elevated pedestals; in *Le Corbusier and Pierre Jeanneret: Oeuvre Complète 1929–34*, vol. 2, (Zurich: Editions d'Architecture, 1967), pp. 58–62. See also Paul Nelson, *La Maison suspendue* (Paris: Editions Albert Morancér, 1939). Nelson's house was published in the Museum exhibition catalogue *Art in Our Time*, p. 291; repr., p. 306.

38. Mies's designs for both house interiors and exhibitions in the 1920s and 1930s incorporated sculptures, floor-to-ceiling curtains, and expensive

materials such as marble as room dividers; the Tugendhat House is a good example. Mies may have been inspired by contemporary German innovations in exhibition technique as well. As pointed out by the late John Coolidge, Professor Emeritus, Department of Fine Arts, Harvard University, and former director of the Fogg Art Museum, The Museum of Modern Art lacked the money in its first decades to take the Miesian model *ad litteram,* and instead made do with less costly materials (interview with the author, July 5, 1994).

39. Helen Appleton Read, "'Art in Our Time,'" *Magazine of Art* 19 (June 1939), pp. 339–41; quotation, p. 339. The innovations in exhibition technique at the Museum in 1939 are discussed in Ricciotti, "The 1939 Building," pp. 55–58.

40. On the new exhibition techniques, see Monika Flacke-Knoch, *Museums-Konzeptionen in der Weimarer Republik: Die Tätigkeit Alexander Dorners im Provinzialmuseum Hannover* (Marburg: Jonas, 1985). I owe this reference to Peter Nisbet, Curator of the Busch-Reisinger Museum, Harvard University.

41. Alexander Dorner, *The Way Beyond "Art": The Work of Herbert Bayer* (New York: Wittenborn, Schultz, 1947), p. 205. For Bayer's exhibition designs at The Museum of Modern Art (in 1938, 1942, and 1943) and elsewhere in America in the 1940s, see pp. 197–216.

42. From Herbert Bayer, "Fundamentals of Exhibition Design," *P.M. Magazine* 14 (1939), pp. 17–24; cited in Dorner, *The Way Beyond "Art,"* p. 201.

43. Dorner, *The Way Beyond "Art,"* p. 201.

44. Hudnut, *Modern Sculpture,* p. 29 (chapter 3, "France, Since Rodin: Bernard, Hernandez, Maillol, Despiau, Bourdelle") and p. 89 (conclusion in chapter 4, "America").

45. Letter, Barr to Goodwin, March 1942. Department of Painting and Sculpture, The Museum of Modern Art, New York: Museum Collections/Sculpture Garden, folder 1 (1942–85).

46. "The Museum of Modern Art: Advisory Committee Report on Museum Collections" (April 1941), p. 31. MoMA Archives: Committee Minutes, Box 1.

47. "With nine works each by Despiau and Maillol, five by Lehmbruck, ten by Lachaise, five by Kolbe as well as examples of the work of Zorach, Sintenis, Ben-Shmuel, Epstein, Henry Moore, Brancusi, Lipchitz, Haller, Duchamp-Villon and others in various sculptured media . . . the Museum's sculpture [collection] is without doubt the most important collection of modern work in the world" (Goodyear, *The Museum of Modern Art,* p. 88).

48. Ibid., p. 130.

49. Letter, Barr to Goodwin, March 1942. Department of Painting and Sculpture, The Museum of Modern Art, New York: Museum Collections/Sculpture Garden, folder 1 (1942–85). Barr suggested that the Museum also consider plans by Alice Carson, a graduate of the Cambridge School of Landscape Architecture, adjacent to Harvard, and Edward Durell Stone, but neither appears to have been approached for plans.

50. "The sculptor and the painter once participated in gardens; nowadays they are thus outside, in spite of the fact that the best of modern sculptors are designing for open spaces . . . Sculpture, which relies for its appeal on intricacy and subtlety of detail, is best placed in relation to plain undecorated surfaces such as walls, level lawns or water" (Tunnard, *Gardens in the Modern Landscape* [1938], p. 74).

51. Christopher Tunnard, "Modern Gardens for Modern Houses: Reflections on Current Trends in Landscape Design," *Landscape Architecture* 6 (January 1942), pp. 57–64.

52. The restaurant garden is illustrated in Kassler, "Sculpture Garden," p. 2; and in newspaper clippings in MoMA Archives: Goodyear Papers, V.39.

53. Letter, Barr to Goodwin, March 1948. Department of Painting and Sculpture, The Museum of Modern Art, New York: Museum Collections/Sculpture Garden, folder 1 (1942–1985).

54. Alicia Legg Oral History (1991), p. 65. MoMA Archives: The Museum of Modern Art Oral History Project.

55. *The Museum of Modern Art Bulletin* 13, no. 17 (February 1946). "The proposed addition [by Goodwin] . . . will be three stories in height, and in the same architectural style as the existing building" ("New Museum Wing," *Architectural Record* 101, no. 4 [April 1947], p. 10). For the dates and design of the new wing and the Rockefeller donation of the site, then valued at one million dollars, see Stern et al., *New York 1960,* pp. 473 (repr.) and 475.

56. For the proposed garden, see Tunnard, *Gardens in the Modern Landscape* (1938), p. 174; and Tunnard, "Art and Landscape Design," *Landscape Architecture* 39, no. 3 (April 1949), p. 104. On Tunnard's career, particularly in planning, see Lance M. Neckar, "Strident Modernism/Ambivalent Reconsiderations: Christopher Tunnard's Gardens in the Modern Landscape," *Journal of Garden History* 10, no. 4 (October–December 1990), pp. 237–46.

57. The forms recall both Tunnard's own private garden designs since the 1930s, illustrated in his book, and those of James Rose since 1939.

58. Like many of his private garden designs of the late 1930s and the 1940s, Tunnard's proposal was influenced by the work of modern French garden designers of the 1920s but manifested also a regionalist strain. In fact, it was the perfect complement to the full-scale house with "cypress tongue-and-groove vertical boarding" that Breuer designed for the site of the sculpture garden in spring of 1949 (illustrated in *Arts + Architecture* 66 [May 1949], pp. 33–35).

59. Lehmbruck's *Standing Youth,* an imposing figure in cast stone almost eight feet high, had been exhibited in the Museum's third-floor gallery since 1939; Lachaise's *Floating Figure,* over four feet high on its pedestal, had been installed in the garden against a bare brick wall around 1944–46. Information about their locations comes from published photographs of the Museum collection. See, for example, *Painting and Sculpture in The Museum of Modern Art,* ed. Alfred H. Barr, Jr. (New York: The Museum of Modern Art, 1942), and subseqent catalogues edited by Barr, such as *Supplementary List* (1945), *Painting and Sculpture in The Museum of Modern Art* (1948), and *Masters of Modern Art* (1954).

60. Tunnard, *Gardens in the Modern Landscape* (1938), p. 174. One year before Tunnard's publication of his proposed sculpture garden, Johnson had illustrated several of Mies's projects that used photomontage images of sculptures in the exhibition catalogue *Mies van der Rohe* (New York: The Museum of Modern Art, 1947), pp. 176–77, 180. As seen below, Johnson himself would be inspired by one of these projects.

61. The photographs, accompanied by a two-page text on the project, are housed in the Department of Architecture and Design, The Museum of Modern Art, New York. The caption on the verso of the view reads: "JOHNSON, Philip. Project—The Glass House, Museum of Modern Art Garden, 1948. MMA 12677;" and, on the verso of the plan, "JOHNSON, Philip. Project for Museum of Modern Art garden. The Glass House. 1948." I thank Peter Reed for generously bringing these documents to my attention.

62. On the House of Glass, see, most recently, the synthetic chapter in Schulze, *Philip Johnson,* pp. 188–98, and notes.

63. Johnson, "Project for Museum of Modern Art Garden" (1948), p. 1.

64. The House of Glass project of 1948 was directly inspired by an important project by Mies, Museum for a Small City (1942), intended for a hypothetical site. It fuses to that project many ideas that had occupied Johnson in commissions for houses, both brick and glass containers, since 1942, when he built the Ash Street house in Cambridge. Its gridded paved courts, with a minimum of figurative statues; the use of sculptures reclining and standing, seen especially in profile; and high brick walls with cascading greenery can be seen in Mies's 1934 design for his own house in the Tyrol as well as Johnson's Glass House in New Canaan. In Johnson's proposed House of Glass for the Museum garden, the plantings were kept to a minimum: There is no pool or groves of trees, which Mies had poetically arranged in the Museum for a Small City and which Johnson would use equally poetically in the sculpture garden of 1953. However, Mies's transposition of gridded pavements, sculptures, and glass cages from his courtyard houses into an urban museum project was a fundamental programmatic precedent, which Johnson later adopted for both his garden projects at the Museum, in 1948 and in 1953.

Numerous unpublished schemes for houses in the 1940s and early 1950s were shown by David Mohney and Stover Jenkins, who are preparing a book on Johnson's house designs, in a seminar on Johnson given by Professor Neil Levine at Harvard in the fall of 1993. Among the published work, see also Johnson's 1951 House Project for Kootz Gallery Exhibit (model, fig. 17 in Jacobus, *Philip Johnson*); and the Wiley House of 1953.

65. John McAndrew, *Guide to Modern Architecture: Northeast States* (New York: The Museum of Modern Art, 1940), p. 77. In a letter to the author of August 5, 1994, John Coolidge noted of McAndrew, with

whom he shared an office at Vassar College in 1937–38: "John was trained as an architect and would have practiced professionally had he not graduated in the depths of the depression…I believe that he was responsible for all the architectural features in the garden [of 1939]."

66. In the Museum Archives, the three drawings are filed in a large, white envelope mislabeled in pencil "John McAndrew. Blue prints for the first [sic] Museum garden. Received from Marga [Margaret Scolari] Barr, June 21, 1979." The blueprint drawings, with garden elements and the decorative surfaces of the buildings highlighted in colored chalk, include a plan, two sections, the east elevation, and the north elevation of the proposed West Wing. The style of the building and garden elements suggests that the drawings belong to 1946–48.

67. For the Ministry in Rio de Janeiro, see *Le Corbusier: Oeuvre complète,* vol. 4: 1938–1946, ed. W. Boesiger (Zürich: Erlenbach, [1947]; 6th ed., 1971), pp. 80–89. Other details of McAndrew's proposals show that he also remained interested in Aalto's architecture.

68. Images of these columns can be found in Sima Eliovson, *The Gardens of Roberto Burle Marx* (New York: Harry N. Abrams/Sugapress, 1991). I thank Anita Berrizbeitia for pointing out the connection to Burle Marx's floral columns. Marc Treib believes these columns appeared only later in Burle Marx's work (personal communication with the author); as the chronology of Burle Marx's work becomes more clearly established, the dates of these floral columns should become documented. McAndrew may also have been inspired by the 1943 Museum exhibition *Brazil Builds. Architecture New and Old 1652–1942;* Goodwin wrote the exhibition catalogue, in which Burle Marx's current work was discussed. One should keep in mind, as well, the connection of the Rockefellers to Venezuela and Brazil at that time. In 1940, Nelson A. Rockefeller was appointed Coordinator of Inter-American Affairs by President Franklin Delano Roosevelt. The work on the Brazilian exhibition of 1943 was guided by two associates of the Museum, Wallace K. Harrison and René d'Harnoncourt, who were then attched to the Coordinator's office. A trustee of the Museum in 1939–40, Harrison would be re-elected to the board in 1945, serving until his death in 1981. D'Harnoncourt would join the Museum staff as Director of Manual Industries and Vice-President in Charge of Foreign Activities in 1944, and would succeed Barr as Director in 1949, holding this position until his retirement in 1968. For a concise history of their early association with both the CIAA and the Museum, see Helen M. Franc, "The Early Years of the International Program and Council, in *Studies in Modern Art 4. The Museum of Modern Art at Mid-century: At Home and Abroad* (1994), pp. 109–12.

69. Unidentified newspaper clipping of April 1953. MoMA Archives: Johnson Papers, II.15. With additional study, one may be able to investigate whether a "Rockefeller" building style was developed, with the opening of Rockefeller Center in the mid-1930s, and

applied thereafter to building projects supported by the Rockefeller family in mid-Manhattan, including The Museum of Modern Art and its sculpture garden of 1953.

70. The project consists of a portfolio containing three perspective views (View North, View East, and View East, which is really northeast) and three plans (Old Garden Plan, New Garden Design, Planting Plan), signed "Christopher Tunnard Landscape Architect." The verso of the View East (northeast to Fifty-fourth Street) is dated September 19, 1949. The portfolio is labeled "New Garden Design. For The Museum of Modern Art. Christopher Tunnard Landscape Architect," and housed in the Architecture and Design Study Collection, The Museum of Modern Art, New York. Many thanks to Marc Treib, who, assisted by Peter Reed in the Department of Architecture and Design, located Tunnard's project drawings.

71. In 1947–48, Kiley's scheme in the winning design for the Gateway Arch in St. Louis, with Eero Saarinen as architect, was anchored around a grid of magnificent trees planted beneath the arch, all strictly ordered and crossed by regular allées.

72. Schulze, *Philip Johnson,* p. 182. See Alfred H. Barr, Jr. "Opening Remarks," *The Museum of Modern Art Bulletin* 16 (Spring 1948), pp. 6–7, 14; cited in Marc Treib, ed., *An Everyday Modernism: The Houses of William Wurster* (San Francisco: San Francisco Museum of Modern Art, 1995), pp. 58, 60, 75, 166. Later that year, Johnson and Blake collaborated on the article "Architectural Freedom and Order," *Magazine of Art* 41 (October 1948), pp. 228–31.

73. Cited in Treib, *An Everyday Modernism,* pp. 58, 60.

74. Letter, Eckbo to Wheeler, June 24, 1946. MoMA Archives: René d'Harnoncourt Papers, file 704.

75. Letter, Wheeler to Eckbo, July 11, 1946. MoMA Archives: d'Harnoncourt Papers, file 704.

76. Letter, Eckbo to Wheeler, September 3, 1946. Ibid.

77. The seminal contributions of Eckbo's *Landscape for Living,* ultimately published by the Architectural Record with Duell, Sloan, and Pearce, New York, in 1950, are examined in Reuben M. Rainey, "'Organic Form in the Humanized Landscape': Garrett Eckbo's Landscape for Living," in *Modern Landscape Architecture: A Critical Review,* ed. Marc Treib (Cambridge, Mass.: MIT Press, 1993), pp. 180–205.

78. Johnson would remain at the Museum as head of the department until 1954. Elizabeth Bauer Mock (later Kassler) succeeded McAndrew, serving as acting director of the Department of Architecture and Design from 1943 to 1946. As Elizabeth Kassler, she would publish *Modern Gardens and the Landscape* (New York: The Museum of Modern Art, 1964; 2nd ed., 1984). For further information on Johnson's earlier career at the Museum, see "The International Style at Fifty" (Special Section), *Progressive Architecture,* 63 (February 1982), pp. 87–109, in particular Helen Searing, "International Style: The Crimson Connection," pp. 88–91; and Terence Riley, "Portrait of the Curator as a Young Man," pp. 34–69 of the present volume.

79. Franz Schulze has recorded that Landis Gore, in his memoirs, spoke of a plan for the new annex in 1949; see Schulze, *Philip Johnson,* pp. 205–06.

80. *The New Yorker,* April 25, 1953, op. cit.

81. "Up-to-date Annex for Modern Museum," *Interiors* (August 1950), p. 10; and Hitchcock, "Philip Johnson," p. 245.

82. The model was published in "New Sculpture Garden," *Interiors* 3 (July 1952), p. 14; a few little models of sculptures are visible in the photograph. Museum curator Alicia Legg later recalled that, for the extension in 1962–64, Johnson "had a big plan of the new garden, as it was to be; it was a scale model and his office had made little sculptures of some of the existing things. . . . I made little models of all the stuff" (Alicia Legg Oral History [1991], p. 65). MoMA Archives: The Museum of Modern Art Oral History Project.

83. "Up-to-date Annex for Modern Museum," p. 10.

84. For example, in an angry memorandum to Barr of March 10, 1952, Dorothy C. Miller, who had been Curator of Museum Collections since 1947, denounced the "Plans for Reconstructing [the] Garden." She began by saying: "I can't tell you how unhappy I am about this [new garden] plan." Her displeasure centered on the reduction of space and especially the plan to pave the garden area, which she feared would be excessively costly, difficult to maintain, psychologically wearing, and very hot in the summer. She wanted to preserve "the original garden in 1939 [which had] had certain uniquely valuable aspects which I think we would be foolish indeed to throw away." For Miller, these were spaciousness, privacy, informality, variety and surprise, an open-work fence on Fifty-fourth Street, a first-rate sculpture exhibition, and flexibility. Department of Painting and Sculpture, The Museum of Modern Art, New York: Museum Collections/Sculpture Garden, Folder 1 (1942–1985). Miller, who joined the Museum's curatorial staff in 1932, was Assistant Curator of Painting and Sculpture from 1935 to 1941, Associate Curator in 1942, and Curator from 1943 to 1947. From 1947 until her retirement in 1967, she served as Curator of Museum Collections.

85. In June 1952, the Museum's plans to publicize its new garden included: "July 3: News paper story . . . with pictures of new model . . . to go on view in Museum. City desks and real estate editors. Model on TV"; "Oct: Model on TV with Ritchie, perhaps, or D'H[arnoncourt], stressing advantages for sculpture exhibitions"; "March [1953]: Stories in Times and Tribune Special Garden Section. Feature story"; "May: Garden Club Tours—be a garden to visit"; "Summer: Fashion photo. See if *Vogue* would shoot an entire issue or a section of an issue in the garden." MoMA Archives: d'Harnoncourt Papers, file 924.

86. *The New Yorker,* April 25, 1953, op. cit.

87. Johnson in an interview with the author, June 6, 1994. In listing the seven key aspects of his design in 1955, Johnson also noted: "5. Chinese idea of sunken area to increase size of court" (Hitchcock, "Philip Johnson," p. 245).

88. Henry McBride, in an unidentified clipping

(presumably *Garden News*), ca. April 25–29, 1953. MoMA Archives: Johnson Papers, II.15.

89. "With plane trees nearby, it will be as continental as a boulevard restaurant in Paris" (unidentified newspaper clipping, Associated Press Newsfeatures, ca. April 29, 1953). MoMA Archives: Johnson Papers, II.15.

90. *The New Yorker*, April 25, 1953, op. cit., p. 25.

91. Ibid. In 1964, the cryptomerias were replaced by European weeping beeches; see the planting plan of 1964 by Zion and Breen in Kassler, "Sculpture Garden," p. 8. Johnson listed this grove as the sixth of the seven key design features cited above: "'Anchor' accent of asymmetrically placed clump of Japanese cedars around which every other feature 'revolves'" (Hitchcock, "Philip Johnson," p. 245).

92. "Our biggest problem wasn't planting; it was unplanting—cleaning out the plane trees and lindens in the old garden. Twenty-three of them were sent to Fort Jay" (Fanning, quoted in *The New Yorker*, April 25, 1953, op. cit., pp. 24–25).

93. Cited in Hitchcock, "Philip Johnson," p. 245.

94. Of the open grille Johnson said: "This gives emotional release from the inside, and keeps street passersby from feeling excluded" (Hitchcock, "Philip Johnson," p. 25).

95. Clay Lancaster, *The Japanese Influence in America* (New York: W. H. Rawls, 1965), pp. 165–66.

96. John Coolidge, *Patrons and Architects: Designing Art Museums in the Twentieth Century* (Fort Worth, Texas: Amon Carter Museum, 1989), pp. 80–81.

97. *The New Yorker*, April 25, 1953, op. cit., p. 25.

98. Ricciotti, "The 1939 Building," pp. 58–59.

99. See, for example, "Museum Garden Is an Outdoor Living Room for Sculpture Display," *Architectural Forum* 99 (July 1953), pp. 136–37. The modern conception of the garden as an outdoor room had been embraced by Johnson since 1932 (for which, see below).

100. *The New Yorker*, April 25, 1953, op. cit., p. 25; and *Interiors*, July 1952, p. 14.

101. By the winter of 1953, as photographs show, the pieces were already moved about, emphasizing the nature of the sculpture garden as an outdoor gallery for temporary exhibitions. Jacques Lipchitz's bronze *Mother and Child II* (1941–45) was at first placed in the southeastern corner of the garden, in a fairly hidden spot; it then was moved to a prominent place outside the main door from the museum to the garden. A 1962 drawing of the proposed new extension of the garden, by Helmut Jacoby, shows four or five of the original set pieces, but moved to different locations: Lachaise's *Floating Figure* now stood below the new grand staircase on the east; Aristide Maillol's *The River* had returned to the head of the longer canal; Renoir's *Washerwoman* faced that canal, but now on its northwestern bank, as opposed to the southeastern or northeastern one; Lipchitz's *Figure* guarded the rear doors leading from the Museum to the garden terrace. See *The Museum of Modern Art: Annual Report 1962–1963*, p. 14 (repr.).

102. Letter, Ritchie to Monroe Wheeler, September 26, 1951. Department of the Registrar, The Museum of Modern Art, New York: Exh. #526, Sculpture of the Twentieth Century.

103. The few pieces that could be called abstract were Max Bill's *Tripartite Unity* (1947–48) of chrome-nickel steel, lent by the Museu de Arte Moderna, São Paulo; Raymond Duchamp-Villon's *Horse* (1914; cast 1930–31); and Lipchitz's *Mother and Child II* (1941–45).

104. Nevertheless, there were complaints. One critic felt that there was not enough room to look at the sculptures, and, stepping back to get a better view of the *Maja* by Gerhardt Marcks, which is seven feet tall, he nearly fell into a pool. Wrote Otis Gage: "In spite of all the apparent space, there seems to be no proper place for the sculpture. Three reliefs in bronze by Matisse fit well against the brick wall, but the sculptures in the round stand about uncomfortably like people in a large room looking for chairs to sit down on. Cool, chic, Italianate, the garden seems very distant from most of the sculpture, welcoming only the stylized horse of Marini and the stylish abstraction of Max Bill" (Gage, "The Reflective Eye," *Arts Digest* 27 [June 1953], p. 4).

105. For the sculptures shown in 1953, see the catalogue of the exhibition by Andrew Carnduff Ritchie *Sculpture of the Twentieth Century* (New York: The Museum of Modern Art, [1952]).

106. Johnson, *Mies van der Rohe*, p. 30.

107. The isolation of the Picasso figure and of others in the sculpture garden probably led Gage to make the further remark that works of sculpture, "like people, need a certain amount of privacy, a neighboring wall or screen to retain the view. Most free-standing sculpture is not nearly as free-standing as it is thought to be" (Gage, "The Reflective Eye," p. 4).

108. For example, Elie Nadelman's bronze *Man in the Open Air* (ca. 1915), acquired in 1948, was exhibited in the garden in 1967.

109. Hitchcock, "Philip Johnson," p. 245.

110. I thank John Dixon Hunt and Marc Treib, reviewers of an early draft of this text, for raising questions such as these.

111. Coolidge in an interview with the author, July 5, 1994. Coolidge was referring here to the gallery on the property of Johnson's Glass House, which the architect built in 1970 for his own sculpture collection; see Coolidge, *Patrons and Architects*, pp. 14–17.

112. Describing the reactions to Johnson's installation of the exhibition *Machine Art* at the Museum in 1934, A. Conger Goodyear wrote: "All of the commentators were enthusiastic over the installation. . . . Philip Johnson was 'our best showman and possibly the world's best. . . . He has such a genius for grouping things together and finding just the right background and the right light'" (Goodyear, *The Museum of Modern Art*, p. 48).

113. Hitchcock, "Philip Johnson," p. 244.

115. In 1932, as a curator at the Museum and as a coauthor, with Hitchcock, of *The International Style*, Johnson had already taken a position on the relationship of modern sculpture to its architectural settings: "It should retain its own character quite separate from that of its background. . . . It is particularly important today that sculpture should be isolated" (Henry-Russell Hitchcock and Philip Johnson, *The International Style: Architecture Since 1922* [New York: W. W. Norton, 1932], pp. 73–74).

115. Ibid.

116. *The New Yorker*, April 25, 1953, op. cit., p. 25.

117. "[7.] General idea same as furnishing a room such as my own glass house: creating barriers high or low, wide or thin, within a rigid, undecorated rectangle" (cited in Hitchcock, "Philip Johnson," p. 245).

118. The architects of the new Museum, Goodwin and Stone, had chosen a long rectangle for that sculpture gallery and not a round or square room, thereby evoking the narrow width of the classical sculpture gallery, as in the Vatican museums, where statues are lined up enfilade. This long gallery (and the ones nearby, used for temporary installations of sculpture) were described in 1939 as follows: "Sculpture galleries are top-lighted, with illumination varied by the use of cement asbestos sheets. Flexibility of background treatment is obtained with curtains of different colors" (caption to photographs of the third-floor gallery by Robert Damora, reproduced in *The Architectural Forum*, 71 [August 1939], p. 122).

119. Epstein's *Madonna* is a curious piece for the garden, since it clearly was created for the interior of a chapel. But it was probably chosen in 1953 because its large size made it suitable for an outdoor setting. As Barr wrote in his annual report in 1941, "we have an outdoor garden which is in almost continuous need of more good large pieces" ("The Museum of Modern Art: Advisory Committee Report on Museum Collections," typescript, April 1941), p. 31. Fine Arts Library, Harvard University.

120. Coolidge in an interview with the author, July 5, 1994. Helen Appleton Read described the main entrance to the sculpture gallery in 1939: "The visitor enters through a narrow door directly in front of which Lehmbruck's celebrated *Kneeling Woman* is shown against a grey blue curtain" ("Art in Our Time," op. cit., p. 339).

121. Just as with the sculptures installed indoors at the Modern and at other museums of modern art, all of the works in the sculpture garden were placed on pedestals, which gave them a fixed character (although they would be moved about). Yet the disparate heights of the pedestals, which ranged from five inches to four feet, denied potential associations with traditional garden sculptures, say, those at the Villa d'Este at Tivoli or at Versailles, where the pedestals and sculptures were of uniform heights and serially arranged. Both indoors and out at the Modern, many of the pedestals were low enough (as with Marini's *Horse* and the statues by Despiau, Maillol, Renoir, and Moore in the garden) that visitors could see the sculptures up close and get a direct sense of their dimensions and materials.

123. When he went to study architecture at Harvard and Mies was working in Chicago, Johnson kept in touch with him; see Martin, "From the Courthouses," p. 6. Later, Johnson became Mies's collaborator, and he and those who wrote about him clearly

acknowledged his indebtedness to Mies. See Vincent J. Scully, "Archetype and Order in Recent American Architecture," *Art in America* 22 (December 1954), pp. 254–55, especially p. 254; Hitchcock, "Philip Johnson," p. 238; and William Jordy, "The Mies-less Johnson," *Architectural Forum* 111, no. 3 (September 1959), p. 115. Hitchcock also noted that Johnson's important 1947 exhibition and monograph on Mies at the Museum "made Johnson in some sense an official spokesman for Mies."

123. Martin, "From the Courthouses," pp. 14–15; and Olin, unpublished paper (1991), *passim.*

124. The drawing for the Wolf House is reproduced in *The Mies van der Rohe Archive* (New York: Garland Publishers, 1987), p. 20.

125. My thanks to Franz Schulze for pointing out the *Rosengarten* in the Werder drawing and, above all, for a stimulating conversation about Mies and garden design, which Professor Schulze also believes was not a major focus of study for Mies. For the two versions of the Werder project, see Philip C. Johnson, *Mies van der Rohe* (New York: The Museum of Modern Art, 1947), pp. 18 (repr.) and 20; and the discussion in Schulze, *Mies van der Rohe: A Critical Biography* (Chicago: University of Chicago Press, 1985), pp. 75–77. In the Werder project, Mies's concept of the garden is an architectural and a formal one, that of seventeenth-century French gardens, and I believe that his approach in this project should be seen in the context of the "architectural garden" advocated in Germany around 1905–15 by architects and landscape architects such as Leberecht Migge, Hermann Muthesius, and Heinrich Tessenow. This notion of the Architekturgarten was actively promoted and published in 1908, when Migge, Muthesius, and Tessenow, among others, participated in the competition *Hausgärten: Skizzen und Entwürfe aus dem Wettbewerb der Woche* (Berlin, 1908). For comparisons with Mies's Werder project, see Migge, *Gartenkultur des XX. Jahrhunderts.*

126. At this point in his work, Johnson's approach is perhaps closest to that of Mies in his courtyard house projects, as in Group of Court-Houses project of 1938, reproduced in Johnson, *Mies van der Rohe*, p. 105. Jacobus also noted that in the Cambridge house Johnson "actually built this Miesian type for the first time" (Jacobus, *Philip Johnson*, p. 25).

127. For Johnson's departure from Miesian vocabulary at the Glass House, see Jacobus, *Philip Johnson*, pp. 22–27; and Schulze, *Philip Johnson*, pp. 188–98. At the Glass House, Johnson placed a sculpture by Lipchitz out-of-doors as part of the overall composition of the site, and not in a Miesian way, which would have had this statue relate primarily to the spatial composition of the house. Hitchcock noted Johnson's attention to the site as a whole: "The site plan is still further elaborated by the large Lipchitz state in between [the two pavilions] and, just lately, by the circular swimming pool beyond. . . . In a special sense, this is 'landscape architecture'" (Hitchcock, "Philip Johnson," p. 240).

128. This approach changed somewhat in his project Museum for a Small City (1942), discussed below. Unlike Mies, who applied his personal and philosophical discourse about architecture consistently to all of his projects, Johnson was by training and also by inclination more flexible and more eclectic, able to approach each project with respect to its own disciplinary category.

129. Ludwig Mies van der Rohe, "Museum," *Architectural Forum* 78 (May 1943), pp. 84–85. This project was one of several requested by the magazine from contemporary American architects for a medium-sized American city of the future. See Schulze, *Mies van der Rohe: A Critical Biography*, pp. 230–31. Mies's project is discussed and illustrated in Johnson, *Mies van der Rohe*, pp. 163–64, 174–79, with two additional interior perspective drawings by Mies.

130. Although Mies included only one sculpture, a reclining figure, in his photocollage for the great plaza in front of the museum, his stated intent to explore "a garden approach for the display of sculpture" implies a potential multiplication of sculptural pieces on the outdoor terraces.

131. From Mies's description and his drawings, we see that the interior-exterior spatial dialogue of the compound included a large outdoor pool at one end (no. 9 on the plan; repr. in Johnson, *Mies van der Rohe*, p. 174), and at the other, a garden enclosed by a great wall (no. 1) and two inner courts designed as atrium gardens open to the sky (nos. 3 and 7).

132. The great mountains drawn in the background of Mies's "Museum" also bring to mind associations with the Acropolis complex in Athens.

133. Some of these issues are addressed in a recent article by Sarah Ksiazek, "Architectural Culture in the Fifties: Louis Kahn and the National Assembly Complex in Dhaka," *Journal of the Society of Architectural Historians* 52 (December 1993), pp. 416–35.

134. This text was then published with the papers of another symposium, including presentations by Louis I. Kahn and Philip Goodwin on sculptural monuments in the city, in *New Architecture and City Planning: A Symposium*, ed. Paul Zucker (New York: Philosophical Library, 1944). See also Christiane C. and George R. Collins, "Monumentality: A Critical Matter in Modern Architecture," *Harvard Architecture Review* 4 (Spring 1984), pp. 15–35. Kahn shared these concerns for urban character in architecture, and described an approach akin to Johnson's in the Museum sculpture garden when he said during his years at Yale in the 1950s that the "paving block is the grass of the city" (quoted in Vincent J. Scully, *Louis I. Kahn,* [New York: Braziller, 1962], p. 20).

135. James Johnson Sweeney, "Sculpture and the Core of the City," in *The Heart of the City: Towards the Humanisation of Urban Life, 8th International Conference for Modern Architecture,* ed. J. Tyrwhitt, J[osé] L[ouis] Sert, and E. N. Rogers (New York: Pellegrini and Cudahy, 1952), p. 59. Le Corbusier presented "The Core as a Meeting Place of the Arts."

136. "A Symposium on How to Combine Architecture, Painting, and Sculpture," *Interiors* 110 (May 1951), pp. 100–105. Sert, among others, called for new urban sites for public art, to be made on the model of "the agora, the forum, the cathedral square, which were also meeting places and constituted the heart of the city" (p. 103). On the debates about public art in the 1950s, see Harriet F. Senie, *Contemporary Public Sculpture: Tradition, Transformation, and Controversy* (New York: Oxford University Press, 1992), pp. 62–69.

137. *The New Yorker,* April 25, 1953, op. cit., p. 25. Johnson and Giedion probably discussed Johnson's design for the Museum garden in relation to the contemporaneous debate on civic spaces in New York, because at that time Giedion was writing on the Italian piazza, for example "Space and the Elements of the Renaissance City," *Magazine of Art* 45, no. 1 (January 1952), pp. 3–10. A link between these urban images and Mies's work of around 1957 was made by Vincent Scully, who stated that it "now offers the images of the Renaissance townscape and the permanent order of the urban piazza" (Scully, "Modern Architecture: Toward a Redefinition of Style," *Perspecta* 4 [1957], p. 8).

138. See the many press reports of 1953 in MoMA Archives: Johnson Papers, II.15; for example, Gage, "Modern Backyard," p. 4, and "The Museum's Marble Piazze," pp. 136–37. Already in the 1950s, landscape architects as well as architects were drawn to the urban quality of the Museum's sculpture garden. John Ormsbee Simonds used it as a key example in discussing design theories of boundaried open spaces in his comprehensive book *Landscape Architecture: The Shaping of Man's Natural Environment* (New York: McGraw-Hill, 1961), in which he stated: "This magnificent urban space extends the limits and function of the museum and serves in all seasons as an exhilarating exhibition area" (p. 177).

139. When Johnson used the grid of marble paving in order to associate his sculpture garden with the larger urban setting of paved malls and walks, he may have been recalling a specific moment in the development of the Museum's site. In 1936, when the trustees were searching for a site for the new Museum building, one proposal considered placing the museum on Fifty-fourth Street at the head of a long, north-south plaza, with a gridded pavement, leading directly to Fiftieth Street and Rockefeller Plaza itself. This project, never realized, is outlined and illustrated in Paul J. Sachs, "The Museum of Modern Art, New York," *Chart,* no. 8 (September 1939), p. 34. Sachs wrote: "What may be of greater importance is the possibility of the continuation of the new street (now extending from 49th to 51st Streets between 5th and 6th Avenues in Rockefeller Center) through 52nd Street to 53rd Street. In this event the Museum would be situated at the head of a boulevard five blocks long, making the site one of the most prominent in New York City" (p. 31).

140. The plan and a view of the sculpture garden to the west were included in Henry-Russell Hitchcock's "Three Approaches to Architecture 2: Modern Classicism," *Architectural Forum* 102 (May 1955), pp. 146–49; no discussion of the garden, or of what is meant by "classicism," is included. The issue of classicist tendencies in modern architecture is a complex one, and there is by no means any consensus as to its

exact definition. The following are helpful in developing the issue further: Henry Millon, "Rudolf Wittkower, Architectural Principles in the Age of Humanism: Its Influence on the Development and Interpretation of Modern Architecture," *Journal of the Society of Architectural Historians* 31, no. 2 (May 1972), pp. 83–91; Colin Rowe, "Neo-'Classicism' and Modern Architecture I–II," in his *The Mathematics of the Ideal Villa and Other Essays* (Cambridge, Mass.: MIT Press, 1976), pp. 119–58; and Alan Colquhoun, "Classicism and Ideology," in his *Modernity and the Classical Tradition: Architectural Essays, 1980–1987* (Cambridge, Mass.: MIT Press, 1989), pp. 201–05.

141. Hitchcock, "Philip Johnson," pp. 236–37, 243. See also Scully, "Archetype and Order in Recent American Architecture," p. 251.

142. On the house of Loreius Tiburtinus and other examples of ancient Roman garden design, see the articles by Eugenia Salza Prina Ricotti and Nicholas Purcell in *Ancient Roman Villa Gardens,* Dumbarton Oaks Colloquium on the History of Landscape Architecture, ed. Elisabeth B. MacDougall (Washington, D.C.: Dumbarton Oaks Research Library and Collection, 1987). In a conversation with the author on December 2, 1992, Vincent Scully recalled his visit to Italy with Johnson in the early 1950s and suggested, evocatively, that the sheet of water with adjacent sculptures at Hadrian's Villa, the Canopus Canal, may have inspired Johnson; see also Scully, "Archetype and Order," on how "a direct experience of Hadrian's Villa, as of Palladio and of the Baroque, has played a large part in Johnson's recent growth" (p. 256).

143. For these years at the Graduate School of Design, see Klaus Herdeg, *The Decorated Diagram: Harvard Architecture and the Failure of the Bauhaus Legacy* (Cambridge, Mass.: MIT Press, 1983), pp. 2–5.

144. Neckar, "Strident Modernism," pp. 241–42.

145. "The elaborate formal garden has no place in connection with the international style" (Hitchcock and Johnson, *The International Style,* p. 77).

146. It is important to note the complexity of Le Corbusier's attitude toward the modern garden and landscape; it was not only of the "Virgilian Dream" type but included very refined gardens in such projects as the villas for the Meyer and Stein families in the mid-1920s.

147. "Trees and vines are a further decoration for modern architecture. Natural surroundings are at once a contrast and a backbground emphasizing the artificial values created by architects" (Hitchcock and Johnson, *The International Style,* p. 77).

148. Hitchcock and the architect Richard Neutra took the same position in their essays for the *Contemporary Landscape Architecture* exhibition in San Francisco in 1937: Hitchcock could only imagine terraces and "outdoor living rooms" for modern houses; otherwise the landscape must remain essentially untouched, as in the English landscape park. His "primary principle" was "that modern gardening should preserve all the values of the existing natural environment, adding only the necessary features for convenient human use." Neutra viewed garden elements only as appendages to the modern house, among numerous other "ingredients of truly contemporary design." (*Contemporary Landscape Architecture* [San Francisco: San Francisco Museum of Art, 1937], pp. 19, 21).

149. Hudnut's brief text, "The Modern Garden," appeared in the second, revised edition of Tunnard's book, *Gardens in the Modern Landscape* (1948), pp. 175–78; the citation here is from pp. 175–76 and p. 178. The text was a reprinting of his article "Space and the Modern Garden," *Bulletin of the Garden Club of America* (May 1940), pp. 16–24, which was illustrated with works by Tunnard.

150. Jean C.N. Forestier (1861–1930) published his work in *Jardins: Carnet de plans et de dessins* (Paris: Powis Picard, 1920), which was translated into English as *Gardens: A Note-book of Plans and Sketches* (New York: Scribner's, 1928). For a recent, comprehensive view of the French modernists, see Dorothée Imbert, *The Modernist Garden in France* (New Haven, Conn.: Yale University Press, 1993).

151. Le Corbusier took the roof terrace paved with regular slabs from Garnier's designs and placed it both on roofs and on the ground in his villas of the 1920s and 1930s; one of the earliest examples is the Villa La Roche-Jeanneret of 1923–24, illustrated in Tim Benton, *The Villas of Le Corbusier, 1920–1930* (New Haven, Conn.: Yale University Press, 1987), p. 211. Mies began using grids of rectangular slabs around 1929–30, in the Tugendhat House and in the Krefeld Country Club project, reproduced in Johnson, *Mies van der Rohe,* pp. 79 and 87, respectively.

152. By the time of the exposition of 1937, the *jardin dallé* was one of the major modes of garden design associated with modernism; Jean-Jacques Haffner had included it in courses at Harvard in the 1920s and 1930s, Tunnard after 1939. Haffner's hybrid style, mixing elements of Beaux-Arts composition and Forestier's gardens, was passed on to his students in his book *Compositions de Jardins,* published in Paris in 1931; the English translation, *Garden Compositions,* appeared in the same year. The predominance of the *jardin dallé* is evident in the April 1937 issue of *L'Architecture d'aujourd'hui,* which was devoted to modern gardens in Europe. Examples of these juxtapositions of pavement and plantings can be seen in private work such as Church's Kirkham garden, built 1948 in San Francisco (fig. 12); and Canneel-Claes's Garden of a Small Country House, built 1935 at Dendre in Flanders (fig. 14).

153. James C. Rose, "Space Composition for the Display of Plant Forms," *Pencil Points* (April 1939), pp. 226–27; citation on p. 226.

154. Like Johnson, Rose was particularly interested in modern painting and sculpture. The sources of his illustrations in articles of 1938–39 show that he was following recent exhibitions such as Barr's *Cubism and Abstract Art* (1936) at The Museum of Modern Art and reading various books on contemporary sculpture such as Carola Giedion-Welcker's *Modern Plastic Art: Elements of Reality, Volume, and Disintegration,* trans. Philip Morton Shand (Zürich: H. Girsberger, 1937).

155. Two compendia of images that give the range of landscape architecture in America and Europe around 1950 are the exhibition catalogue *Landscape Architecture,* ed. Lester Collins and Thomas Gillespie (Cambridge, Mass.: Department of Landscape Architecture, Graduate School of Design, Harvard University, 1951); and Peter Shepheard, *Modern Gardens* (London: Thames and Hudson, 1953).

156. Canneel-Claes's work was published in French architecture magazines in the 1930s, and Tunnard had illustrated the designer's own house and modernist garden near Brussels; see Tunnard, *Gardens in the Modern Landscape* (1948), p. 65. For Eckbo, reviewing modernist theory and practice in landscape design before World War II, Canneel-Claes, Le Corbusier, and Guevrékian "all produced interesting and relevant work" (Eckbo, *Landscape for Living,* p. 23).

157. The ultimate origins of this design component still await research; such relations between pavement and planting also appear in early twentieth-century—and later, modernist—Japanese gardens, which themselves may have contributed to the development of the configuration and its variations. In an interview with Elizabeth Kassler in 1975, Johnson had said of the border between pavement and ground cover at the Museum garden: "Japan, don't you think? . . . There had been something of this in the courtyard of my Cambridge house, but in that case the trees were already there, and all I did was push the pavement up to them" (Kassler, "Sculpture Garden," p. 4).

158. For illustrations of these houses, see Hitchcock, "Philip Johnson," pp. 243–44; Jacobus, *Philip Johnson,* figs. 27–28, 43–47; and Johnson, *Philip Johnson: Architecture 1949–1965,* pp. 46–50.

159. Quoted in Kassler, "Sculpture Garden," p. 3.

160. Since the time of Frank Lloyd Wright and then of Bruno Taut, Mies, and others of their generation, features of the traditional Japanese house, such as white surfaces, wood screens, and garden courts, came to represent, paradoxically, aspects of modernity and modern life. On this and the Modern's dissemination of knowledge about Japanese buildings and gardens, see Arthur Drexler, *The Architecture of Japan* (New York: The Museum of Modern Art, 1955); and Lancaster, *The Japanese Influence in America.*

As we prepared companion essays for this volume, Peter Reed pointed out to me a photograph made in 1951 of Johnson's office at the Museum, in which the coffee table displays a book, *Masterpieces of Japanese Art.* This title was published in three folio volumes in 1940–48, one of which regarded architecture and gardens. See Central Federation of Nippon Culture, Bunka Koryu Kurabu. *Masterpieces of Japanese Art,* 3 vols. (Tokyo, 1940–48). The image is reproduced on p. 77 of the present volume.

164. Tunnard, *Gardens in the Modern Landscape*, pp. 85–92, and *passim.* Interest in Japanese houses, gardens, and their culture—abetted by World War II—appears strongly in the work of the landscape architect Rose as well. Rose wrote an article pairing the Museum's Japanese Exhibition House with his own residence, which he had just designed that year

in New Jersey; see "A Traditional Japanese House: The Esthetic Discipline; A Contemporary American House: The Spatial Discipline," *Progressive Architecture* 34 (December 1954), pp. 108–13.

162. *Japanese Exhibition House,* MoMA Exh. #559, June 16–October 21, 1954.

163. Like the two previous exhibition houses built in the Museum garden,one by Gregory Ain and one by Breuer, the Japanese house was to serve as a model for modern architecture. See "Museum Garden Is Site for a Japanese House," *Architectural Record* 116 (November 1954), pp. 332–33; and Drexler, *The Architecture of Japan,* pp. 262–286, in which he stated: "A Japanese building was chosen by the Museum for its third House in the Garden because traditional Japanese design has a unique relevance to modern Western architecture" (p. 262).

164. Mumford, "Windows and Gardens," p. 130; see also pp. 121–29, 131, quotation on p. 130. The quotation continues: "its variety of form, which, because of its miniature scale, seems as rich in contrasts as several rambling acres of natural woodland." Except for the slabs of concrete that function as bridges, miniaturization is not really used by Johnson, and his sculpture garden's plantings evoke groves but not acres of woodland.

165. Martin, "From the Courthouses," pp. 7–8.

166. Hitchcock, "Philip Johnson," p. 238.

167. "New Canaan: Commentary by P[hilip] Johnson on the Glass House Designed for his Own Occupation," *Architectural Review* 108 (September 1950), pp. 152–59; cited in Schulze, *Philip Johnson,* p. 196.

168. "Expansion and Remodeling Plans for Museum of Modern Art," *Architectural Record,* 134 (September 1963), p. 11.

169. For the new planting plan, see Kassler, "Sculpture Garden," pp. 7–8.

170. There have since been renovations of the sculpture garden, notably in 1989, undertaken with grant support from the Rockfeller family. These include: "1. Reconstruction of the Garden wall, with a structurally improved re-creation of the existing design; 2. Reconstruction of the ornamental pools, with a design modification—a false floor of polished black granite—to conceal piping and lighting systems; and 3. Redesign and reconstruction of the stair landing at the entrance to the Garden from the Garden Hall, to enhance the view of the Garden from that entrance. John Burgee Architects, with Philip Johnson continuing in his long-standing role as consultant for the Garden, are the architects for these renovations" (memorandum from James Snyder, Deputy Director, The Museum of Modern Art, New York, December 13, 1988). Departmentof Architecture and Design files, The Museum of Modern Art, New York.

Appendix

Selected Gifts of Philip Johnson to The Museum of Modern Art

Since 1930, when he joined the Advisory Committee of the new Museum of Modern Art, Philip Johnson has donated to the Museum collections, or provided funds for, more than twenty-two hundred paintings, sculptures, drawings, prints, photographs, posters, design objects, and architectural models and drawings. This total does not include approximately five hundred books and periodicals given by Johnson to help establish the Museum Library in 1932–33.

Listed herein is a selection of works drawn from each curatorial department within the Museum, arranged alphabetically by artist; the works of each artist appear in chronological order. The date of a work is enclosed in parentheses if it is not inscribed by the artist on the work itself. Dimensions are given in inches, followed in parentheses by centimeters; height precedes width precedes length. The Museum accession number indicates the year in which a work was acquired; for example, 2.61 is the number assigned to the second work acquired in 1961. The words "by exchange" in the credit line indicate that the work was acquired in exchange for one previously owned by the Museum. Unless otherwise noted, all works cited are the gift of Philip Johnson.

Department of Painting and Sculpture

133 works

Armand P. ARMAN. American, born France, 1928

Valetudinarian. (1960). Assemblage of pill bottles in a white painted wood box with glass top, 16 x 23¾ x 3⅛" (40.4 x 60.2 x 7.9 cm). 494.70

Boom! Boom! (1960). Assemblage of plastic water pistols in a plexiglass case, 8¼ x 23¼ x 4½" (21 x 59 x 11.2 cm). 495.70

Richard ARTSCHWAGER. American, born 1923

Tower. (1964). Painted formica and wood, 6'6" x 24⅛" x 39" (198.1 x 61.1 x 99 cm). 671.71

Key Member. (1967). Formica veneer and felt on wood, 11⅞ x 29⅛ x 8⅝" (30.1 x 74 x 21.9 cm). 220.68

Jo BAER. American, born 1929

Primary Light Group: Red, Green, Blue. 1964. Oil and synthetic polymer paint on canvas, triptych, a: 60⅜ x 60¼" (153.1 x 153 cm) (red); b: 60⅜ x 60⅜" (153.1 x 153.2 cm) (green); c: 60¼ x 60⅛" (153 x 152.6 cm) (blue). Philip Johnson Fund. 495.69.a–c

Robert BART. American, born 1923

Untitled. 1964. Aluminum, 66½ x 28¾ x 28¾" (168.7 x 73 x 73 cm). 766.69

Lee BONTECOU. American, born 1931

(Untitled). 1959. Construction of canvas, cloth, wire, and steel, 36⅜" (92.3 cm) high x 39¼" (99.7 cm) wide x 5" (12.7 cm) diameter. 769.69

Scott BURTON. American, 1939–1989

Pair of Rock Chairs. (1980). Gneiss, two pieces, a: 49¼ x 43½ x 40" (125.1 x 110.5 x 101.6 cm); b: 44 x 66 x 42½" (111.6 x 167.7 x 108 cm). Purchase. Acquired through the Philip Johnson, Mr. and Mrs. Joseph Pulitzer, Jr., and Robert Rosenblum Funds. 56.81.a–b

Pol BURY. Belgian, born 1922. To France 1961

Erectile Entity (Red and White). 1962. Motor-driven construction of metal wires in wood panel, painted, 36 x 35¾ x 13½" (91.2 x 90.6 x 34.2 cm). 770.69

White Points. 1964. Motor-driven construction of plastic-tipped nylon wires in wood panel, 39¼ x 19⅝ x 4¾" (99.6 x 49.7 x 12.1 cm). Philip Johnson Fund. 566.64

John CHAMBERLAIN. American, born 1927

Tomahawk Nolan. (1965). Assemblage: welded and painted metal automobile parts, 43¾ x 52⅛ x 36¼" (111.1 x 132.2 x 92 cm). 677.71

Dan CHRISTENSEN. American, born 1942

PR. 1967. Synthetic polymer paint on canvas, 8'4⅛" x 10'½" (254.3 x 306.1 cm). 951.79

Bernard COHEN. British, born 1933

Mutation Whitsun Series 2. (1960). Oil and enamel on canvas, 54⅜ x 66¼" (138 x 168 cm). Philip Johnson Fund. 360.60

Bruce CONNER. American, born 1933

Child. 1959–60. Assemblage: wax figure with nylon, cloth, metal, and twine in a high chair, 34⅝ x 17 x 16½" (87.7 x 43.1 x 41.7 cm). 501.70

William COPLEY. American, born 1919

The Common Market. 1961. Oil on canvas, 31⅞ x 51¼" (81 x 130.1 cm). 772.69

Edward CORBETT. American, 1919–1971

Lejos de Socorro. 1957. Oil, enamel, and bronze paint on canvas, 48 x 50" (122.1 x 127.1 cm). 255.57

DADO (Miodrag Djuric). Yugoslav, born 1933. In France since 1956

(Untitled). 1959. Oil on canvas, 44⅞ x 63⅞" (113.8 x 162 cm). 773.69

Salvador DALI. Spanish, 1904–1989. Active in Paris and New York

Retrospective Bust of a Woman (Buste de femme rétrospectif). (1933; some elements reconstructed 1970). Painted porcelain, bread, corn, feathers, paint on paper, beads, ink stand, sand, and two pens, 29 x 27¼ x 12⅝" (73.9 x 69.2 x 32 cm). Acquired through the Lillie P. Bliss Bequest and gift of Philip Johnson (by exchange). 301.92

François DALLEGRET. French

(Untitled). 1961. Painted metal plate, 3¼ x 11½" (8.1 x 29.1 cm). 774.69

Jim DINE. American, born 1935

Still Life Painting. 1962. Oil on canvas with twelve partly painted toothbrushes in plastic glass on metal holder, 35⅞ x 24¼ x 4¼" (91.2 x 61.7 x 10.8 cm). 504.70

Otto DIX. German, 1891–1969

Dr. Mayer-Hermann. 1926. Oil and tempera on wood, 58¾ x 39" (149.2 x 99.1 cm). 3.32

Jean DUBUFFET. French, 1901–1985

Soil Ornamented with Vegetation, Dead Leaves, Pebbles, Diverse Debris (Sol historié de végétation, feuilles mortes, cailloux, débris divers) from the Tableaux d'assemblages series. 1956. Assemblage of oil on canvas, 35⅛ x 30⅜" (89.3 x 77.1 cm). Purchased from the proceeds in the Mr. And Mrs. Ralph F. Colin Fund in honor of Ralph F. Colin with additional funds from a gift of Philip Johnson (by exchange). 303.92

Marcel DUCHAMP. American, born France. 1887–1968

Box in a Valise (Boite-en-valise). 1958, after the original edition of 1941. Cloth-covered cardboard box containing miniature replicas, photographs, and color reproductions of works by Duchamp, 3⅝ x 14⅞ x 15¾" (9.2 x 37.8 x 40 cm). 505.70.1–17

Dusan DZAMONJA. Yugoslav, born 1928

Metallic Sculpture. (1959). Welded iron nails with charred wood core, 16⅜" (41.5 cm) high x 10" (25.5 cm) diameter. Philip Johnson Fund. 2.61

Paul FEELEY. American, 1910–1966

Alniam. (1964). Synthetic polymer paint on canvas, 59⅜ x 59⅜" (150.6 x 150.7 cm). 507.70

Herbert FERBER. American, 1906–1991

If I Touch Them They Bleed (Game I). (1949). Lead and brass moveable parts on a wood base, overall 15⅛ x 20 x 8⅜" (38.2 x 50.8 x 21.1 cm). 775.69.a–d

Eric FISCHL. American, born 1948

Portrait of a Dog. 1987. Oil on canvas in four parts, overall 9'5" x 14'2¾" (287 x 433.7 cm). Gift of the Louis and Bessie Alder Foundation, Inc., Seymour M.

Klein, President; Agnes Gund; President's Fund Purchase (1987), Donald B. Marron, President; Jerry I. Speyer; the Douglas S. Cramer Foundation; Philip Johnson; Robert and Jane Meyerhoff; Robert F. and Anna Marie Shapiro; Barbara Jakobson; Gerald S. Elliott; and purchase. 190.87.a–d

Dan FLAVIN. American, 1933–1996
Pink Out of a Corner—To Jasper Johns. (1963). Pink fluorescent light in metal fixture, 8' 6" x 5⅜" (243.8 x 15.2 x 13.6 cm). 67.79

Untitled. (1968). Fluorescent light bulbs and metal fixtures, 25 x 25 x 5¾" (63.5 x 63.5 x 14.6 cm). 114.75

Lucio FONTANA. Italian, born Argentina. 1899–1968
Spatial Concept: Expectations. (1959). Synthetic polymer paint on slashed burlap, 39⅜ x 32⅛" (100 x 81.5 cm). Philip Johnson Fund. 413.60

Spatial Concept: Expectations Number 2. (1960). Slashed canvas and gauze, unpainted, 39½ x 31⅝" (100.3 x 80.3 cm). 508.70

Sue FULLER. American
String Composition #336. 1965. Polypropalene thread embedded in plexiglass, 21" (53.3 cm) high x 21⅛" (53.4 cm) wide x 1⅛" (2.6 cm) diameter. 776.69

Mathias GOERITZ. German, 1915–1981. To Mexico 1949
Message Number 7B, Ecclesiastes VII. 1959. Assemblage of nails, metal foils, oil, and iron on wood panel, 17⅞ x 13⅝ x 3⅜" (45.1 x 34.5 x 8.4 cm). 779.69

Adolph GOTTLIEB. American, 1903–1974
Blast, I. (1957). Oil on canvas, 7'6" x 45⅛" (228.7 x 114.4 cm). Philip Johnson Fund. 6.58

Robert GRAHAM. American, born Mexico 1938
Untitled. (1968). Three miniature figures of pigmented wax, fur, and paper; two beds, platform, ramp, and pole of balsa wood with foam and paper bedding, pole fixtures of metal, plastic, glass, and wire in plexiglass vitrine. Vitrine: 10 x 20 x 20" (25.4 x 50.8 x 50.8 cm) including base 1 x 20 x 20" (2.6 x 50.8 x 50.8 cm). 115.75

Philip GUSTON. American, born Canada. 1913–1980
Painting. 1954. Oil on canvas, 63¼ x 60⅛" (160.6 x 152.7 cm). Philip Johnson Fund. 7.56

Günter HAESE. German, born 1924
High Noon. (1963). Construction of clockwork parts, brass screening, and wire, 7⅞" (19.7 cm) high including wood base ¾" (1.8 cm) high x 13½" (34.2 cm) wide x 11½" (29.1 cm) diameter. 781.69

Raymond HAINS. French, born 1926. Lives in Venice
Saffa Super Matchbox. (1965). Synthetic polymer paint on plywood, 45½ x 34¼ x 3" (115.5 x 86.9 x 7.5 cm). 782.69

Robert INDIANA. American, born 1928
Moon. 1960. Assemblage: wood beam with iron-rimmed wheels and white paint, 6'6" (198.1 cm) high, on base 5 x 17⅛ x 10¼" (12.7 x 43.5 x 26 cm). Philip Johnson Fund. 288.61

Law. (1961). Assemblage: painted wood and metal, 44⅛ x 10⅞ x 3⅛" (111.9 x 27.6 x 7.8 cm) including wood base 3¼ x 10¾ x 10⅝" (8 x 27.2 x 26.7 cm). 783.69

Neil JENNEY. American, born 1945
Implements and Entrenchments. 1969. Synthetic polymer paint on canvas, 54¼ x 74¼" (137.8 x 178.5 cm) including painted wood frame with title "Implements and Entrench-ments." 412.77

Jasper JOHNS. American, born 1930
Flag. (1954–55; dated on reverse 1954). Encaustic, oil, and collage on fabric mounted on plywood, 42¼ x 60⅝" (107.3 x 153.8 cm). Gift of Philip Johnson in honor of Alfred H. Barr, Jr. 106.73

Donald JUDD. American, 1928–1994
Untitled. (1967). Stainless steel, 6⅛ x 36⅛ x 26⅛" (15.5 x 91.6 x 66.2 cm). 682.71

Untitled. (1968). Brass, 22 x 48¼ x 36" (55.9 x 122.6 x 91.4 cm). 687.80

Untitled. (1969). Brass and plexiglass, 6⅛ x 27⅛ x 24⅛" (15.4 x 68.8 x 61.1 cm). 681.71

Untitled. (1973–75, refabricated after 1967 version). Lacquer on galvanized iron, 25⅝" x 6'4¾" x 14¾" (65.1 x 194.6 x 37.2 cm). Gift of Philip Johnson (by exchange). 375.75

Horst-Egon KALINOWSKI. German, born 1924. To Paris 1952
The Gate of the Executed (La Porte des supplices). 1963. Assemblage: leather over wood with a chain and other metal and wood parts, 6'6¾" x 58½" x 11⅝" (200 x 148.6 x 29.5 cm). Philip Johnson Fund. 1129.64

The Guillotine of Dreams (La Guillotine des Songes). 1963. Assemblage: construction of leather over wood with metal, string, and other wood parts, 54½" (138.4 cm) high x 32⅛" (81.3 cm) wide x 6" (15.2 cm) diameter. 784.69

Ellsworth KELLY. American, born 1923
Curve, II. (1973). Weathering steel, 9'9¾" x 10'3½" x 29" (299 x 313.7 x 73.7 cm). 500.84

R. B. KITAJ (Ronald Brooks Kitaj). American, born 1932. Lives in London
The Ohio Gang. (1964). Oil and graphite on canvas, 6'1⅛" x 6'1¼" (183.1 x 183.5 cm). Philip Johnson Fund. 109.65

Yves KLEIN. French, 1928–1962
Untitled. (1957). Sponge, painted blue, on brass-rod stand, 22⅝ x 12½ x 4⅝" (57.3 x 31.7 x 11.5 cm) including brass rod 15" (37.9 cm) high x ¾" (1.8 cm) diameter and brass base ⅛" x 5¼" x 6" (.4 x 13.1 x 15.2 cm). 786.69

Franz KLINE. American, 1910–1962
White Forms. (1955). Oil on canvas, 6'2⅜" x 50¼" (188.9 x 127.6 cm). 413.77

Gabriel KOHN. American, 1910–1975
Tilted Construction. (1959). Laminated wood, 31 x 18½ x 12⅝" (91.4 x 46.7 x 31.9 cm). Philip Johnson Fund. 606.59

Ilhan KOMAN. Turkish, born 1921. Lives in Sweden
My Country's Sun. (1957). Antique wrought iron, reconstructed, 66⅛" x

6'4⅛" x 17½" (168 x 193.2 x 44.6 cm). Philip Johnson Fund. 13.59

Ronnie LANDFIELD. American, born 1947
Diamond Lake. (1969). Synthetic polymer paint on canvas, 9'1¼" x 14'1¼" (274.8 x 427.3 cm). 301.75

Octave LANDUYT. Belgian, born 1922
Purification by Fire. 1957. Oil on composition board, 47⅞ x 35⅞" (121.7 x 91 cm). Philip Johnson Fund. 128.58

Essential Surface, Eye. (1960). Oil on canvas, 51⅜ x 63⅛" (130.5 x 160.3 cm). Philip Johnson Fund. 122.61

John LATHAM. British, born Northern Rhodesia (modern-day Zambia) 1921
Shem. 1958. Assemblage: hessian-covered door, with books, scrap metals, various paints, plasters, and cements, 8'4½" x 46" x 12½" (255.2 x 116.8 x 31.7 cm). Philip Johnson Fund. 298.61

Julio LE PARC. Argentine, born 1928. To Paris 1958
Double Concurrence—Continuous Light, 2. (1961). Black wood box 21 x 19¾ x 5⅝" (53.4 x 50 x 14.1 cm) with illuminated aperture 7⅞ x 8" (20 x 20.2 cm), in which fifty-four plastic squares 1½ x 1½" (3.6 x 3.6 cm) are suspended from eighteen nylon threads; mirror backing 11⅞ x 16" (30.1 x 40.4 cm), two reflectors, three sets of interchangeable pierced metal screens, and two glass filters. Philip Johnson Fund. 199.63.a–l

Mon LEVINSON. American, born 1926
Summer 1961—White. (1961). Construction of illuminated plastic sheets in painted wood box, 50⅞" (129.1 cm) high x 21⅜" (54.1 cm) wide x 14¼" (36.2 cm) diameter. 787.69

Roy LICHTENSTEIN. American, 1923–1997
Girl with Ball. (1961). Oil and synthetic polymer paint on canvas, 60¼ x 36¼" (153 x 91.9 cm). 421.81

Drowning Girl. 1963. Oil and synthetic polymer paint on canvas, 67⅝ x 66¾" (171.6 x 169.5 cm). Philip Johnson Fund and gift of Mr. and Mrs. Bagley Wright. 685.71

Banner, "Pistol." (1964). Banner in red, black, and white felt, 82⅞ x 44⅛" (210.4 x 112.1 cm). 599.65

Pistol. 1964. Banner in red, black, and white felt, 82⅞ x 44⅛" (210.4 x 112.1 cm). 512.70

Seascape with Dunes. 1965. Plastic and paper mounted on cardboard, 11⅛ x 23⅛" (28.1 x 58.6 cm). 513.70

Richard LINDNER. American, born Germany. 1901–1978. To U.S.A. 1941
Construction. (1962). Assemblage: plastic mask, printed paper, and cloth on painted wood panel, 11⅞ x 13 x 3¾" (29.9 x 33 x 9.5 cm). Philip Johnson Fund. 7.63

Robert MALLARY. American, 1917–1997
Earth Mother. 1958. Relief of composition stone in resin base over wood supports, 6'5⅛" x 48" x 4½" (195.8 x 121.8 x 11.4 cm). 524.71

Agnes MARTIN. American, born Canada 1912. To U.S.A. 1933
Red Bird. 1964. Synthetic polymer paint and colored pencil on canvas, 71⅛ x 71⅛" (180.5 x 180.5 cm). 514.70

Henri MATISSE. French, 1869–1954
Black Chasuble. Designed Nice, late 1950–52; executed 1955. Black crepe with white crepe appliqué, 6'4 (193 cm) wide across top; 47¾" (121.3 cm) in length, front; 48" (121.9 cm) in length, back. 375.55. NOTE: This is one of a set of silk liturgical vestments, made after maquettes of cut-and-pasted paper, designed for the Chapel of the Rosary of the Dominican Nuns of Venice. Manufactured by Atelier d'Arts Appliqués, Cannes, France

Tomio MIKI. Japanese, 1937–1978
Untitled (Ears). (1964). Cast aluminum relief, 21⅜ x 19 x 1½" (54.3 x 48.2 x 3.7 cm). Philip Johnson Fund. 607.65

László MOHOLY-NAGY. American, born Hungary. 1895–1946. In Germany 1921–34; U.S.A. 1937–46
Telephone Picture EM 2. (1922). Porcelain enamel on steel, 18¾ x 11⅞" (47.5 x 30.1 cm). Gift of Philip Johnson in memory of Sibyl Moholy-Nagy. 91.71

Telephone Picture EM 3. (1922). Porcelain enamel on steel, 9½ x 6" (24 x 15 cm). Gift of Philip Johnson in memory of Sibyl Moholy-Nagy. 92.71

Piet MONDRIAN. Dutch, 1872–1944. Worked in Paris, 1912–14, 1919–38; in New York 1940–44
Composition , II. (1929; original date partly obliterated; mistakenly repainted 1925 by Mondrian when he restored the painting in 1942). Oil on canvas, 15⅞ x 12⅝" (40.3 x 32.1 cm). 486.41

Robert MORRIS. American, born 1931
Document. 1963. Typed and notarized statement on paper and sheet of lead over wood mounted in imitation leather mat, overall 17⅝ x 23¾" (44.8 x 60.4 cm). Inscribed: . . . *The undersigned* ROBERT MORRIS, *being the maker of the metal construction entitled* LITANIES, *described in the annexed Exhibit A, hereby withdraws from said construction all esthetic quality and content.* . . . 516.70

Litanies. 1963. Lead over wood with steel key ring, twenty-seven keys, and brass lock, 12 x 7⅛ x 2½" (30.4 x 18 x 6.3 cm). 517.70. NOTE: The twenty-seven keys are each inscribed with individual words from the Green Box, facsimile notes for the Large Glass.

Magnified and Reduced Inches. (1963). Stamped and incised lead over wood painted with metallic powder in synthetic polymer, ⅝ x 11¼ x 4⅞" (1.6 x 28.6 x 12.4 cm). 518.70

Untitled. (1963). Knotted rope on tin box covered with encaustic, on wood base painted with metallic powder in synthetic polymer, overall 7½ x 10¼ x 5¾" (19 x 26 x 14.6 cm). 521.70.a–b

Untitled. (1963). Lead over wood panel painted with metallic powder in synthetic polymer, 1⅛ x 8⅛ x 5" (2.8 x 20.5 x 12.6 cm). 522.70

Untitled. 1963–64. Glass case on wood base painted with metallic powder in synthetic polymer containing cracked glass case on painted wood base, stamped lead, mirror, and two metal rulers, 3¾ x 16⅛ x 4⅝" (9.5 x 41 x 11.8 cm). Inscribed: REJECTED 9–23–63 11:35 AM; BREAKAGE ACCEPTED 6–24–64 2:20 PM. 519.70

Untitled. 1964. Molded sheet lead over wood with painted wood pieces and steel wire, 10½ x 12⅜ x 2" (26.6 x 31.4 x 4.9 cm). 520.70

Rope Piece. (1964). Rope and wood, painted, 18'3" x 10" x 10" (556.2 x 25.5 x 25.5 cm). 70.79

Untitled (Tangle). (1967). Felt, 9'8" x 8'10" x 58" (296.7 x 269.3 x 147.4 cm), variable. 64.95

(Untitled). (1968). Felt, asphalt, mirrors, wood, copper tubing, steel cable, and lead, 21½" x 21'11" x 16'9" (54.6 x 668 x 510.5 cm), variable. 504.84

Robert MÜLLER. Swiss, born 1920. To Paris 1950
Ex-Voto. (1957). Forged iron, 6'11⅞" x 13⅞" x 14¾" (213 x 33.8 x 37.9 cm). Philip Johnson Fund. 18.59

Bruce NAUMAN. American, born 1941
Composite Photo of Two Messes on the Studio Floor. (1967). Gelatin-silver print, 40½ x 10'3" (102.9 x 312.4 cm). 505.84

Barnett NEWMAN. American, 1905–1970
Abraham. 1949. Oil on canvas, 6'10¾" x 34½" (210.2 x 87.7 cm). Philip Johnson Fund. 651.59

Claes OLDENBURG. American, born Sweden 1929. To U.S.A. 1936
Two Cheeseburgers, with Everything (Dual Hamburgers). 1962. Burlap soaked in plaster, painted with enamel, 7 x 14¾ x 8⅝" (17.8 x 37.5 x 21.8 cm). Philip Johnson Fund. 233.62

Floor Cake (Giant Piece of Cake). (1962). Synthetic polymer paint and latex on canvas filled with foam rubber and cardboard boxes, 58⅜" x 9'6¼" x 58⅜" (148.2 x 290.2 x 148.2 cm). 414.75

Floor Cone (Giant Ice-cream Cone). (1962). Synthetic polymer paint on canvas filled with foam rubber and cardboard boxes, 53¾" x 11'4" x 56" (136.5 x 345.4 x 142 cm). 425.81

Pablo PICASSO. Spanish, 1881–1973. To France 1940
Repose. (Spring 1908). Oil on canvas, 32 x 25¾" (81.2 x 65.4 cm). Acquired by exchange through the Katherine S.

Dreier Bequest and the Hillman Periodicals, Philip Johnson, Miss Janice Loeb, Abby Aldrich Rockefeller, and Mr. and Mrs. Norbert Schimmel Funds. 575.70

Bearded Faun. 1956. Painting on tile, 8 x 8" (20.3 x 20.3 cm). Philip Johnson Fund. 274.56

Head of a Faun. 1956. Painting on tile, 8 x 8" (20.3 x 20.3 cm). Philip Johnson Fund. 275.56

Liubov Sergeievna POPOVA. Russian, 1889–1924
Painterly Architectonic. 1917. Oil on canvas, 31½ x 38⅝" (80 x 98 cm). Philip Johnson Fund. 14.58

Richard POUSETTE-DART. American, 1916–1992
Chavade. 1951. Oil and pencil on canvas, 53⅜ x 8'½" (135.6 x 245 cm). Philip Johnson Fund. 503.69

Robert RAUSCHENBERG. American, born 1925
First Landing Jump. 1961. Combine painting: cloth, metal, leather, electric fixture, cable, and oil paint on composition board; overall, including automobile tire and wood plank on floor, 7'5⅛" x 6' x 8⅞" (226.3 x 182.8 x 22.5). 434.72. NOTE: This piece is lit by a small blue light enclosed in a tin can. The electric cable connecting it to a socket is intended to be part of the work.

Bridget RILEY. British, born 1931
Fission. (1963). Tempera on composition board, 35 x 34" (88.8 x 86.2 cm). 793.69

Current. 1964. Synthetic polymer paint on composition board, 58⅜ x 58⅞" (148.1 x 149.3 cm). Philip Johnson Fund. 576.64

Mark ROTHKO. American, born Latvia. 1903–1970. To U.S.A. 1913
Number 10. 1950. Oil on canvas, 7'6⅜" x 57⅛" (229.6 x 145.1 cm). 38.52

Lucas SAMARAS. American, born Greece 1936. To U.S.A. 1948
Book 4. (1962). Assemblage: partly opened book with pins, razor blade, scissors, table knife, metal foil, piece of glass, and plastic rod, 5½ x 8⅞ x 11½" (14 x 22.5 x 29.2 cm). 525.70

Fred SANDBACK. American, born 1943
Untitled. (1967). Elastic rayon cord and metal sleeve clamps, stretched in installation to 69" x 14' x 24" (175.2 x 426.7 x 60.9 cm). 692.71

Oskar SCHLEMMER. German, 1888–1943
Bauhaus Stairway. (1932). Oil on canvas, 63⅞ x 45" (162.3 x 114.3 cm). 597.42

Julius SCHMIDT. American, born 1923
(Untitled). 1961. Bronze, 13¼" (33.6 cm) high x 5¾" (14.4 cm) wide x 5¾" (14.5 cm) diameter. 794.69

George SEGAL. American, born 1924
The Bus Driver. (1962). Figure of plaster over cheesecloth; bus parts including coin box, steering wheel, driver's seat, railing, dashboard, etc. Figure: 53½ x 26⅞ x 45" (136 x 68.2 x 114 cm); overall 7'5" x 51⅝" x 6'4¾" (226 x 131 x 195 cm). Philip Johnson Fund. 337.63.a–u

Jason SELEY. American, 1919–1983
Flip. (1963). Assemblage: welded chromium-plated steel automobile bumpers, 30⅝ x 25¼ x 14⅜" (77.8 x 64 x 36.4 cm), on wood base 2⅛" (5.2 cm) high x 11⅞" (30.1 cm) wide x 11⅞" (30.1 cm) diameter. 795.69

Richard SERRA. American, born 1939
Cutting Device: Base Plate Measure. (1969). Lead, wood, stone, and steel, overall 12" x 18' x 15'7¾" (30.5 x 549 x 498 cm), variable. 974.79.a–cc

Francesco SOMAINI. Italian, born 1926
Sanguinary Martyrdom (Grande Martirio sanguinante). (1960). Cast iron, 52⅛ x 26⅛ x 17½" (132.3 x 66.4 x 44.5 cm). 1534.68

Keith SONNIER. American, born 1941
Untitled. (1967). Satin over foam rubber on wood with felt, 3⅜" x 9'11" x 3¾" (8.4 x 302.3 x 9.3 cm). 526.70

Jesus Rafael SOTO. Venezuelan, born 1923
(Untitled). (1959). Tempera on wood panel with painted wire construction, 9½" (24 cm) high x 7½" (19 cm) wide x 5⅝" (14.1 cm) diameter. 796.69

Daniel SPOERRI. Swiss, born Rumania 1930
Kichka's Breakfast I. 1960. Assemblage:
wood chair hung on wall with board
across seat, coffee pot, tumbler, china,
egg cups, eggshells, cigarette butts,
spoons, tin cans, etc., 14⅜ x 27⅜ x 25¾"
(36.6 x 69.5 x 65.4 cm). Philip Johnson
Fund. 391.61

Richard STANKIEWICZ. American, 1922–1983
Urchin in the Grass. (1956). Iron and
steel, 23⅝ x 16½ x 13" (59.9 x 41.7 x 32.8
cm) including steel base ¼" (.6 cm) high x
16½" (41.7 cm) wide x 11⅛" (28.1 cm)
diameter. 797.69

City Bird. (1957). Iron and steel, 27⅛ x
12¼ x 7¼" (68.9 x 31.1 x 18.4 cm)
including base. Philip Johnson Fund.
16.58

Instruction. (1957). Welded scrap iron
and steel, 12½ x 13¼ x 8⅝" (31.7 x 33.6 x
21.8 cm). Philip Johnson Fund. 17.58

Frank STELLA. American, born 1936
Astoria. 1958. Enamel on canvas, 8'¾" x
8'¾" (245.7 x 245.7 cm). 431.81

Abra Variation I. (1969). Fluorescent
alkyd on canvas, 10' x 9'11⅞" (304.8 x
304.5 cm). Gift of Philip Johnson in
honor of William Rubin. 695.80

Nasielk III. 1972. Synthetic polymer
paint and felt on corrugated cardboard,
9'1¾" x 7'5½" (278.7 x 227.3 cm). 432.81

Harold STEVENSON. American, born 1929
Fingers, Left Hand. (1963). Oil on canvas, 39⅜ x 31¾" (100 x 80.6 cm). 798.69

Myron STOUT. American, 1908–1987
Number 3, 1954. (1954). Oil on canvas,
20⅛ x 16" (50.9 x 40.6 cm). Philip Johnson Fund. 25.59

Mark DI SUVERO. American, born 1933
Ladderpiece. (1961–62). Wood and steel,
6'2½" x 15'3" x 10'10" (189.2 x 464.8 x
330.2 cm), irreg. 510.84

Yves TANGUY. American, born France.
1900–1955. To U.S.A. 1939
*Slowly Toward the North (Vers le Nord
lentement).* 1942. Oil on canvas, 42 x 36"
(106.7 x 91.4 cm). 627.43

Wayne THIEBAUD. American, born 1920
Pink Cones. 1961–62. Oil on canvas, 16 x
20" (40.6 x 50.8 cm). 799.69

Jean TINGUELY. Swiss, 1925–1991
Puss in Boots. 1959. Motor-driven construction of painted steel and wire, 30½ x
7¾ x 18⅛" (77.5 x 19.7 x 46.1 cm).
Philip Johnson Fund. 369.60

Bradley Walker TOMLIN. American,
1899–1953
Number 20. (1949). Oil on canvas, 7'2" x
6'8¼" (218.5 x 203.9 cm). 58.52

Tomonori TOYOFUKU. Japanese, born 1925.
Lives in Milan
Adrift, 3. 1960. Wood on iron supports,
finished with wax and traces of red pig-
ment, figure 6'3¼" (191.2 cm) high; boat
10' (304.8 cm) long. Philip Johnson
Fund. 14.61.a–b

Albert TUCKER. Australian, born 1914
Explorers, Burke and Wills. 1960. Oil and
sand on canvas, 48⅛ x 61½" (122.1 x
156.1 cm). Philip Johnson Fund. 124.60

Jaap WAGEMAKER. Dutch, 1906–1972
Metallic Grey. 1960. Assemblage: wood
panel relief with aluminum egg slicer
and scrap metal, painted, 24 x 19⅝ x
2¾" (61 x 50 x 6.9 cm). Philip Johnson
Fund. 304.61

Andy WARHOL. American, 1928–1987
Gold Marilyn Monroe. 1962. Synthetic
polymer paint, silkscreened, and oil on
canvas, 6'11¼" x 57" (211.4 x 144.7 cm).
316.62

Orange Car Crash Fourteen Times. (1963).
Synthetic polymer paint and silkscreen
ink on canvas, two panels, overall 8'9⅞" x
13'8⅛" (268.9 x 416.9 cm). 234.91.a–b

Campbell's Soup. (1965). Oil, silkscreened
on canvas, 36⅛ x 24" (91.7 x 60.9 cm).
Philip Johnson Fund. 111.66

Campbell's Soup. (1966). Felt banner,
90½ x 56¼" (229.7 x 142.9 cm). 527.70

Tom WESSELMANN. American, born 1931
Still Life Painting, 30. 1963. Assemblage:
oil, enamel, and synthetic polymer paint
on composition board with collage of
printed advertisements, plastic artificial

flowers, refrigerator door, plastic replicas
of "7-Up" bottles, glazed and framed color
reproduction, and stamped metal, 48½ x
66 x 4" (122 x 167.5 x 10 cm). 578.70

Peter YOUNG. American, born 1940
Untitled. (1966). Synthetic polymer
paint on canvas, 42⅛" x 9'8⅝" (107 x
296.1 cm). 118.75

Number 7. (1967). Synthetic polymer
paint on canvas, 9' x 9' (274.5 x 274.5
cm). 105.76

YVARAL (Jean Pierre Vasarely). French, born
1934
Acceleration 19, Series B. (1962). Construction of plastic cord, plexiglass, and
wood, 23⅞ x 24⅜ x 3⅛" (60.5 x 61.8 x 8
cm). 20.63

Hossein ZANDEROUDI (Hossein Zendh-
Roudi). Iranian, born 1937. In France since
1961
K + L + 32 + H + 4. 1962. Felt-tip pen and
colored ink on paper mounted on composition board, 7'5" x 58⅝" (225.9 x 148.7
cm), irreg. Philip Johnson Fund. 317.62

Department of Drawings
25 works

Peter AGOSTINI. American, 1913–1993
Wax Drawing No. 2. 1962. Wax on paper,
38⅛ x 25⅜" (96.8 x 64.3 cm). Philip
Johnson Fund. 177.63

Jean (Hans) ARP. French, born Alsace.
1887–1966. Lived in Switzerland 1959–66
*Squares Arranged According to the Laws
of Chance.* (1917). Cut-and-pasted
papers, ink, and bronze paint on paper,
13⅛ x 10¼" (33.2 x 25.9 cm). 496.70

Marcel DUCHAMP. American, born France.
1887–1968. In U.S.A. 1915–18, 1920–23,
1942–68
L.H.O.O.Q/Shaved. (1965). Playing card
pasted on folded note paper, 8¼ x 5½"
(21 x 13.8 cm). 506.70

John FAWCETT. American, born 1939
"Algiers Motel—Detriot [sic]." (1968).
Pen and ink, rubber stamp and red and
black ink, cut-and-pasted photographs
and printed papers, and pencil on paper,

22¼ x 29" (56.7 x 73.7 cm). Philip Johnson Fund. 433.71

Dan FLAVIN. American, 1933–1996
Pink Out of a Corner from No. 1 of December 19, 1963. 1965. Pencil and crayon on gray paper, 10 x 13" (25.2 x 32.9 cm). 619.71

Charles Ray FRAZIER. American, born 1930
Chinese Gate. 1970. Charcoal on paper, 19 x 24" (48.3 x 61 cm). Philip Johnson Fund. 97.71

Joseph GLASCO. American, born 1925
Blessed are the Meek. 1949. Pen and ink on paper, 31 x 22½" (78.7 x 57.1 cm). 778.69

Donald JUDD. American, 1928–1994
Untitled. (1971). Felt-tipped pen on yellow paper, 17⅛ x 22" (43.5 x 55.9 cm). 617.71

Untitled. (1971). Felt-tipped pen on yellow paper, 17⅛ x 22" (43.5 x 55.9 cm). 618.71

Horst-Egon KALINOWSKI. German, born 1924. To Paris 1952
May Night. 1961. Gouache, velvet, and metal thread on paper, 12½ x 22" (31.7 x 55.7 cm). Philip Johnson Fund. 297.61

Paul KLEE. German, 1879–1940. Born and died in Switzerland
Sacred Islands. 1926. Pen and ink and watercolor on paper mounted on cardboard, 18⅝ x 12⅜" (47 x 31.3 cm). 457.81

Yayoi KUSAMA. Japanese, born 1929. To U.S.A. 1957
Accumulation of Stamps, 63. 1962. Collage of pasted labels with watercolor, 23¾ x 29" (60.3 x 73.6 cm). 510.70

Barry LE VA. American, born 1941
Strips, Sheets and Particles. 1967–68. Pen and ink and cut-and-pasted photograph on graph paper, 17⅛ x 22⅝" (43.5 x 55.1 cm). Philip Johnson Fund. 101.71

Richard LIPPOLD. American, born 1915
The Four Seasons. 1958. Pen and ink and pencil on paper, 30½ x 30¼" (77.3 x 76.6 cm). 788.69

André MASSON. French, 1896–1987. In U.S.A. 1941–45
Praying Mantis. n.d. Pen and ink on paper, 13¾ x 23" (34.9 x 58.4 cm). 595.70

Henri MATISSE. French, 1869–1954.
Self-Portrait. 1945. Pen and ink on paper, 20½ x 15¾" (52 x 40 cm). Gift of Philip Johnson (by exchange). 837.69

Claes OLDENBURG. American, born Sweden 1929. To U.S.A. 1936
Hamburger. 1962. Lithographic crayon on paper, 14 x 17" (35.3 x 43 cm). Philip Johnson Fund. 328.62

Jackson POLLOCK. American, 1912–1956
Untitled. (ca. 1945). Crayon, colored pencil, brush and pen and ink, and watercolor on paper, 20¼ x 25" (51.5 x 63.5 cm). Gift of Philip Johnson, Abby Aldrich Rockefeller, Curt Valentin and Edward M.M. Warburg (by exchange). 662.83

Kurt SCHWITTERS. British subject, born Germany. 1887–1948. In England 1940–48
Untitled. (1919). Cut-and-pasted cloth, papers, and pencil on paper, 8 x 6⅝" (20.2 x 16.7 cm). 321.80

One One (Eins Eins). (1919–20). Cut-and-pasted papers and oil on paper, 10¼ x 9¼" (25.9 x 23.5 cm). 322.80

Merz 461: Goldmark. 1922. Cut-and-pasted papers on paper, 6⅞ x 5⅝" (17.5 x 14.2 cm). 321.80

Untitled. (1923). Cut-and-pasted papers on paper, 8¾ x 7¼" (22 x 18.4 cm). 319.80

Untitled. (1930). Crayon on paper, 5⅝ x 4⅜" (14.2 x 11 cm). 318.80

Sonia SEKULA. Swiss, 1918–1963
Untitled sketchbook with seven drawings. 1957. Pen and ink, gouache, colored pencil, and metallic paint on paper, each 5¾ x 4⅛" (14.6 x 10.5 cm). Joseph M. and Dorothy B. Edinburg Charitable Trust Fund and Philip Johnson Fund. 147.73.1–7

Marian WARZECHA. Polish, born 1930
Number 50. 1960. Cut-and-pasted papers on paper, 13¾ x 21⅝" (34.7 x 54.7 cm). Philip Johnson Fund. 274.61

Department of Prints and Illustrated Books
16 works

Alberto GIACOMETTI. Swiss, 1901–1966
Head of a Horse II (Tête de cheval II). (1954). Lithograph, printed in black, composition: 14⅞ x 10⅞" (37.8 x 27.7 cm); sheet: 20¹⁵⁄₁₆ x 17³⁄₁₆" (53.3 x 43.7 cm). 607.70

Stanley William HAYTER. British, 1901–1988
Amazon. 1945. Engraving, soft-ground etching, and embossing, printed in black, plate: 24½ x 15⅞" (62.2 x 40.3 cm); sheet: 29⅞ x 20¼" (76 x 51.4 cm). Philip Johnson Fund. 161.45

Jasper JOHNS. American, born 1930
No. 1969. Lithograph, printed in color, with embossing and lead collage additions, composition: 46¹⁵⁄₁₆ x 28¹¹⁄₁₆" (119.2 x 72.9 cm); sheet: 56 x 35⅞" (142.2 x 91.1 cm). Gift of Philip Johnson (by exchange). 449.71

Alphabet. 1969. Embossing, composition (irreg.): 28⅝ x 34¼" (72.7 x 87 cm); sheet: 29⅝ x 37" (75.3 x 94 cm). 325.73

Donald JUDD. American, 1928–1994
Untitled (6–L) from an untitled series. 1961–69. Woodcut, printed in color, composition (irreg.): 25⅝ x 15¹⁵⁄₁₆" (65.1 x 40.5 cm); sheet: 30⁹⁄₁₆ x 22" (77.6 x 55.9 cm). 329.73

Untitled (11–L) from an untitled series. 1961–69. Woodcut, printed in color, composition (irreg.): 26³⁄₁₆ x 16" (66.5 x 40.6 cm); sheet: 30⅝ x 22¹⁄₁₆" (77.8 x 56 cm). 330.73

Vasily KANDINSKY. French, born Russia. 1866–1944
Etching for Circle of Friends of the Bauhaus (Radierung für den Kreis der Freunde des Bauhauses). 1932. Drypoint, printed in black, plate: 7¹³⁄₁₆ x 9⅜" (19.9 x 23.9 cm); sheet: 13¹⁄₁₆ x 16⅛" (33.2 x 41 cm). 179.34

Paul KLEE. German, 1879–1940. Born and died in Switzerland
Head (Kopf) or *Bearded Man (Bärtiger Mann).* 1925, published 1930. Lithograph, printed in black, composition: 8¾ x 5¹⁵⁄₁₆" (22.2 x 15.2 cm); sheet:

17¹⁵⁄₁₆ x 12¹¹⁄₁₆" (45.5 x 32.2 cm). Philip Johnson Fund. 122.46

Roy LICHTENSTEIN. American, born 1923
Brushstrokes. (1967). Screenprint, printed in color, composition: 21¹⁵⁄₁₆ x 30" (55.7 x 76.2 cm); sheet: 22¹⁵⁄₁₆ x 30¹⁵⁄₁₆" (58.4 x 78.7 cm). 347.73

Edward RUSCHA. American, born 1937
1984. 1967. Lithograph, printed in black, with watercolor additions, composition: 14 ¹⁄₁₆ x 17⅞" (35.7 x 45.4 cm); sheet: 20 x 24⅞" (50.8 x 63.2 cm). 389.73

Andy WARHOL. American, 1928–1987
Self-portrait. (1967, dated 1966). Screenprint, printed in black, composition: 22¹⁄₁₆ x 20¾" (56 x 52.8 cm); sheet: 23¹⁄₁₆ x 22¹⁵⁄₁₆" (58.6 x 58.3 cm). 413.73

Flash—November 22, 1963 by Philip Greer. Briarcliff Manor, Racolin Press, 1968. Twelve screenprints, including folder, one printed in black and eleven printed in color, page: 21½ x 21¼" (54.6 x 54 cm). 440.73.1–12

Campbell's Soup I. (1968). Portfolio of ten screenprints, printed in color, composition (each approx.): 31⅞ x 18¾" (81 x 47.6 cm); sheet (each approx.): 35 x 22¹⁵⁄₁₆" (88.9 x 58.4 cm). 638.73.1–10

Campbell's Soup II. (1969). Portfolio of ten screenprints, printed in color, composition (each approx.): 31⅞ x 18¾" (81 x 47.6 cm); sheet (each approx.): 35 x 22¹⁵⁄₁₆" (88.9 x 58.4 cm). 639.73.1–10

Electric Chair. 1971. Portfolio of ten screenprints, printed in color, composition: 35⁷⁄₁₆ x 47⅞" (90 x 121.6 cm); sheet: 35⁷⁄₁₆ x 47⅞" (90 x 121.6 cm). 412.73.1–10

Vote McGovern. (1972). Screenprint, printed in color, composition (irreg.): 41⁵⁄₁₆ x 41⅛" (105 x 104.4 cm); sheet: 42 x 41¹⁵⁄₁₆" (106.7 x 106.6 cm). 415.73

Department of Photography
6 works

T. Lux FEININGER. American, born Germany 1910
From the Roof of the Bauhaus. (ca. 1929). Gelatin-silver print, 11½ x 8½" (29.2 x 21.6 cm) (sight). 562.39

Carts. (ca. 1929). Gelatin-silver print, 7 x 9⅜" (17.8 x 23.8 cm). 113.40

Untitled (Male Torso). (ca. 1929). Gelatin-silver print, 9⅜ x 6¾" (23.8 x 17.1 cm). 114.40

Ladder. (ca. 1929). Gelatin-silver print, 9⅜ x 7" (23.8 x 17.8 cm). 115.40

The Bauhaus Jazz Band. (ca. 1929). Gelatin-silver print, 9⅜ x 11¾" (23.8 x 29.8 cm). 116.40

Bauhaus or *Bauhaus Balconies (Balkons im Sommer).* (ca. 1929). Gelatin-silver print, 9¼ x 7" (23.5 x 17.8 cm). 549.67

Department of Architecture and Design

Johnson has donated approximately two thousand works to the Museum's Department of Architecture and Design, including architectural drawings and models, design objects, and, in 1950, part of the Jan Tschichold Collection of graphic ephemera, which is currently being catalogued. Gifts to the department not selectively described herein include four hundred and eighteen works on paper not formally accessioned as part of the collection; these include elevations, sections, perspective views, plans, and sketches for architectural projects with which Johnson was involved from 1947 to 1982, among them, the Glass House, New Canaan, Connecticut, 1947–49; the Rockefeller Guest House, New York, 1948–51 (with Frederick C. Genz and Landis Gores Associated); the William A.M. Burden House, Mount Kisco, New York, Project, 1951–58; the Roofless Church for Robert Lee Blaffer Trust, New Harmony, Indiana, 1960; and the Fort Hill Square/Boston Center, Boston, 1982 (with John Burgee). An additional four hundred and ninety-eight elevations, sections, plans, and isometric views, all relating to Mies van der Rohe's design of the Joseph E. Seagram and Sons Office Building, 375 Park Avenue, New York, 1954–58, were given by Johnson to the Mies Archive in 1988. Lastly, the architect's

gift of one hundred and fifty works on paper relating to various architectural projects ca. 1940–70 are now housed in the Study Collection; these include elevations, sections, perspective views, and plans for Johnson's own Harvard School of Design Project, Cambridge, Massachusetts, 1940–42; Ash Street House, Cambridge, 1943; New London Hospital (addition), New London, Ohio, 1946; and Glass House, New Canaan (ninety-three preliminary studies executed 1945–47), as well as furniture and lighting designs ca. 1950–52. The department also maintains a collection of 825 drawings for major expansions and minor improvements to The Museum of Modern Art—built as well as unbuilt projects—designed by Johnson ca. 1949–85.

Architectural Drawings and Models
Twenty-nine selected works

Raimund ABRAHAM. Austrian, born 1933
City Transformation. 1964. Montage mounted on board, 10¼ x 7" (26 x 17.7 cm). Philip Johnson Fund. 281.65

Linear City. Plan. 1964. Pen and ink and pencil on paper, 24¾ x 17½" (62.8 x 44.4 cm). 282.65A

Linear City. Perspective view. 1964. Pen and ink and pencil on paper, 24¾ x 17½" (62.8 x 44.4 cm). 282.65B

Earth-Cloud House. 1970. Pencil and colored pencil on paper, 34⅜ x 53½" (87.3 x 135.9 cm). 19.80

Jason CRUM. American, born 1935
Project for a Painted Wall, Houston Street at Broadway, New York City. 1969. Photomontage and gouache, 20 x 27½" (50.8 x 69.9 cm). Philip Johnson Fund. 372.69

Project for a Painted Wall, 15 Layfayette Street, New York City. 1969. Photomontage and gouache, 30 x 20" (76.2 x 50.8 cm). 373.69

Project for a Painted Wall, Fox Department Store, Hartford, Connecticut. 1969. Photomontage and gouache, 13¾ x 16⅞" (34.9 x 42.9 cm). 374.69

Michael GRAVES. American, born 1934
Aspen House. 1978. Pen and ink on paper, 23½ x 23⅝" (59.7 x 60 cm). 25.80

French and Co. Façade study. 1978. Pencil, pen and ink, and colored pencil on tracing paper, 10³⁄₁₆ x 12⁵⁄₁₆" (25.9 x 31.3 cm). 26.80

Hines House Fireplace. 1978. Pencil and colored pencil on tracing paper, 7½ x 7⁹⁄₁₆" (19.1 x 19.2 cm). 27.80

Hans HOLLEIN. Austrian, born 1934
Studies of Building Forms, Project. Perspective view. 1962. Pencil on paper, 9⅜ x 12¾" (23.8 x 32.4 cm). 565.63

Monument to Victims of the Holocaust, Project. Perspective view. 1963. Photomontage and pencil, 5⅞ x 11½" (14.9 x 29.2 cm). 564.63

Beach House, Project. Aerial perspective view. 1963. Photomontage, pen and ink, and pencil on tracing paper, 15½ x 21⅞" (39.3 x 55.5 cm). Philip Johnson Fund. 432.67

Urban Renewal in New York, Project. Aerial perspective view. 1964. Photomontage, 8⅛ x 10" (20.6 x 25.4 cm). Philip Johnson Fund. 433.67

Aircraft-Carrier-City, Project. Perspective view. 1964. Photomontage mounted on board, 8½ x 39⅜" (21.6 x 100 cm). Philip Johnson Fund. 434.67

Aircraft-Carrier-City, Project. Perspective view. 1964. Photomontage, 4½ x 7¼" (11.4 x 18.4 cm). Philip Johnson Fund. 435.67

Aircraft-Carrier-City, Project. Section and perspective view. 1964. Photomontage and pen and ink on glazed paper, 6⅜ x 15⅝" (16.1 x 39.7 cm). Philip Johnson Fund. 436.67

Aircraft-Carrier-City, Project. Aerial perspective view. 1964. Photomontage mounted on board, 4¾ x 14½" (12 x 36.8 cm). Philip Johnson Fund. 437.67

Highrise Building: Sparkplug, Project. Perspective view. 1964. Photomontage, 4¾ x 7¼" (12 x 18.4 cm). Philip Johnson Fund. 438.67

Highrise Building: Theodolite, Project. Perspective view. 1964. Photomontage mounted on board, 6¾ x 17½" (17.1 x 44.4 cm). Philip Johnson Fund. 439.67

Philip JOHNSON. American, born 1906
Glass House, New Canaan, Connecticut. 1947–49. Model by Paul Bonfilio with Edith Randel and Leon Kaplan, 1985. Scale: ⅜":1'. 42½ x 55½ x 67" (108 x 170.2 x 141 cm). 439.67

Walter PICHLER. Austrian, born 1936
Underground Building. Perspective view. 1963. Pen and ink and wash on paper, 12⅝ x 11¾" (32.1 x 29.8 cm). Philip Johnson Fund. 566.63

Entrance to an Underground City. Aerial perspective view. 1963. Photomontage and pencil on paper, 15¼ x 17½" (38.7 x 69.8 cm). 567.63

Nucleus of an Underground Building, Project. 1962. Pencil and colored pencil on tracing paper, 16¾ x 19½" (42.5 x 49.5 cm). 568.63

Nucleus of an Underground Building, Project. 1962. Pencil and colored pencil on white tracing paper, 18⅞ x 19⅜" (47.8 x 49.2 cm). 569.63

Aldo ROSSI. Italian, 1931–1997
Regional Government Office, Trieste, Italy. Elevation and section. 1974. Rubbed ink and pastel on print, 28½ x 36" (72.4 x 91.4 cm). Philip Johnson Fund. 28.80

Friedrich ST. FLORIAN. Austrian, born 1932
New York Birdcage—Imaginary Architecture. 1968. Colored pencil on print, 33½ x 36" (85.1 x 91.4 cm). Philip Johnson Fund. 1252.74

Imaginary Icicles (Over the Charles River, Boston). 1972. Printed acetate overlays, 13 x 18" (33 x 45.7 cm). Philip Johnson Fund. 1253.74

Lauretta VINCIARELLI. Italian, born 1943
Variations and Interferences of 3 Non-homogenous Grids in a 32 x 32 cm Square. n.d. Gouache on paper, 17½ x 17⅛" (44.4 x 43.5 cm). Philip Johnson Fund. 1255–63.74

Design Collection
One hundred and twenty-three works, including

Carl AUBÖCK. Austrian, born 1924
Cocktail Shaker. (1959). Chromed metal, 8¼" (20.9 cm) high x 3⅛" (7.9 cm) diameter. Philip Johnson Fund. 699.59.a–c

Peter BEHRENS. German, 1868–1940
Glasses. n.d. Glass, gold; set of four, 3¹¹⁄₁₆–7½" (9.4 –19 cm) high x 1¹⁵⁄₁₆–3" (4.9–7.6 cm) base diameter. Philip Johnson Fund. 343.61.1–4

Max BILL. Swiss, born 1908
Wall Clock (Model 32/0389). (1957). Chrome-plated metal frame and hands, painted metal face, 2⁷⁄₁₆" (6.2 cm) deep x 11⅞" (30.2 cm) diameter. Philip Johnson Fund. 347.61

Delores Dembus BITTLEMAN. American, born 1931
"Entrance II" Wallhanging. (1964). Wool, 76 x 72" (193 x 182.8 cm). Philip Johnson Fund. 598.65

Marcel BREUER. American, 1902–1981
Table (Model B10). (1927). Tubular-steel frame, and wood, 25³⁄₁₆ x 29⁵⁄₁₆ x 29³⁄₁₆" (66.5 x 74.5 x 74.1 cm). Philip Johnson Fund. 625.80

Luigi CACCIA DOMINIONI. Italian, born 1913
Pier Giacomo CASTIGLIONI. Italian, 1913–1968
Knife, Fork, and Soup Spoon. (1938). Hand-wrought silver, knife: 9¼" (23.5 cm) long; fork: 8" (20.5 cm) long; spoon: 7⅞" (20 cm) long. 554.53.1–3

Gino COLOMBINI. Italian, born 1915
Covered Pail (Model KS 1146). (1954). Polyethylene metal, 10½" (26.7 cm) high x 11" (27.9 cm) diameter. 514.56.a–b

Hans COPER. British, 1920–1981
Vase. (ca. 1958). Glazed ceramic, 9¼ x 6¼ x 4¾" (23.5 x 15.9 x 12.1 cm). Philip Johnson Fund. 407.60

Andries Dirk COPIER. Dutch, 1901–ca. 1990
Bowl. (Manufactured 1930). Glass, 4⁹⁄₁₆" (11.6 cm) high x 9⅞" (25.1 cm) diameter. 182.47

Gunnar Cyrén. Swedish, born 1931
Vase. (1960). Glass, 7" (17.8 cm) high x
5¾" (14.6 cm) diameter. Philip Johnson
Fund. 351.61

Daum Frères. Nancy, France
Vase. (ca. 1900). Painted glass, 23¼"
(59 cm) high x 5½" (14 cm) diameter
(approx.). Philip Johnson Fund. 707.59

Christian Dell. German, 1893–1974
Adjustable Desk Lamp. (1929). Painted
metal, 17⅞" (45.5 cm) high x 7⅛" (18
cm) base diameter. Philip Johnson Fund.
7.83.SC

Desny. Paris, France
Cocktail Goblets. (ca. 1930). Silver; set
of two, each 4¾" (12.1 cm) high x 3"
(7.6 cm) diameter. Philip Johnson Fund.
346.61.1–2

Sheila Hicks. American, born 1934
"Blue Letter" Weaving. (1959). Wool,
handwoven, 17¾ x 17" (41.5 x 43.2 cm).
Philip Johnson Fund. 338.60

Josef Hoffmann. Austrian, 1870–1956
Silver Footed Bowl. (Manufactured ca.
1920). Silver, 5⅝" (14 cm) high x 5⅞₆"
(13.8 cm) diameter. Philip Johnson
Fund. 162.77

Philip Johnson. American, born 1906
Richard Kelly. American, 1910–1977
Floor Lamp. (1950). Brass and painted
metal, 42" (106.7 cm) high x 25" (63.5
cm) diameter. 265.58.a–b

Karl J. Jucker. German, born 1902
Wilhelm Wagenfeld. German, born 1900
Table Lamp. (1923–24). Glass, chrome-
plated metal, and silver-bronze wiring
tube, 16¾" (42.5 cm) high x 5⅛" (14 cm)
base diameter. 490.53

Nil Landberg. Swedish, born 1907
Vase. (1957). Glass, 13¾" (34.9 cm) high x
7" (17.8 cm) diameter. Philip Johnson
Fund. 352.61

Gerhard Marcks. German, 1889–1981
Wilhelm Wagenfeld. German, 1900–1990
"Sintrax" Coffee Machine. (ca. 1925).
Heat-resistant glass, wood, rubber, and
metal, overall 11¾" (30 cm) high. Philip
Johnson Fund. 114.76

Enzo Mari. Italian, born 1932
Perpetual Calendar. (1962). Anodized
aluminum and plastic, 12⅜ x 12⅜" (31.4 x
31.4 cm). Philip Johnson Fund. 352.66

Ludwig Mies van der Rohe. American,
1886–1969
"Brno" Chair. (1929). Chrome-plated
tubular steel and calf parchment, 30⅞ x
21⅝ x 28⅜" (78.4 x 54.3 x 72.1 cm).
411.76

Umberto Nason. Italian
Tumbler. (1954). Glass, 2⅜" (6 cm) high x
2⅜" (6 cm) diameter. 473.56.9

Josef Maria Olbrich. Austrian, 1867–1908
Candelabrum. n.d. Pewter, 14¼" (36.2
cm) high x 6¹³⁄₁₆" (17.3 cm) diameter.
Philip Johnson Fund. 344.61

Owo. Germany
Water Tumbler. (ca. 1954). Plastic, 3½"
(8.9 cm) high x 2¾" (7 cm) diameter.
Gift of Philip Johnson Fund. 545.56

Sven Palmqvist. Swedish, 1906–1984
Bowl. (1960). Glass, 7⅝" (19.4 cm) high x
14¼" (36.2 cm) diameter. Philip Johnson
Fund. 350.61

Ezio Pirali. Italian, born 1921
Electric Fan. (1953). Aluminum,
chromed steel, and rubber, 8¼" (21 cm)
high). 459.56

Claus Josef Riedel. Austrian, born 1925
"Exquisit" Stemware. (1958). Glass; set of
nine, 6¾–9¾" (17.2 x 24.8 cm) high x
2¼–5" (5.7–12.7 cm) diameter. Philip
Johnson Fund. 710.59.1–9

Gerrit Rietveld. Dutch, 1888–1964
"Red and Blue" Chair. (ca. 1918). Wood,
painted, 34⅛ x 26 x 33" (86.5 x 66 x 83.8
cm). 487.53

Magnus Stephensen. Danish, born 1903
Ice Bucket. (1951). Sterling silver and raf-
fia, 4⅜" (11 cm) high x 7¾" (17 cm)
diameter. 485.53.a–b

Nanny Still. Finnish, born 1926
Platter. n.d. Glass, 2" (5.1 cm) high x
11⅝" (29.5 cm) diameter. Philip Johnson
Fund. 261.62

Gebruder Thonet. Vienna
Armchair (Model 6009, later B9). (ca.
1904). Steam-bent beechwood, 28⅜ x
20⅞ x 21⁵⁄₁₆" (74.5 x 52.7 x 55.7 cm).
Philip Johnson Fund. 667.80

Wilhelm Wagenfeld. German, 1900–1990
Cup and Saucer. (1932). Heat-resistant
glass, cup: 1½" (3.8 cm) high x 4⁵⁄₁₆" (11
cm) diameter; saucer: 5¾" (14.6 cm)
diameter. 471.56.a–b

Wolfgang von Wersin. German, 1882–1976
Tea Caddy. (Manufactured ca. 1954).
Polished brass, 4⅛ x 2⅞ x 2⅛" (10.5 x
7.3 x 5.4 cm). 489.56.a–c

Jan Tschichold Collection
Partial gift of Philip Johnson, 1950

*The Tschichold Collection comprises approxi-
mately 780 examples of graphic ephemera and
posters by leading artists and designers of the
1920s and 1930s; currently being catalogued, it
includes the following selected works:*

Herbert Bayer. American, born Austria.
1900–1985
Invitation to Das Weisse Fest (The
White Festival). (1926). Letterpress, 8¼ x
11⅜" (20 x 29 cm). 541.77

Max Bill. Swiss, born 1908
Menu for the 28th Annual Meeting of
the Bund Schweitzer Architekten (Federation of Swiss Architects). (1935). Letterpress, 8¼ x 3" (21 x 7.6 cm); extended,
11¾ x 16½" (29.8 x 41.9 cm). 547.77

A. M. Cassandre. French, 1901–1968
Poster: "Chateau de la Roche Vasouy."
n.d. Lithograph, 47¼ x 30¼" (120 x 76.8
cm). 363.50

Walter Dexel. German, 1890–1973
Brochure: "Fotografie der Gegenwart"
(Today's Photography). 1929. Letter-
press, 8¼ x 11¾" (20.9 x 29.8 cm). 551.77

Gustav Klutsis. Russian, 1895–1944
Cover for *The Daily Life of Airplane Pilots*
by N. Bobrow. Moscow, 1928. 8¹⁵⁄₁₆ x
12¼" (22.7 x 31.2 cm). 557.77

El LISSITZKY (Lazar Markovich Lissitzky). Russian, 1890–1941

Of Two Squares. Leipzig, 1920 (designed 1922). Letterpress, 11 x $8\frac{3}{4}$" (28 x 22.3 cm). 562.77

Program: "Merz-Matineen" (Merz Matinee). (1923). Letterpress, 11 x 9" (27.9 x 22.8 cm). 561.77

Filippo Tommasso MARINETTI. Italian, 1876–1944

Scrabrrrrraanng. (1919). Illustration from *Les Mots en Liberté Futuriste.* Letterpress, $13\frac{3}{8}$ x $9\frac{1}{4}$" (34 x 23.4 cm). 598.77

Herbert MATTER. American, 1907–1984

Advertising brochure for Gebr. Fretz A.G. Zurich. (1933). $11\frac{3}{4}$ x $8\frac{5}{16}$" (29.8 x 21.1 cm). 566.77

László MOHOLY-NAGY. American, 1895–1946

Jacket for *Bauhausbücher 5: Piet Mondrian, Neue Gestaltung* (Bauhaus Books 5: Piet Mondrian, New Design). (1924). Letterpress, $9\frac{5}{16}$ x 15" (23.7 x 38.1 cm). 569.77

Alexander RODCHENKO. Russian, 1891–1951

Novyi Lef (Moscow), no. 8/9. (1927). $8\frac{15}{16}$ x $6\frac{1}{16}$" (22.8 x 15.4 cm). 575.77.a–c

Hajo ROSE. American, born 1909

Invitation to the Drie Stuivers Bal (Three Penny Ball). (1935). Letterpress, $3\frac{7}{8}$ x $7\frac{1}{4}$" (9.9 x 18.4 cm). 576.77.a–b

Paul SCHUITEMA. Dutch

Brochure for Nutricia Powdered Milk. (1927). Letterpress, $14\frac{1}{2}$ x $11\frac{13}{16}$" (36.8 x 30 cm). 584.77

Label for VBP Oil Can. (ca. 1928). Letterpress, $5\frac{7}{8}$ x $11\frac{3}{4}$" (14.9 x 29.8 cm). 588.77

Kurt SCHWITTERS. British subject, born Germany. 1887–1948. In England 1940–48

Mailing Wrapper for the Merz Werbezentrale (Merz Advertising Agency). (ca. 1923). Letterpress, $8\frac{5}{8}$ x $11\frac{5}{8}$" (21.9 x 29.5 cm). 594.77

Letterhead for Die Abstrakten Hannover (The Hannover Abstractionists). (1927). Letterpress, $11\frac{5}{8}$ x $8\frac{5}{16}$" (29.5 x 21 cm). 597.77

Karel TEIGE. Czech

With the Ship Comes Coffee and Tea by Konstantin Biebl. Prague, n.d. Letterpress, $7\frac{7}{8}$ x $3\frac{1}{2}$" (20 x 14 cm). 601.77

Georg TRUMP. German, born 1896

Poster: "Lichtbilder—Vortrag—Gropius" (Photographs—Lectures—Gropius). (ca. 1925). Lithograph, $16\frac{3}{4}$ x $21\frac{1}{2}$" (42.6 x 54.5 cm). 366.50

Jan TSCHICHOLD. Swiss, 1902–1974

Program for the Phoebus-Palast Cinema. (1927). Letterpress, $12\frac{3}{16}$ x $9\frac{3}{16}$" (31 x 23.5 cm). 602.77

Friedrich VORDEMBERGE-GILDEWART. German, 1899–1962

Mailing envelope for Gruppe K (Group K). (ca. 1924). Letterpress, $4\frac{7}{8}$ x $6\frac{3}{16}$" (12.4 x 15.7 cm). 608.77

Piet ZWART. Dutch, 1885–1977

Cover for *De Komische Film* (The Comic Film) by C. J. Graadt van Roggen. Rotterdam, 1931. Letterpress, $8\frac{7}{8}$ x $7\frac{3}{8}$" (22.5 x 18.7 cm). 629.77

Advertisement for NFK Cables, Delft ("Hot Spots"). (1926). Letterpress, $9\frac{7}{8}$ x $6\frac{5}{8}$" (25 x 16.8 cm). 618.77

Photograph Credits

The photographs reproduced in this publication were provided in most cases by The Museum of Modern Art. The following list, keyed to page numbers, applies to photographs for which an additional acknowledgment is due.

Contributors

Mirka Beneš is Associate Professor of the History of Landscape Architecture, Graduate School of Design, Harvard University

Peter Reed is Associate Curator in the Department of Architecture and Design, The Museum of Modern Art, New York

Terence Riley is Chief Curator of the Department of Architecture and Design, The Museum of Modern Art, New York

Kirk Varnedoe is Chief Curator of the Department of Painting and Sculpture, The Museum of Modern Art, New York

A Note to Contributors

Studies in Modern Art publishes scholarly articles focusing on works of art in the collection of The Museum of Modern Art and on the Museum's programs. It is issued annually, although additional special numbers may be published from time to time. Each number deals with a particular topic. A list of future topics may be obtained from the journal office.

Contributors should submit proposals to the Editorial Committee of the journal by January 1 of the year preceding publication. Proposals should include the title of the article; a 500-word description of the subject; a critical appraisal of the current state of scholarship on the subject; and a list of works in the Museum's collection or details of the Museum's program that will be discussed. A working draft of the article may be submitted as a proposal. The Editorial Committee will evaluate all proposals and invite selected authors to submit finished manuscripts. (Such an invitation will not constitute acceptance of the article for publication.) Authors of articles published in the journal receive an honorarium and complimentary copies of the issue.

Please submit all inquiries to:

Studies in Modern Art
The Museum of Modern Art
11 West 53 Street
New York, New York 10019

Trustees of The Museum of Modern Art

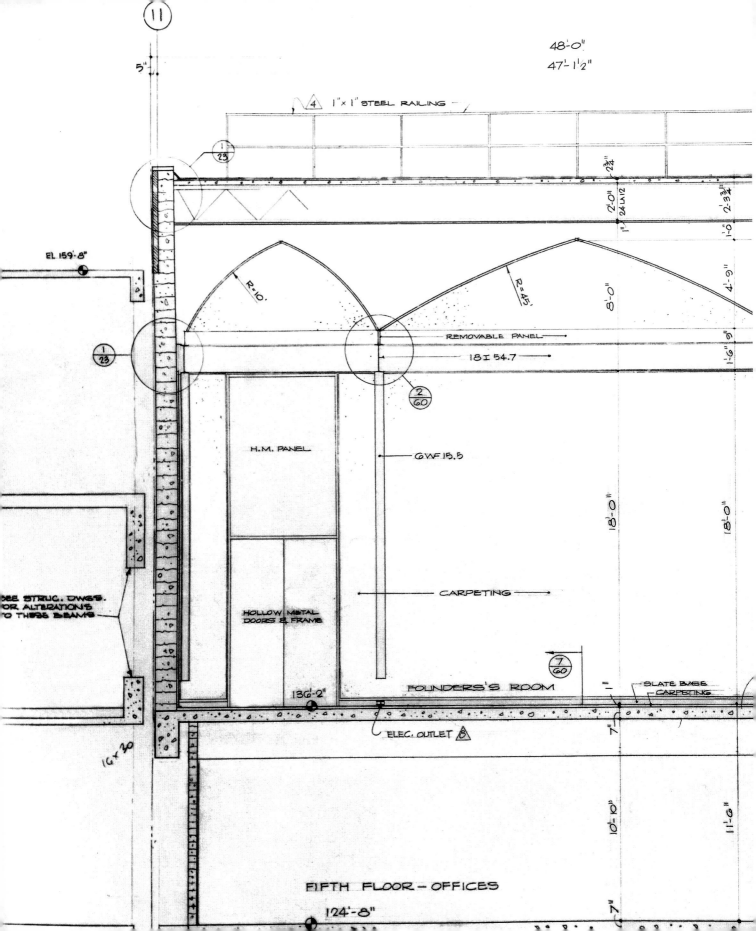

11

48'-0"
47'-1½"

4 1"x 1" STEEL RAILING

1
23

2¾"
2'-0" 24 LA 12
1'-0" 2-3¾"

EL 159'-8"

R=10'
R=45'
8'-0"
4'-9"

1
23

REMOVABLE PANEL
18 I 54.7

2
60

H.M. PANEL

6 WF 15.5

18'-0"   18'-0"

CARPETING

SEE STRUC. DWGS.
FOR ALTERATIONS
TO THESE BEAMS

HOLLOW METAL
DOORS & FRAME

7
60

FOUNDERS'S ROOM

SLATE BASE
CARPETING

136'-2"

1"
7"

16 x 20

ELEC. OUTLET 8

10'-10"   11'-6"

FIFTH FLOOR - OFFICES

124'-8"

7"